A LIFE IN TEARS

A LIFE IN TEARS

Understanding Fethullah Gülen and His Call to Service

Salih Yücel

TUGHRA
BOOKS

Published by Tughra Books
335 Clifton Ave.
Clifton, NJ, 07011, USA
www.tughrabooks.com

978-1-59784-933-3
EPUB 978-1-59784-973-9

Library of Congress Cataloging-in-Publication Data

Names: Yücel, Salih, author.
Title: A life in tears : understanding Fethullah Gulen and his call to
  service / Salih Yucel.
Description: Clifton, NJ : Tughra Books, [2018] | Includes bibliographical
  references and index. |
Identifiers: LCCN 2018023926 (print) | LCCN 2018024878 (ebook) | ISBN
  9781597849739 | ISBN 9781597849333 (pbk.)
Subjects: LCSH: Gülen, Fethullah. | Gülen Hizmet Movement.
Classification: LCC BP80.G8 (ebook) | LCC BP80.G8 Y835 2018 (print) | DDC
  297.092--dc23
LC record available at https://lccn.loc.gov/2018023926

Printed in Canada

Contents

Foreword

In the Name of God, the All-Merciful and the All-Compassionate.

All praise is due to Him, and peace and blessings be upon Prophet Muhammad, his family, all other Prophets, and their companions.

Great men are understood entirely and properly only by great people. It is unimaginable for a murderer to know why a person would walk on the other side of the path in order to avoid harming a trail of ants. It is not possible for those who steal taxpayers' money to understand those who will not even turn on a light in a public building for a personal matter. It is unthinkable for a greedy person to perceive how someone else could donate half of his or her wealth for the common good. It is inconceivable for a politician who has worldly ambitions to quit his position of power as Hasan (r.a.)—the grandson of the Prophet Muhammad (pbuh)—quited his caliphate, the most honorable leadership in order to ensure peace.[1] It is unbelievable for a stone-hearted individual to understand why someone would cry over the death of a bee or the cutting of a branch off a tree. It is not possible for someone who loves to be praised and always seeks fame to relate to a man who sees himself as a servant.

Even through careful study, a person can only understand what the eyes see, what the ears hear, and what reason can comprehend. Mawlana Jalal ad-Din Rumi (1207–1274) said, "Study me as much as you like, you will not know me, for I differ in a hundred ways from what you see me to be. Put yourself behind my eyes and see me as I see myself, for I have chosen to dwell in a place you cannot see." He also said, "When you become like me, you will understand who I am."

Through this research, I have learned that it is not possible to truly understand a great scholar through reading or analysing his texts. The best way to understand him is to be like him, to be at his degree of action, faith, piety, dedication, altruism, compassion and love.

I have been contemplating writing a book about Fethullah Gülen for years, but could not proceed as I did not see myself as the right per-

---

1 The expression (r.a) is an abbreviation of "*radiyallahu anh*", which means, "may Allah be pleased with him." This is used for the Companions of the Prophet to revere them. Pbuh stands for "peace be upon him", which is used after the name of the Prophet.

son to do it. After he was subjected to a torrent of insults, accusations, and slander after December 17, 2013 from a diverse group of Turkish politicians, intellectuals and media, including aggressive secularists, political Islamists, Maoists, atheists, Islamophobes, and ultra-nationalists, I felt a moral obligation to conduct and present this research on Gülen. All his close associates who have been with him throughout this life and those who are near him unanimously stated that Gülen refrains from even killing an ant or pulling a leaf off a tree. However, the Republic prosecutors, after accusing him of heading a terrorist organisation, asked for his sentence to be almost 3,500 years.

As Ali Ünal, author of a Turkish biography of Gülen, says, "It is very difficult task to introduce Gülen to readers." Great scholars' lives are best understood by great people. Gülen can be understood properly by those who are like him in all aspects of life. Therefore, this study of Gülen is a very humble contribution. The primary aim of this book is to encourage scholars of the field to do more research and examine Gülen's life, particularly his Islamic scholarship. Thus far, some books and many articles have been written about his philosophies of education and dialogue, but his Islamic scholarship deserves further research. While it is an arduous task to reflect on Gülen as he is, it is an honour for me to shed light briefly on some aspects of his scholarship.

This research covers over seventy books, 564 sermons, and over 500 talks by Gülen and more than fifty interviews of his close associates and friends which were aired on the Irmak and Mefkure TV channels in Turkey. I have also included my personal observations of Gülen over a total of six months from 1997 to 2007.

My aim is to contribute through this work, which is meant to be an introduction as opposed to a comprehensive biography. Based on my research and the approximately six months I have spent near him, Gülen does not want such a book written about him. He avoids any form of boasting or showing off and detests fame, running from it as from a poisonous scorpion. He has never called himself a scholar, leader, or an intellectual in his talks, works, and media interviews, although he is all of these to his supporters. In one interview, a journalist asked Gülen how he thought he would be remembered. Gülen responded, "I wish to be forgotten when I die. I wish my grave not to be known. I wish to die in solitude with nobody actually becoming aware of my death and hence nobody conducting my Funeral Prayer. I wish that nobody would remember me."

Gülen is one of the rare Muslim scholars who has been widely recognized both in the Muslim world and in the West during his lifetime. Thus far, over a dozen conferences have been held about Gülen, and many more books and articles have been written about him. None were at his instigation but by the efforts of his close associates, who saw the need for academically sound and accurate information on Gülen in order to minimise misconceptions and misunderstandings. I attended one international conference about Gülen and the Hizmet Movement in November 2008 at Georgetown University. After the conference, I visited Gülen with a group of academics. We expected him to ask how the conference went. Yet, in the four days I stayed at the retreat centre where he resides, he did not ask any presenters about the conference.

Those who have been close to Gülen for decades may be critical of this work, which is inadequate and does not show a complete picture of him. Western scholars may view this research as not critical enough. I am an insider, but sometimes I take a step back and look at him as an outsider as well. Being an insider had its advantages and disadvantages for the writing of this book. I accept and welcome all criticisms.

Once, in 1989, I asked my four-year-old son to bring me one of Gülen's video tapes from another room. He brought it and then asked, "Daddy, why is his last name Gülen [which means 'laughing' in Turkish]? He often cries when he talks." That day I was unable to answer my son's question. My son was right. I could not forget his question and it was one of the inspirations for this research.

After months of contemplation, I decided to name this book after the tears of Fethullah Gülen. I do not know of any other man who cries as much as Gülen. What I have found through my research of Muslim scholars and leaders is that the shedding of tears has played a crucial role in their work, whether in the formation of Islamic sciences or the establishment of a civilisation. Islamic civilisation is a product of ideas and works moulded by tears and suffering. It can be said that all notable Islamic scholars and leaders have contributed to Islamic civilisation, not only with their different types of skills but also with their tears, which reflect their concern for the welfare of people in both this life and the Hereafter. There is no great figure in Islamic history who did not shed tears for the love of God, the Prophet, his Companions, and all humanity. If Islamic civilisation is a building, the tears bind the mortar that holds the bricks and keeps the foundations firm. Without these tears, it would not be a compassionate civilisation, nor would it last. Similarly, the tears of Gülen, his close associates and followers are vital ingredients in the foundation of the Hizmet Movement. I have listened to over a thousand of Gülen's sermons and talks, but could not find a single one wherein he does not shed a tear.

Gülen is commonly called by the respectful title "*Hodja Efendi*" or "honorable teacher" in Turkish, but throughout this book, I use his given name (Fethullah Gülen or Gülen).

I have also undertaken the task of translating some parts of his works from Turkish to English. It must be noted that instead of translating literally word by word, I have translated for meaning. I know through my past academic work that it is very difficult to translate his books and speeches, which include eloquent and historical Turkish with many Arabic, Persian and Ottoman Turkish idioms.

Finally, I thank many of his close associates and students who helped me collect information about Gülen and answer my questions over the last twenty years that I have known about him. Special thanks to Ruth Woodhall for her precious editorial contributions to the manuscript.

Salih Yücel
May 1, 2017
Sydney, Australia

CHAPTER 1

A SCHOLAR WITHOUT REST

A Scholar without Rest

Great scholars are products of times of crisis. Their revivalist ideas are often not understood nor welcomed by their contemporaries. Fethullah Gülen is not only a product of a time of crisis but also a fruit of a great family and spiritual environment. His religiously devout grandparents and parents planted the seeds of a future scholar. The spiritual circle of Muhammed Lütfi Efendi (1868–1956) from Alvar in Erzurum became the nourishing soil for this plant. Said Nursi's (1887–1960) works of Qur'anic *tafsir* and focused study circles nurtured Gülen like the water of life and rays of the sun. Studying the biography of Prophet Muhammad (pbuh), his Companions and the *Salaf al-Saliheen*[2] or "Righteous Predecessors," in depth at young age injected spirituality into his soul. Reading the works of major Muslim scholars and intellectuals from the earliest to the modern period laid the foundations of knowledge in his mind. Great vigilance about his five daily Prayers, all types of *nafila* (voluntary) Prayers, including the *Tahajjud* (the night vigil) must have purified his heart, cleared his mind, strengthened his resolve, removed that which could have led him off the straight path and opened a window of wisdom for the spiritual journey towards to the All-Wise.

Reading Western classical books broadened Gülen's understanding of the world. From the age of seventeen, he travelled in the service of Islam (*hijrah*) from city to city in Turkey. Moving to the United States not only detached him from the world but also increased his exposure to different people, ideas, and information and served the growth of his knowledge and experience. On top of that, suffering from various types of illnesses throughout his life kept him sharply aware that this world was not meant for comfort and that he was only a guest in a transitory world. All these circumstances, including his not marrying, motivated him to dedicate himself entirely to his mission.

Serving humanity made him a fruit-bearing tree which scattered its seeds throughout the world. The barrage of insults, rumours, slander,

---

2   *Salaf al-Saliheen* is an honorific which is used for the first three generations of Islamic history, the Companions (*Sahaba*), their successors (*tabiun*), and the successors of the successors (*tabau tabiun*).

and outright tyranny of foes has served as a fertiliser, nourishing his ability to endure and remain patient in the face of injustice. Seeing the products of serving humanity through the Hizmet Movement[3] has become like oxygen for his life. The loyalty, unity, and commitment of his friends and followers gave him hope for tackling the three major problems of the Muslim world: ignorance, poverty, and disunity.

Despite Gülen's powerlessness and lack of desire for worldly ambitions, his unwavering commitment to serving and educating people in every condition, including on the days when his parents and brothers passed away, has made him a formidable leader in the sight of his friends and enemies. His firmness in faith, in even the most difficult situations, has inspired and motivated countless people to strive against ignorance. His compassion towards all creation, including insects and animals, has made him beloved, as he lives by his saying, "You must have a seat for every person in your heart." Regardless of what has been done to him, he forgives those whose ill actions have affected him alone. His desire to remain unknown and then entirely forgotten after death may be what will make him remembered.

I do not know of any contemporary figure who has been as discriminated against, despised, accused, slandered, and insulted by a wide range of political, social and religious groups. He has faced discrimination since birth. Because his father named him "Fethullah", which includes the word "Allah", the secularist authorities did not register his birth for more than two years. During the secularists' military coup in 1960, a military officer wanted to push him from the sixth floor and then claim that he had committed suicide, but a police chief intervened to save him. In 1971, along with almost half of his students, he was arrested for six months after a coup. He was verbally abused and at times

---

3   The Hizmet movement is a civil society movement that arose in the late 1960s in Turkey, initially composed of a loose network of individuals who were inspired by M. Fethullah Gülen. The Hizmet movement established over 2,000 schools, more than 750 tutoring centres, over 1,000 student dormitories and over two dozen universities in over 170 countries. After the attempted military coup on July 16, 2016, over 3,000 institutions comprising about 800 schools, 13 universities, 750 tutoring centers, and over 1000 dormitories, childcare and 16 hospitals were closed by the Turkish government.

For detail of interviews see www.fgulen.com/en/press/news retrieved on 17.04.2016.

was prohibited from using the toilet as torture. After the 1980 military coup, he was listed among the "most wanted" alongside communist terrorists who had killed hundreds of people. This forced Gülen to live as a fugitive for six years. A close friend of Gülen has described him as "a man who does not rest and has not been allowed to rest throughout his life," referring not only to Gülen's dedication to positive action without rest, but to the regular mistreatment he has faced throughout his life. He has combined self-respect with willingness to forgive those who insulted him, caused him harm, and persecuted and imprisoned him. It astounds me how, despite many years of abuse, accusations and trials, Gülen has not given up his mission. During difficult moments, seeing the fruits of sincere service through the Hizmet movement has been a source of motivation for him.

The degree of a believer's faith is as much as his/her level of compassion towards the creation on earth, Gülen asserts. Prophet Muhammad (pbuh) says, "Be merciful to those on the earth and the One in the heavens will have mercy upon you."[4] If Gülen sees a trail of ants, he will walk to the other side of the path or road to avoid treading on them. His compassion towards animals prevents him and his friends from the unnecessary killing of any creature, even insects, for they reflect much of God's Names and magnificence even in their tiny bodies and seemingly insignificant actions. As will be shown in Chapter 2, for Gülen, the environment is the "Lost Paradise" and his idealistic approach to the environment reflects his desire to one day make it resemble a garden of *Firdaws Jannah* (Paradise).

He supplicated at a young age to be tender-hearted or *awwâh*, as Prophet Abraham is described in the Qur'an for praying continuously to God with respect. He requested to be like Prophet Job (Ayyoub) and weep until people think of him as being mad. It looks as if his supplications were accepted by God.

His tears over the condition of creation have led to the spreading of the seeds of this tree throughout the world. His leadership, not only through his philosophy expressed in words, but mainly through his sincere and positive actions, has conquered many hearts and minds. He expresses his sorrow, suffering, pain, love, and compassion by shedding

---

4 Sunan al-Tirmidhi, Hadith no: 1924, www.*sunnah*.com.

his tears to cool down as lovers of God do. I can only comment on the physical tears but cannot see the tears he sheds inside his heart. Physical tears are a form of mercy from the All-Merciful. Weeping is a step in comprehending the beauty of the universe, in understanding the significance of creation in depth.

Each teardrop is a manifestation of a compassionate heart, a reflection of the suffering of body and soul for humankind. Tears are also a lightning conductor protecting us against sins and are steps in spiritual ascension, as Sufis argue. The act of weeping can revive a person who is spiritually ill or dead, are a wonder of a new spiritual station, and the most sophisticated soft power for solving problems through affecting hearts and minds.

Instead of using the language of politics or radicalism, Gülen bursts into tears to express his rage against injustice. Shedding tears is his outlet, enabling him to cool down when facing oppression and tyranny and direct his energy to positive action. As the evil in the world knows no end, neither do Gülen's tears. A close friend of his described him as *yağmur gözlü*, literally translating to "the rainy-eyed one," reflecting the regular dropping of his tears.

His tears can be likened to seeds which are planted. Some of them sprout sooner while others sprout later. Some of them are eaten by animals and never grow. Eventually, the remaining seeds will become a fruitful tree or trees and they will scatter their seeds throughout the land. In Chapter 3, I will shed light on the significance of tears in the Qur'an and *Sunnah* and then analyse Gülen's view and the reasons for the flowing of his tears.

Since the early 1970s, Gülen has been targeted by the Turkish media at different levels. All of his activities have been under the scrutiny of the Turkish Intelligent Service, military, and police. Like his predecessor Said Nursi, he has not been able to have much peace or any worldly pleasure. Yet, like Nursi, who followed the example of Prophet Ayyoub (Job), he does not complain about his suffering.

Since corruption investigations into government ministers in December 2013 in Turkey, powerful sectors of the Turkish government, including the military, judiciary, intelligence service and diplomatic corps around the world, have been mobilised to discredit Gülen and take apart the Hizmet Movement, but they have not yet been successful. Over ninety percent of the Turkish media, most of the Islamist political groups, and non-governmental organisations have been used as a tool to achieve this aim. Over 250 national and local TV channels, more than a thousand radio stations, 30 newspapers, around 500 news websites have been circulating fabricated news in Turkish about Gülen since mid-December 2103. Over twenty times various Turkish media channels have claimed that Gülen has died and his family is preparing his funeral service. There is no one else like Gülen who has faced such fabricated news despite being surrounded by between two or three dozen people and having many visitors daily. Although he avoids stepping on ants, he faces an Attorney General in Turkey who has requested for Gülen a 3500-year sentence, the length of which has never been requested for anyone in the history of Islam.

Despite all the accusation, slander, insults, and tyranny, he continues to act positively and educate people as far as his health allows.

Yet even all of that has not stopped Gülen from preaching what he knows to be right and encouraging others to continue on this difficult path. Those who oppose him thought that by shutting down the educational institutions and media outlets established by Hizmet and usurping their properties, businesses and wealth, Gülen would cave into the pressure and possibly suffer a fatal blow due to his poor health. They expected Hizmet people to disperse and quit their mission of service. It is hard to estimate the hundreds of millions of dollars spent on dismantling the movement through counter-establishments, propaganda, arrests, trials, intelligence services, and other methods. The government has used force to confiscate over 3,000 of the Hizmet Movement's educational institutions, from child-care centres to major universities. Records indicate that over 140,000 Hizmet affiliates have been interrogated while 62,000 have been arrested. Over 150,000 people have been laid off from the public service unlawfully.[5] These victims cannot seek justice because the justice system is rigged against them with lawyers afraid of representing someone being accused with terrorism. Any sign of clemency or understanding towards those in the movement could cost those in the judiciary their livelihoods and reputations.

Despite these Machiavellian political games, following the example of the grandson of the Prophet, who strived against injustice and

---

5   These numbers, which change daily, are from December 1, 2017.

eventually sacrificed his life for it, Gülen did not compromise his position against the government's distortion of Islam, corruption, injustice, oppression, and the denial of fundamental human rights. He did not compromise the leadership principles of *Sayyidhood*, which will be explained in Chapter 4. To do so would be a denial of all the main Islamic and ethical principles he has been striving hard to follow and preach for sixty years.

In the face of all these immense trials, he has piloted the Hizmet Movement like a ship through dangerous waters time and time again, emphasising positive action as opposed to reaction. He remains critical of his failures and takes responsibility for his deeds, but never accepts or claims any success as a result of his own leadership or actions.

One of the key factors in his success is role modelling (*tamthil*), which is elaborated in Chapter 5. Gülen has not succeeded by ordering people around but by leading an exemplary life. Following the example of Prophet Muhammad (pbuh), he would undertake more risk, more work and more difficult tasks than the ones his followers would undertake. As Prophet Muhammad (pbuh) chose to describe himself as a servant Prophet and not a king or leader Prophet, so too does Gülen choose to call himself not a leader but a servant. He believes that there is no leadership position in Islam except that of a public servant. His servanthood criteria and their application in his life have not changed whether he has had two dozen or two million followers.

Although he is considered to be the leader running the largest faith-based movement in the Muslim world, with over 7000 institutions, he does not spend more than four or five hours per day meeting and talking with people. He sets the management principles by role modelling, which leaves its mark in peoples' minds and hearts, including those who assume great leadership responsibility in the movement's projects. Those *khadims*[6] (servants) apply these principles in general and sometimes consult with Gülen when there are new developments or challenges.

As much as he may preach about altruism, his actions precede his words. By strictly applying the examples of *Salaf al-Saliheen* in his life, he has been able to influence and mobilise millions in the cause of education by the grace of God. For Gülen, altruism is an essential principle

---

6   The description of *khadim* is elaborated in Chapter 4.

of Islam. Without it, Muslims cannot overcome the crises that they have been facing for over a century. In Chapter 6, I cover the altruism (*ithar*) of Gülen expressed in his principles and actions, both of which are of a high degree for our modern time.

As someone who is considered an insider in the Hizmet Movement, I estimate that between sixty and seventy percent of Hizmet Movement activities are done by volunteers or as unpaid or voluntary overtime by employees at the movement's institutions. Otherwise, such organisations would need tens of billions of dollars to achieve similar success and such fast growth, although I doubt even more money could produce the same effect. The efforts and activities of volunteers have a different, and arguably stronger, effect on the community and society than those of paid workers.

Over the last twenty-five years, I have spoken to hundreds of people who have been migrating from city to city or country to country after graduating from university or marriage. Their constant movement is for the purpose of serving people from all faiths, cultures and ethnicities. I have met businessmen who have been donating much more generously since they began their affiliation with the Hizmet Movement. Some have given twenty percent of their total wealth. Some have given half of their wealth like Umar (r.a.) the second caliph. I have met those who have given their entire incomes like Abu Bakr as-Siddiq (r.a.), the first caliph. I have heard many stories of women who donated all the jewellery they happened to be wearing when they heard of the need for scholarship funds. I have met many parents who were immensely proud of their children for serving as teachers in every corner of the world, including in countries which were formerly colonized, where they faced great difficulties and risks to life.

Istighna (to be independent of all wants and needs) is a significant principle of all prophets, their companions, saints and great scholars, which is why Gülen has followed it so strictly throughout his life. Gülen has applied this principle in many ways, such as by avoiding indebtedness to anyone, including his siblings. He applies the *mabda-muntaha* principle[7] with *istighna* as well. There have been times when he has had no

---

7   This principle refers to the human condition in which a human comes to this world
    with no possession, and so is he when he dies. The day a leader takes position or office

place of his own to sleep, no money to use, no food to eat, but refused to ask for help. Since he began receiving royalties of ten percent from his seventy books, he has donated ninety percent of his income from these publications and used the remaining amount to host his countless visitors.

Gülen shares the destiny of the great scholars, the *Salaf al-Saliheen*, such as Imam Malik (711–795), Imam Azam Abu Hanifa (699–767), Imam Shafi'i (767–820), Ahmad ibn Hanbal (780–855), Imam Bukhari (810–870), Imam al-Sarakhsi (d.1096), Imam Rabbani (1564–1624) and Said Nursi and many others. The life of Gülen seemed to me similar to Imam Azam when I saw his study circle of fiqh (jurisprudence), hadith and *tafsir* (exegesis of the Qur'an). I believe his life also resembles that of Ahmad ibn Hanbal, who suffered at the hands of most of the Abbasid caliphs and governors. Gülen has been made a fugitive, abused, sued, persecuted, jailed and effectively exiled by almost all governments in Turkey since 1960 and is now accused of leading a violent organisation aiming to topple the government. In his speaking about Prophet Muhammad (pbuh) and his Companions with tearful eyes, Gülen resembles Imam Malik, who would not leave Medina due to his love of the Prophet. In his weeping over his shortcomings, weaknesses and errors, he resembles Hasan al-Basri (642-728), who is considered one of the leading *Salaf al-Saliheen*. Gülen has been in a state of self-exile for the last sixteen years just as Imam al-Ghazali (1058–1111) was at the beginning of the eleventh century for almost ten years in Damascus. As al-Ghazali's books were banned and burned for decades in North Africa, so too have Gülen's books have been banned and burned in Turkey, despite their content in no way threatening the established powers.

The founders of the Hanafi, Maliki, Shafi'i and Hanbali schools of law, the Ash'ari and Maturidi schools of theology and the Qadiri and Naqshbandi orders of Sufism, all suffered unjustly at the hands of rulers for many years, turning to God with their tears. Various type of leaders tried to discredit them and stop or limit their activities. They may have even succeeded to an extent. However, the influence of these great scholars is still continuing today and their principles have been and continue to be applied by hundreds of millions of Muslims. Similarly, this humble study argues that Gülen is striving to revive the way of the *Salaf al-Sa-*

---

and the day he/she leaves the office must be the same financially.

liheen in a form suitable for modern times, his example and principles in serving the needs of humanity will continue to be applied by more people in the future.

All the spiritual or religious movements, schools of thought, and orders with long life spans have been drenched in the tears of their leaders and followers who faced pain and suffering. The sincere tears of Gülen and those affiliated with the movement have nurtured the growth of the movement and will prolong its life span.

A close friend of Gülen calls him "*asrin dertlisi*"—the most grief-stricken person of this century. Indeed, Gülen has faced immense difficulties throughout his life, facing more as he became more passionate about reviving the principles of Islam and pursuing the cause of educa-tion. In this way, he has suffered for others. He has listened to those who are suffering and worked very hard to find solutions for them. He weeps together with those who are weeping. Those who have been near him or with him since the late 1960s have all told me that not a single day would pass wherein Gülen did not weep or grieve for the pain of others. Those similar to Gülen have had more foes than followers in their lifetime such Imam Azam and Imam Rabbani. However, decades or even centuries lat-er, the names of their foes are forgotten but their names have lived on in people's hearts. Their examples and works have enlightened humanity.

Gülen is a scholar who will be known for his tearful eyes. His students describe his devotion to worship as "the room with the light that never dims or turns off." This phrase denotes Gülen's devotion. Not only during the day but throughout the night, Gülen is busy with worship, making *dhikr* (remembering God), reading, writing or con-templating.

His firmness in faith, devotion to worship, crying in anguish over the state of humanity, his compassion towards all creation and his sin-cerity in action have earned him a high degree of heroism in the eyes of many people. This is only strengthened by his altruism, ascetic life and depth of and mastery over religious knowledge.

1.1 Who is Fethullah Gülen?

"Muhammad Fethullah Gülen" is one the most influential and contro-versial spiritual leaders of our time. Even though Gülen sees himself as an ordinary Muslim, many intellectuals, scholars and politicians see him as unique.[8] He is considered the spiritual leader of one of the biggest transnational faith-based movement in the Muslim world, despite Gülen having never accepted any such leadership. He has dedicated his life to the cause of education. Despite all the accusations, persecution and imprisonment, Gülen has never ceased to educate others as long as his health allows. He has had diabetes, heart problems and hypertension since the early 1980s. His pupils view him as a compassionate father. Some intellectuals have referred to Gülen as *"Dhul Janahayn"*, that is, a scholar who excels at both religious and secular sciences. He is also known as "the man whose actions precede his words."

In this section, first, I will very briefly inform the readers about the history of Gülen's family, his childhood and youth. Secondly, I will cover his life journey from being assigned as an imam to the Üç Şerefeli Mosque in Edirne and then the Kestanepazarı Qur'anic Boarding School in Izmir, one of the most populated cities of Turkey. Thirdly, his life period from 1980 to 1999 will be touched upon.

This section has two arguments. First, no individual in the contemporary Muslim world has been as discriminated against, insulted, persecuted, imprisoned and attacked by all camps during his/her whole life as Gülen. Secondly, Gülen has faced the same challenge and fate of all great scholars in the Islamic history in not being understood.

I have been collecting information about him for many years. I have listened to more than one thousand of his sermons and speeches. I have also read most of his works, some more than once. Furthermore, I analysed more than fifty interviews on Irmak TV and Mefkure TV channels in which interviewees spoke about his personality. In addition, this research also includes my personal observations of Gülen.

He is the author of over seventy books and some of them are translated into more than forty languages including English. With the exception of his books, Gülen does not have any worldly possessions. Gülen donates ninety percent of his royalty income to poor students[9] or humanitarian aid organisations. However, since the early 1970s many claims have been made about what he possesses, while questioning the

---

8   Ali Ünal, *M. Fethullah Gülen, Bir Portre Denemesi* (Izmir: Nil Yayınları, 2002), 13.

9   Salih Yücel, ""Fethullah Gülen: Spiritual Leader in a Global Islamic Context"," *Journal of Religion and Society*, Vol. 12 (2010), 8.

transparency of the Hizmet Movement's financial sources. Some media groups even claimed that he has a net value of billions of dollars. Gülen responded to these claims by indicating that all Hizmet institutions operate according to the law of the countries where they are established. Almost all are operated as charitable organisations. The authorities have audited their financial sources every year since they have been established. Neither Gülen nor his relatives own any of these institutions.

He mobilises and inspires millions of people to open educational institutions throughout one hundred and seventy countries. Since 1986 he has spent most of his life in seclusion. He has been under the scrutiny of the Turkish state since the age of eighteen, when he became an imam at the Üç Şerefeli Mosque in Edirne. To date, over two hundred doctoral dissertations have focused on him in various universities. The Muslim World journal published a special issue about him. Thousands of academic and news articles are written about him. Many leading global media groups from various countries have interviewed him, including CNN, BBC, PBS, CBS, ABC, Deutsche Welle, *The New York Times*, *Le Monde*, *The Wall Street Journal*, *The Washington Post*, Sputnik, Reuters, *Politico*, *Foreign Policy*, *The Guardian*, *Al-Hayat*, *Al-Khabar* and many others.[10]

1.2 Childhood and first discrimination

Gülen's official date of birth is April 27, 1941. However, he was born in 1938, in Korucuk Village in Pasinler, Erzurum. According to Gülen's brother Sıbgatullah, his father wanted to name him Fethullah, but the registrar declined due to the name having the word "Allah" in it. There was very strict and aggressive secularist policy against anything related to religion including the naming of an infant. Later, with the assistance of a top sergeant of the military guard post in the village, his father was able to register the name on April 27, 1941. Thus, Gülen was discriminated against from the day of his birth. To attain a better understanding of who Fethullah Gülen is, it is necessary to inform the readers his family background briefly.

Salih Selimoğlu has traced Gülen's family line back seven generations. Gülen's maternal line traces back to Sayyid Hamza, a descendant

---

10 For detail of interviews see www.fgulen.com/en/press/news. Retrieved on 17.04.2016.

of the Prophet. However, Gülen does not want this to be known. When he was asked about it by the researchers, Gülen reluctantly responded a few times with "it is said"[11] and he was hesitant to talk about the issue. From the maternal and paternal side, all of them were well known and respected for their piety, generosity and contribution to society. Sending role-model families to newly conquered regions was a tradition in the Ottoman system. Selimoğlu found out that Gülen's family was sent to Egypt in the sixteenth century, but later, due to a local revolt against the Ottomans, they were settled in Erzurum, a city in northeast Anatolia.[12] Historically, Gülen's family was well known and respected by the Ottoman sultans and the people in the region. Şükrü Pasha and Kurt Ismail Pasha are two highly respected figures from Gülen's maternal line who played an important role in the Ottoman army.

Gülen recalls his lineage like this: "My great-grandfather, Halil, had two sons, Süleyman Efendi and Mullah Ahmad. Mullah Ahmad is the father of my grandfather Şamil Ağa. Mullah Ahmad was a knowledgeable and pious person. In the last thirty years of his life, he never slept on a bed because he spent most of his night in worship. He would have short naps and then resume his worship." Mullah Ahmad was quite keen on reading books. It is noted that he would eat little, sometimes only having a few olives a day and he continued this ascetic lifestyle until he passed away. "My father was somewhat critical of Mullah Ahmad because of his very strict ascetic lifestyle," Gülen continues. "My grandfather Şamil Ağa had similar attributes to those of his father, Mullah Ahmad. Şamil Ağa was also known as a man of God. He appeared not to belong to this world and would always make an effort for life in the Hereafter. During the most difficult times with such aggressive secularism on the rise that it even made it obligatory for men to wear European caps instead of turbans, my grandfather continued to wear his turban.[13] His turban was

---

11 Personal communication, December 27, 2016.

12 Şemsinur Özdemir, *Hoca Anne ve Ailesi* (Istanbul: Ufuk Yayınları, 2014), 19-20.

13 On October 25, 1925, Atatürk introduced the 'Hat Law', which was part of the revolution. Instead of the *turban* or *fez*, it became mandatory for men to wear a hat in Turkey. Those who disobeyed were persecuted and jailed. When many people disobeyed the Hat Law in the Rize region, the city was bombarded by a warship. Seventeen people were killed, over twenty people sentenced to twenty years in prison, and fourteen

similar to that of the founder of the Ottoman Empire, Osman Ghazi's turban. All the residents of the village would respect and honor him as he was a man of dignity. Şamil Ağa would respect scholars who practiced their religion while not being content with non-practising scholars."

According to Osman Şimşek, a student of Gülen, Şamil Ağa would pray one hundred *rakats* (units) *Salat* (ritual Prayer) every night. Gülen would observe his grandfather with admiration and sometimes would pray with him until he fell asleep.[14] Gülen further recalls, "Once my grandfather hugged me and his eyes were full of tears when I was eight years old. I will never forget that experience."

According to Gülen's sister Nurhayat, her grandmother Munise Khatun was very pious, generous and had an ascetic life.[15] Gülen's mother Refia stated that Munise Khatun fasted every day for twelve years.[16] She would eat once a day and talk little. Whenever Munise Khatun read or recited the Qur'an, she would weep. She was also very vigilant about the *Tahajjud* (night vigil) Prayer.[17]

Gülen's father, Ramiz Efendi, was an imam and well respected in the Erzurum region. He had a brilliant memory and was well versed in Islamic sciences. According to Gülen, his father memorised Mehmet Zihni Efendi's *fiqh* book *Ni'matul Islam*[18] which consists more than six hundred pages. Imam Ramiz knew the biographies of the Companions by heart.[19] Memorisation of the Qur'an, hadiths, the most influential scholars' books and poems is a very strong intellectual tradition in the history of Islam. Imam Ramiz was also known for his piety, generosity and witty personality. Imam Ramiz would invoke God's Name or recite the Qur'an when he walked. Sometimes he would recite spiritual poems. Gülen later would indicate that he memorised *Qasida al-Burdah*

---

people were executed. However, the Hat Law was observed less in rural areas due to ineffective control by the state. Nevzat Çiçek, www.timeturk.com/tr/2012/12/12/sapka-yuzunden-rize-bugun-bombaladi.html#.VDfVXhbVh2k retrieved 26.11.2016.

14   Osman Şimşek, *İbretlik Hatıralar* (Izmir: Işık Yayınları, 2010), 235–236.

15   Özdemir, *Hoca Anne ve Ailesi*, 41–43.

16   Ibid., 41.

17   Ibid., 41–43.

18   Ibid., 83–84.

19   Ibid., 97.

from his father. [20] *Qasida al-Burdah* is a thirty-three-page ode of praise for Prophet Muhammad (pbuh) composed by Imam al-Busairi (1211–1294). Gülen's parents were well-known in the region because of their piety.

Gülen recalls, "My dad would put a muzzle on our oxen, cows and horse when they passed by a garden or a planted field due to his piety and sensitivity for caring other people's rights and property. I have applied this principle of my fathers throughout my entire life in relation to piety and other's rights."[21] Gülen's brother, Kutbettin, recollects, "When my father reached the age of sixty-four, he cried. The reason was that he knew that Prophet Muhammad (pbuh) lived sixty-three years and living more than him made him burst into tears." Imam Ramiz would cry while delivering his sermons on Fridays. He viewed the *sahabah*, the Companions of the Prophet (pbuh), as a walking Qur'an. He can be considered as an admirer and lover of the *sahabah*. Gülen would later go on to note that his father inspired in his heart the love of the *sahabah*. Due to his father's influence on him, at a very young age Gülen saw every *sahabah* as a great hero. This would lead Gülen to study the biographies of approximately ten thousand of them and he memorised their names at a young age.[22]

Gülen's mother, Refia Hatun, was a very pious, devoted and generous woman. She taught the Qur'an voluntarily in the morning and did the housework for the rest of day until she passed away. In addition, she would feed or give sweets to her students and care about their needs. Gülen recalls his childhood days in the village: "Due to aggressive secularism, the gendarme raided our house two times because my mother was teaching the Qur'an."[23] Any day when she did not have a guest in her home would be a day that left her heartbroken. Refia would spend two hours on *dhikr* daily.[24] She would not breastfeed her children without performing an ablution first. While Refia suckled her children, she would make *dhikr* or recite *salawat* (blessings on the Prophet) and ab-

---

20 Ibid., 85.

21 Fethullah Gülen, *Kalbin Zümrüt Tepeleri* (Izmir: Nil Yayınları, 2011), 107.

22 It is said that there were more than hundred thousand *Sahabah*. However, the names of only ten thousand of them are in the record books.

23 Özdemir, *Hoca Anne ve Ailesi*, 67.

24 Ibid., 27.

stain from worldly talk.[25]

Gülen's grandmother and mother would sometimes shed tears when the Qur'an was recited or *dhikr* was performed in their homes.[26] According to Gülen and his brother Kutbettin's testimonials, their parents would often host the great scholars, imams, travellers and Sufi sheikhs of northeast Turkey. At the age of four or five, Gülen would love and have great respect for these special guests. He was keen to listen and learn from them during their visits. According to Gülen's brother Sıbgatullah, from his early childhood Gülen preferred to sit with those who were older than him. Imam Ramiz and Refia taught the Qur'an to all their children before the age of five.[27]

According to Selimoğlu, both Imam Ramiz and Refia were very devoted to the daily obligatory Prayers. For them, not praying was equal to commit a murder.[28] This is a highly idealistic expression in Turkish culture which shows the importance of the daily ritual Prayer. Otherwise, not praying cannot be equal to killing in Islam. They paid attention to their children's performing their obligatory Prayer even before the age of seven. Thus, Kutbettin states that none of his brothers and sister can remember the date they began to perform the obligatory Prayer because of they were so young at the time. Gülen began to pray at the age of five. He has never abandoned his daily Prayers since then.

Gülen attended primary school in his village in 1946. Although his primary school teacher loved Gülen and she was very kind to him, the principal punished him for praying at school. This led Gülen to leave formal education and pursue a traditional *madrasa* education. Gülen would never forget his primary school teacher and still from time to time would call her and send gifts. Gülen was a child prodigy with a photographic memory. While herding the family flock, he read all the books his father had at home and finished memorising the entire Qur'an by the age nine.[29] It was a tradition in that region to organise a ceremony of thanksgiving for a child who had memorised

---

25   Ibid., 71.

26   Ibid., 81.

27   Ibid., 73.

28   Ibid., 63.

29   Mehmet Özalp, "Muhammad Fethullah Gülen", in *Great Spiritual Leaders: Studies in*

the Qur'an. Consequently, Gülen's parents held a ceremony and invited neighbours, relatives and all people in the village for the ceremony of mastering the Qur'an. It was similar to a wedding. Delicious food was served as a banquet, supplications made and everyone congratulated Gülen. His mother told Gülen at the ceremony, "My darling, this is your wedding." Gülen's face turned red with embarrassment. However, it was one of the happiest days for Gülen's family. He also took Arabic lessons from his father and learned the art of Qur'anic recitation from al-Qari (a person who recites the Qur'an with the proper rules of recitation) Sıtkı Efendi.

Gülen was not just excellent at reading but also at helping at home. He would help his mother at home in all types of work and would receive special treatment in the family, particularly from his parents. Then, with his parents' permission, he moved to Erzurum to study Islamic sciences. Gülen recalls his early days: "I was studying in Erzurum and few students plus myself lived in a small room in the vicinity of a mosque. It was difficult even to find a place to lie down to sleep at night. I would not stretch my leg towards the Ka'ba direction when I slept." He thought that this would be disrespectful to the Ka'ba. Some scholars in history practised a similar tradition. Imam Malik (711–795) and Ahmad ibn Hanbal (780–855) are two prominent examples.

Gülen studied Arabic, all Islamic *usul* (methodology) sciences, theology, and the major *tafsirs* (Qur'anic exegesis) at a young age in depth and knows by heart almost all hadiths, biographies of the Companions and Said Nursi's work *Risale-i Nur*. Later on, he also studied the theories of modern social and physical sciences. Gülen has a solid grasp of Islamic history and Sufism as well. He is not a Sufi, nor does he belong to any order but as Zeki Sarıtoprak argues "he is Sufi in his own way"[30] like Imam al-Ghazali (1058–1111).

Gülen reads a lot, from six to seven hours per day. According to Mehmet Eldem a friend of Gülen since 1974, he would read over three

---

Leadership for a Pluralist Society, ed. Seforosa Carroll and William W. Emilsen (Canberra: Barton Books, 2014), 35.

30 Zeki Sarıtoprak, "Fethullah Gülen: A Sufi in His Own Way", in *Turkish Islam and the Secular State: the Gülen Movement*, ed. M. H. Yavuz and J. L. Esposito (Syracuse: Syracuse University Press, 2003), 169.

hundred pages per day. However, after he became permanently ill, he had to reduce his daily reading to 150–200 pages a day.

Gülen memorised the poems of Mehmet Akif Ersoy and some poems of prominent poets such Imam Busairi (1211–1294), Mawlana Jalal Din Rumi (1204–1273), Abd al–Rahman Jami (1414–1492), Sheikh Sa'di Shirazi (1193–1291), Sayyid Nasimi (1369–1417), Dhun Nun al–Misri (796–859) and many others. Memorising poems is part of the Islamic intellectual tradition, and many great scholars knew many poems by heart. According to Ali Ünsal, who attended Gülen's study circles for many years, once Gülen stated that he could recite poems by heart for twenty hours without a break. In addition to Islamic sciences, he studied Western classics such as Aristotle (384–322 BC), Marcus Aurelius (121–180), Immanuel Kant (1724–1804), Albert Camus (1913–1960) and Jean-Paul Sartre (1905–1980).[31]

After completing his studies in Islamic sciences, he attended Muhammed Lütfi's study circle in 1954. Muhammed Lütfi was a descendant of Prophet Muhammad (pbuh),[32] a Naqshibandi sheikh and a poet and well educated in Islamic sciences. He left a permanent mark on Gülen's spiritual life. He guided him in matters of spirituality, gnostic knowledge and religious practices. It can be argued that he was the first person after his parents who injected the importance of education in Gülen's soul. Gülen recalls: "Muhammed Lütfi Efendi valued education so much once he said that even if he heard the Ka'ba was damaged, he would still prefer to donate to a scholarship instead of the Ka'ba's reconstruction."[33] When the Russians occupied Erzurum, Muhammed Lütfi fought against the occupation with sixty volunteers from his village. Gülen often refers to him in his speeches, and he knows most of Muhammed Lütfi's poems by heart.

After Muhammed Lütfi had passed away, Gülen continued to study traditional Islam in *madrasa* under leading scholars in Erzurum. Some of his close associates say that Gülen has a photographic memory. He would almost memorise or learn inside out any book that he read.

---

31 Ali Ünal and Alphonse Williams, *Advocate of Dialogue: Fethullah Gülen* (Fairfax: The Fountain, 2000), 16.

32 Özdemir, *Hoca Anne ve Ailesi*, 25.

33 Ibid., 29.

However, later, Gülen stated that after a certain age, he had to read twice to know a book inside out. This photographic memory can be observed in his daily conversations in his study and private circles. I attended his study circle of *hadith*, *tafsir* and *fiqh* on numerous occasions as part of the audience. I was very impressed by how Gülen knew by heart the biographies of Companions, hadith narrators (*rijals*) and details of their life, and Said Nursi's work *Risale-i Nur*, as well as many Arabic, Turkish and Persian poems.

One of his pupils said that "Gülen knows the Companions of Prophet and Hadith narrators' (*rijal*) lives as he knows his own family members and relatives." All of those who attend his study circles are aware and can understand his level of knowledge. Therefore, Ali Bulaç states that this degree of knowledge and expertise in the methodology of all Islamic disciplines, as well as his understanding of modernity and the modern world, makes Gülen a *Dhul Janahayn* scholar.[34] Gülen does not only write or talk but his ideas have also been institutionalised in over one hundred and seventy countries. Aydın Bolak, the former chairman of the Turkish Industrialists' and Businessmen's Association, says that "Gülen injected idealism into the soul of the Turkish youth."[35]

During the six months that I spent near him, I did not cease to be amazed by his prodigious memory. He would remember an event that others would quickly forget. When a man who had hosted him overnight from Colorado approximately ten years before came to visit him, Gülen recalled the names of all of his children. In addition to remembering the names of many visitors, he also often remembers their children's names as well, even after only having met them once or twice. I have witnessed many other cases of Gülen's prodigious memory.

One of the turning points of his life was when he met Said Nursi's student, Muzaffer Aslan, who exposed him to the theological writings and the non-political, non-violent religious activism of Said Nursi[36] in 1956. He began to attend Nur study circles where Nursi's works were studied collectively and which were organised by Mehmet Kırkıncı, known as Kırkıncı Hodja, who was one of Nursi's disciples in Erzurum.

---

34 A scholar who is very good at religious and worldly sciences.

35 Ünal and Williams, *Advocate of Dialogue*, 22.

36 Mehmet Özalp, "Muhammad Fethullah Gülen", 35.

Gülen was inspired by the deep spiritual life of Nursi and his golden rules for serving humanity and would later apply them as principles of the Hizmet Movement. His greatest objective and achievement was to educate the younger generation in both secular and religious sciences, in order to solve the issue of ignorance and protect them from spiritual diseases.[37] Gülen said, "I was very impressed with *Risale-i Nur* and have continued to study it." To this day, he reads *Risale-i Nur* almost daily together with his students.

There is a historical tradition that was initiated by Pir Ali Baba approximately five hundred years ago in Erzurum. Every Ramadan the congregation reads 1001 *khatim* (reading the entire Qur'an) and the supplications of the *khatims* are done collectively in the mosque. Gülen stayed in that mosque one night before the 1001 *khatim* ceremony and cried the whole night. He prayed to be accepted by the Nur Group, not just for physical participation, but also spiritually in the sight of God. After the Morning Prayer, he listened to the preacher of the mosque. When he sought to leave the mosque, his close friend, Hashmet Hodja, appeared at the gate. He spoke to Gülen, indicating that he had seen Said Nursi in his dream. In the dream, Nursi sent a letter to Gülen and gave Hashmet some walnuts. Gülen was so excited and wept for a while. He interpreted this dream as an indication of spiritual acceptance into the Nur study circle. Gülen preached voluntarily for three years in Erzurum, Amasya, Tokat and Sivas provinces from 1955 to 1958. Gradually, he became well known in the region.

1.3 Youthful mosque imam

In 1959, Gülen was assigned by the Turkish Presidency of Religious Affairs to be a deputy imam at the Üç Şerefeli Mosque in Edirne, a historical city. Abdullah Aymaz, who has been close to him since 1967, recalls: "Accepting such a position was a bit of a mystery. Why did Gülen insist on being an imam in Edirne when there were other and better opportunities in Erzurum or nearby cities?" Later, Aymaz found out that at the age of seventeen Gülen saw Said Nursi in his dream. Nursi asked him to go and serve Islam in Edirne. After that dream, Gülen wished to go. However, his parents did not want him to go to Edirne as it was a

---

37 Personal communication, April 4, 2006

city situated on the western border of Turkey and approximately 1,800 kilometres away from his hometown. Edirne was a cosmopolitan city, and no imam at the time would want to go there. In addition, culturally speaking, it would not have been acceptable in Erzurum at that time for someone to leave their hometown at the age of seventeen and to live in a faraway town. Gülen did not want to disobey his parents and break their hearts. However, he had a plan in his mind. According to Aymaz, one day Gülen's mother prepared breakfast and called him, but he opened the Qur'an and began reading and did not respond to his mother's call. Similarly, he did not respond his mother at dinner time and next day at breakfast time again. Then his parents understood that Gülen was committed to a cause and allowed him to go to Edirne.

One of his close associates, Professor Suat Yıldırım, the former Dean of the Faculty of Divinity at the University of Sakarya, shared the same house with Gülen in Edirne for six months. He recalls:

> I have known Gülen since he was an imam in the beginning of 1959. He would read many books and devoted himself to education. He reads Eastern and Western classics. This is Gülen's defining characteristic that set him apart from the contemporary imams and religious leaders. With a portion of his salary, he would buy books and journals, read them and then give to others to read… Gülen would spend a portion of his time daily in Edirne's library where he would read historical books. He had and still has an ascetic lifestyle; he would eat little, sleep only a few hours and spent a significant part of his day in worship.[38]

While serving as an imam in Edirne, from time to time, the police would interrogate him because he was conducting study circles at the mosque with a few youth in the evenings. Despite these obstacles, Gülen would not abandon his support of the young people in these activities. Gülen notes that since that time he has been under scrutiny and surveillance by the police and Turkish National Intelligence Service.

According to Yıldırım, Gülen would give some of his salary to poor students. Later, Gülen would move to the Üç Şerefeli Mosque and lived in one of the window alcoves, which was approximately two by one-and-a-half metres, just big enough to sleep in. All he owned

---

38 Yücel, "Fethullah Gülen: Spiritual Leader in a Global Islamic Context", 1–19.

at that time was two blankets, two plates, a teacup and a spoon.[39] He would use one blanket to sleep on and the other one to cover himself. The region had very low temperatures during the winter period. Gülen would eat little, sleep less, and spend most of his time reading books and performing supererogatory Prayers. Sometimes he would voluntarily not eat anything for a few days, aiming to attain an ascetic lifestyle and purification of his *nafs* (carnal soul). Osman Şimşek, who has been in Gülen's study circle for more than sixteen years, narrates from Gülen's memories in his book *İbretlik Hatıralar* (Exemplary Recollections), which is dedicated to Gülen's life. He asserts that Ottoman Sultan Murad II (1404–1451)[40] would call Gülen in his dream or sometimes in a vision saying, "Wake up, Fethullah, for the *Salat* (Prayer)."[41] Gülen used the mosque window as his accommodation for two-and-a-half years. Those years can be considered as a retreat for him. While residing there Gülen would pay an amount of money for the mosque's electricity and the water which he consumed. Generally, none of the imams of any mosques would pay or were required to pay for these utilities. This two-and-a-half-year retreat was a turning point in his spiritual journey.

Right after the aggressive secularists' military coup in 1960, he was interrogated by the military. A secularist officer sought to push him down the stairway of a building, murder him, and then declare his death as a suicide. However, the Police Chief of Edirne intervened and saved Gülen.[42] Later, Gülen said that the sudden appearance of the police chief was unexpected at that time in the army building.

At the age of twenty, Gülen was conscripted into the army. He was a volunteer imam in the regiment's *masjid* (Prayer hall) while he was performing his national service. During the mandatory military service in Iskenderun, Gülen would not eat the food served there. He would purchase his food from the canteen. On the issue of using public places, *waqf* (charitable) institutions and tax payers'

---

39 Şimşek, *İbretlik Hatıralar*, 85.

40 According to some sources Üç Şerefeli Mosque was built by the Ottoman Sultan Murad II when Edirne was the capital city before the conquest of Istanbul.

41 Şimşek, *İbretlik Hatıralar*, 241.

42 Personal communication, 26.12.2016

money, Gülen is very sensitive. He does not use or, if he has to use it out of necessity, then he pays for it. For Gülen, this is the vital and uncompromisable principle of "*istighna*"; it will be examined later in Chapter 7.

In 1963, a military coup was attempted by a Marxist group led by Colonel Talat Aydemir. Gülen was an ordinary soldier in Aydemir's regiment with more than three thousand troops. Although he had no relation with the coup, he was arrested but later released. After he completed his national service, he was assigned as a Qur'an teacher at the Dar ul-Hadis mosque in Edirne in 1964.

1.4 The seeds of Hizmet

In 1966, Gülen was assigned by the Director of Presidency of Religious Affairs to Izmir as a preacher and Qur'an course teacher. Gülen would teach during daytime as required and after hours and at weekends work voluntarily at Kestanepazarı Qur'anic Boarding School. He would not accept any payment for his overtime. In a short period, Gülen built strong relationships with the students. Aymaz, who was a student at the Qur'anic course, recalls how all the students respected and loved him: "Gülen was teaching through his actions more than words. In a short period, Gülen was able to conquer the hearts and minds of students. He treated and looked after them as his though they were his younger brothers. He would attend to their needs." Aymaz states that "Gülen would spend half of his salary on the poor students but no one knew at the time." Years later, these students who received financial help revealed how Gülen supported them in a confidential way and asked them not to discuss this with anyone. This was because by doing so he would refrain from any showing off and he wanted to be known just as an ordinary Muslim. Furthermore, in Islam, sometimes giving charity in secret is better than giving it openly.

Residing in a small timber hut in the garden of the institution, Gülen began to form the foundation of the Hizmet Movement with a small group of benefactors and dedicated students.[43] Aymaz remembers the significant effort of Gülen in educating students in all Islamic sciences: "He was so eager to teach us and many of the students were eager to

---

43 Özalp, "Muhammad Fethullah Gülen", 36.

learn. Gülen was not just a teacher but also a role model for the students." Before Gülen's arrival and teaching, the students would learn how to read Qur'an and memorise a part of it without understanding the meaning. Mehmet Ali Şengül, one of the students at the Qur'anic course recalls:

> Once Gülen gathered all of us. I told him that I had been *hafidh* (one who has memorised the entire Qur'an) for fourteen years. Gülen asked me to recite some chapters which I did and then asked me to provide the meaning of three Qur'anic verses but I could not. Then, he asked about two hundred students the same question and none of them could tell the meaning of the three verses. He turned to me and said, "You have been reading a book for fourteen years but you don't know the meaning." So, he began to teach Arabic to some of us to understand the Qur'an. Following this event, he educated some students in secular sciences to succeed in the university exams. In about two years, sixteen students were able to study in the universities. He sent each student to a different faculty.

But such religious activities meant the risk of being sentenced to a minimum of two years in jail in that era of Jacobin secularism in Turkey.

Hasan Üzümcü, who has been near Gülen since then and was a Board Member of Kestanepazarı Qur'anic Boarding School in the late 1960s, recalls: "A year after his arrival, Gülen called the board members and asked us to rent sixteen apartment units for the university students in a week. I told him we have sixteen students only and four units will be sufficient." Initially, Üzümcü could not understand his plan. Gülen added, "Hasan Bey, you did not understand. I would like to put each of these students in charge of one unit. Then we will provide free accommodation for poor students who come to Izmir to study." Üzümcü continued, "so we rented sixteen units but had no money to furnish them. Gülen visited me at home and asked how many bedrooms I had. I said three. He said, 'since you have only one child, two bedrooms is sufficient. Please take the furniture of the third room for the students' units. Also, you have extra kitchenware, donate it to a unit as well.' So he visited all the board members' homes and similarly told them to donate some furniture to the students' units. The students who were studying medicine would stay in one unit; education would live in another unit and so on."

They were able to accommodate more than sixty students that year.

Gülen then asked Üzümcü to provide the basic needs of these students such as rice, sugar, fruit, oil, and so on. Each board member would look after two or three units and attend to the needs of the students. Gülen himself took care of each student. He cooked for them, washed their dishes, vacuumed the units, and organised volunteer tutors for their studying. Furthermore, he educated them in private study circles in the Islamic sciences, specifically in faith. In less than one year, all sixty students were ready to serve Islam and the community voluntarily. Üzümcü says, "Gülen was a role model for them. He taught moral values through his actions more than in words." The following year the number of students tripled and this growth continued every year afterwards. Then Gülen assigned the well-educated and dedicated ones to other cities after they had graduated from different universities. The same system has been applied in other towns, and the Hizmet Movement continued to grow in this way in Turkey in the early 1970s.

Enver İlhami Küçüktepe, who has known Gülen since 1956, recalls how those who served religion were persecuted. It was even forbidden to read some religious books such as Said Nursi's works. From 1927 to 1960, in over 1,500 cases, people who read Nursi's books were prosecuted and sentenced to jail. To serve religion meant to take the risk of the minimum two-year sentence. He further recalls, "Once I was travelling by bus. The gendarme stopped the bus and searched our luggage. They found Said Nursi's work, *Küçük Sözler*, a small book with sixty pages, in my case. There is nothing related to politics in this book. However, the gendarme interrogated me, followed by an arrest. I spent two months in jail for carrying that small booklet." Despite all the pressure, Gülen was reading Nursi's works to us in his little temporary hut next to the mosque. Abdullah Ünal Birlik, the son of Said Nursi's student, Mustafa Birlik, remembers how the police raided their home on numerous occasions. He stated that "the police would search even inside our beds at home. Many times, they interrogated my father for reading Nursi's works. But still, Gülen and my dad continued to teach Nursi's works in study circles."

Immediately after the 1971 coup, Gülen and more than fifty of his students were arrested on charges of attempting to alter the secular regime and bring *sharia* law to Turkey. He was released on all charges after six months of imprisonment. When Gülen was released from jail, none of his friends and students greeted him at the gate. It was a difficult time and being near or around Gülen meant taking the risk of being sentenced. It was a heartbreaking day for Gülen. He went to Erzurum to visit his parents and his family but did not stay for a long period as he returned to Izmir and continued his service.

In 1972, the Presidency of Religious Affairs assigned Gülen as a preacher to Edremit, a small town over 220 kilometres from Izmir. While he was working there, Gülen would return frequently to Izmir to continue his voluntary Islamic service. Once, he had a gathering with the people who had helped him in the Islamic service before the military coup. He mentioned the importance of helping students and educating them for the future and the benefit of society. Some of them were very hesitant to be affiliated with Gülen for fear of the military. He was very upset and suffered for them. Shedding tears, he asked them how they could possibly discontinue performing the *hizmet*. Yusuf Pekmezci, a middle-class businessman and a dedicated and pious Muslim, stood up and said, "Sir, I would sacrifice everything, including my soul, in the service of Islam."[44] A few more endorsed Pekmezci. Gülen would never forget those few people who took the risk of being sentenced to jail and dedicated themselves despite the pressure from the military. They kept on sacrificing their time and money for the service, and those who are still alive are continuing to perform the service. With those few dedicated middle-class businessmen and Gülen's students, the Hizmet Movement rapidly grew, with the spread of student boarding facilities throughout the Aegean Region in the late 1970s.

1.5. First hajj in 1968

Gülen recollects: "In 1968, I was teaching at the Kestanepazarı Qur'an Course. I had a very strong desire to go on hajj and it was a great dream for me. I was very eager to visit the holy places [in Mecca and Medina]. I was hoping to be called or invited." However, financially, he was not able to go. Whenever he heard someone was going on hajj, Gülen would visit him and send his greetings to the Prophet and request that they supplicate in his place. Gülen recalls:

Once I was thinking about hajj during my teaching and unexpectedly one of

---

44 Şimşek, *İbretlik Hatıralar*, 281–282.

the students (most likely it was İbrahim Çalışkan) asked me, "Are you thinking about going on hajj?" Upon hearing this, I could not stop my tears and left the class. I went to my room and continued weeping for a while. After a few hours, I received a phone call from Lütfi Doğan, the Deputy of the Presidency of Religious Affairs, and he told me that I was assigned to lead pilgrims as cleric that year. I thought I was dreaming. It was the first time in Turkey's history, the Presidency of Religious Affairs was sending three members of the clergy on hajj as a guide and I was one of them.

Gülen continues: "At the Hajj, I almost never left the Ka'ba except on a few occasions. I devoted my time to performing *umrah*s (minor pilgrimage), worshipping and supplications. I performed three *umrah*s per day. I performed an *umrah* for the Prophet, four for each of the four Rightly Guided Caliphs, some great scholars and my grandparents." According to some of his companions on hajj, Gülen would touch the wall of the Ka'ba (at *multazam*) and cry a lot. They called him "*çok ağlayan hoca*" or "the imam who cries a lot." Touching the wall of the Ka'ba at the *multazam* section, supplicating and crying is considered a *sunnah* of the Prophet.

1.6 Why Gülen did not marry

It was, and still to a certain extent is, a tradition for men to get married after completing one's education and military service, which is mandatory in Turkey. After his military service, Gülen's parents and his Uncle Enver wanted him to marry. His mother, Refia, told Gülen, "My darling, I would like you to get married before I die." This is an expression in Turkish culture for a mother to demonstrate how she loves and care for her child who is at the age of marriage. However, Gülen did not accept due to his intention to dedicate himself entirely to the service of Islam, despite his parents and uncle's insistence. His uncle told him, "Now we have insisted you get married, but you declined. Keep it in mind. There will be one more attempt when you are at the age of thirty. After that, there will be no more."

Gülen recollects that when reached thirty, the Mufti of Izmir, Yaşar Tunagür, who loved Gülen very much and cared for him as his son, once came to his office. His aim was to persuade Gülen to get married. He spoke to him fervently and even mentioned the name of a pious girl whose family Tunagür had known for a long time. Gülen kindly declined but Tunagür insisted. Gülen hugged him with tearful eyes and told him. "Sir, if you cannot understand me [why I am not marrying], then who can understand me?" Next day, in the early morning, one of Gülen's close friends came to his office in a rush and told him: "I saw Prophet Muhammad (pbuh) in my dream last night. He sent his salaams (greetings) to you and then he said that 'If Fethullah gets married, he will die on the day of the wedding and I will not attend his funeral service.'"[45] It may be difficult to understand for many why he did not marry. However, for those who have seen the Prophet in a dream, it is not difficult to comprehend. His uncle Enver was right, and after Tunagür's attempt, no one has asked Gülen for marriage again.

This dream issue is subjective and may not be understood by some people. Even some are critical of Gülen because he has not married, which is one of the *sunnah* of the Prophet. There is no vow of celibacy in Islam. However, there are some Companions of the Prophet among the *Ashab Suffa* (the People of the Bench) who lived next to the mosque and never got married because they dedicated their lives to the cause of Islam. Similarly, some great scholars and figures in Islamic history never married. Rabia al-Adawiyyah (713–801), Bishr al-Hafi (767–850), Bayazid Bastami (804–874), Al-Tabari, (838–923), al-Zamakhshari (1070–1143), Imam Nawawi (1233–1277), Ibn Taymiyyah (1263–1328), Ahmad al-Badawi (1199–1276), and Said Nursi are just a few examples.

Osman Şimşek argues that Gülen followed in his spiritual master Said Nursi's footsteps and preferred *fard* (obligation) over *sunnah* in relation to marriage. Şimşek asserts that serving Islam is *fard* but marriage is *sunnah*. If he had married, Gülen would not be able to dedicate his entire life to serving Islam. When asked about marriage, many times Gülen has answered in the same way as Said Nursi, who said, "The suffering of the Islamic community is more than enough. I have not found time to think of myself."[46] Like Said Nursi, Gülen has led a celibate life not out of his own will, but as forty-six-year associate Nevzat Türk, who has been with Gülen since the early 1970s, puts it, he simply did not have the time.[47]

---

45 Ibid., 86.

46 Ibid., 86–88.

47 Özalp, "Muhammad Fethullah Gülen", 37.

If he had married, he would not be able to dedicate all of his time to the cause of Islam. Also, he has suffered during most of his life because of persecution, imprisonment, exile and illnesses. If he had a wife who was not as strong spiritually, physically and psychologically as Gülen, it would be impossible for her to bear such a life. In addition, Gülen has lived an ascetic life for many years.

1.7 Fugitive in the 1980s

Hasan Üzümcü, who has been close to Gülen since the early 1970s, recalls, "After the military coup in September 1980, Gülen was among the wanted. His picture was hung on the walls throughout Turkey next to pictures of terrorists and communists. This meant that if he did not surrender, law enforcement could kill him wherever they found him and no one may ask them why he was killed." Gülen had to hide like a fugitive for six years. Later, Gülen told Üzümcü that once in the early 1980s he had no place to live and no money to spend. Sometimes, he slept in parks for many nights. His friends could provide accommodation for him in their houses but he did not want to put them at risk. If he were caught in someone's place, the owner of the house would be arrested and sentenced to more than two years in jail. Gülen had no salary but a little income from some of his publications. He would never ask for any help from anyone due to applying strictly *istighna*, the principle of indebtedness and serving without expectation. He sold his coat and tape recorder to pay for his basic needs. He had to leave Izmir, went to a nearby mountain, and lived in a cave for more than a month. Gülen had only bread and water in his time in the cave because he could not afford to buy anything else. The police and military were looking for him everywhere. They frequently raided his relatives, students and friends' houses in the attempt to arrest him. A few times he was about to be caught in the raids but at the last minute, he was able to escape.

Although he was on the wanted list, Gülen did not give up serving the cause of Islam. He became more active, not in public, but in private circles. He visited some of his friends and students and consulted with them throughout Turkey. Despite his fugitive status, Gülen was able to meet secretly with some of Hizmet's regional and local leaders and middle-class people in business. He visited key persons in the Hizmet Movement and met with them face to face or in small groups. He was able to visit some of his friends and students in more than forty cities while on the run. Observing Gülen's dedication and observing his fearless mentality boosted the morale of Hizmet leaders known as *khadim*.[48] Gülen does not complain about those difficult days in his public or private speeches or his writings. According to his brother Kutbettin, not complaining about the challenges he has faced since his childhood is an ethical principle for Gülen. The author spent more than six months near him at times between 1999 and 2007, and sometimes he talked about the oppression and difficulties which he confronted in those years but, interestingly, he never blamed anyone, nor complained about those painful days.

While he was on the run for about six years, the Hizmet Movement would spread from twelve to over fifty cities throughout Turkey. New dormitories and students' houses[49]opened. Even a couple of high schools began educating pupils in the major cities such as Istanbul, Ankara, Izmir, Bursa, Konya and Kayseri. The circulation of *Sızıntı* monthly magazine of scientific and spiritual thought climbed to over 40,000 copies from 2,000. More tutoring centres opened to prepare lower- and middle-class families' children to pass their university exams. Mehmet Ali Şengül, a close associate of Gülen, recalls, "Despite all oppression, the Hizmet Movement spread faster than we expected. As part of Hizmet since the late 1960s, I see that Hizmet always expanded during the difficult times." Şengül argues that "Hizmet people become sincerer during the difficult times, and with little work much more is achieved. This is a

---

48 The details of *khadimhood*, leadership in the Hizmet Movement, will be explained in Chapter 4.

49 The students' houses are called ışık evleri which means "light houses." There are between five and seven students in each house. One of them who is better educated and altruistic will be in charge of the others. While studying in different universities, these students are educated in Islamic sciences to a certain extent, specifically about faith, jurisprudence, the life of the Prophet and his Companions through study circles. They perform their daily Prayer in congregation when they are at home. Also, the one who knows better will give voluntary tutorials. Some religious books, particularly Said Nursi's works are studied together. Students perform the Tahajjud and do dhikr for spiritual purification on a daily basis. Also, the local middle-class businessmen will provide for their basic needs, such furnishing the house, food, etc.

blessing from God."

In January 1986, Gülen was captured in Burdur by police and interrogated. He was sent to the State Security Court in Izmir, but no charge was laid against him. So, he was not arrested and finally, the court dismissed his case.[50] The main reason he was wanted was the military pressure on the judiciary. However, after the 1983 election, the law granting freedom of expression changed and gradually the military pressure eased. This gave the opportunity to judges to act according to the law.

1.8 Second hajj in 1986

Gülen missed Mecca and Medina very much. So he went on hajj again, this time with a few Hizmet-affiliated individuals. However, the description of him as "the man who has no rest and not allowed to rest" was true even in Medina. Gülen recalls, "When I was in the Prophet's mosque in Medina during hajj in 1986, I saw an institution in one of the corners of the mosque which was called "'amr bi'l ma'ruf, nahy ani'l munkar." It means the institution which "enjoins goods and forbids the unlawful." Similar institutions have been established in the history of Islam with the same purpose. Initially, he could not understand why such institutions existed in the Prophet's mosque. Since the people who visit there have a love of the Prophet and the sacred city, Gülen said, "I will never forget police arrested me during my visit to the grave of the Prophet. I could not understand why they did it. It might have been because of a few people around me asking questions. It looked like a small gathering, or perhaps because I had a few prayer beads in my hand, or it may have been because I was reading the Qur'an besides the tomb of the Prophet. It may be difficult for you to understand. Outside the Prophet's mosque, hundreds of shops were selling beads but I was not allowed to carry them with me in the mosque."[51] In the Wahhabis' view, visiting the grave of the Prophet is *bid'a* (innovation) and supplicating or reciting anything near a grave is also considered a sin and forbidden. In addition, for security reasons, the police do not allow even a few people to gather in the Prophet's Mosque or Ka'ba. So, Gülen was not even allowed to rest on hajj. However, he does not explain in detail what they did to him.

---

50 Ünal, *Bir Portre Denemesi*, 509.

51 Fethullah Gülen, *Fasıldan Fasıla* 3 (Izmir: Nil Yayınları, 2011), 252.

Despite pressure from the military, Prime Minister Turgut Özal was able to carry out many economic, political and social reforms in the mid-1980s. From 1983 to 1993, Gülen was in touch with him indirectly and advised him on certain issues. During the Özal era, Gülen had limited freedom but it was much better than previous years. He was able to give sermons which attracted congregations of tens of thousands in Istanbul and some other cities. After the unexpected death of President Özal, the militant secularists increasingly promoted anti-Gülen and anti-Hizmet propaganda in the media. It appeared as though preparation was being made for a military coup. The aim was to create conflict between secularists and religious groups and then use this conflict to justify the military intervention. Gülen's approach was to minimise tension between secularists and religious groups. Therefore, he initiated the idea of dialogue at least with some secularists and non-Muslims in Turkey. Gülen met some secular political, community leaders, actors and journalists and heads of non-Muslim organisations at *iftar* dinners that were organised by the Journalists and Writers Foundation of which Gülen was honorary president. He received severe criticism from some secularists, ultra-nationalists, and political Islamists. Giving *iftar* during Ramadan later became a tradition for almost all government departments, military, educational institutions, political parties, non-governmental organisations and religious bodies throughout Turkey. It can be said that this initiative was a successful *ijtihad* of Gülen and the Hizmet Movement to break a taboo in Turkey.

Indeed, having a dialogue with non-Muslims was a big taboo in those years. On a visit to my hometown in 1995, I saw that a picture, with Gülen and the head of the Orthodox Church, Patriarch Bartholomew in the same shot, was being displayed in a large shop on one of the main streets in Adıyaman. I asked the owner why he was displaying the photograph. He said to me, "I wanted to show how Gülen is a bad man." To be in the same shot with a non-Muslim religious leader was sufficient evidence to be called an "infidel" by some political Islamists and Muslim groups in Turkey. Since the establishment of the Turkish Republic and the creation of a secular nationalistic Turkish identity, there have been two scapegoats, religious groups and ethnic minorities. Although Gülen was aware of this situation, he continued to have a dialogue with secular and non-Muslim groups. Dialogue with non-Muslim leaders later became a state policy which has been applied by the Presidency of Religious Affairs in Turkey.

Gülen's life progressed from 1999 onward in self-exile, preferring seclusion in Pennsylvania. In Chapter 8, however, I will give very brief details about accusations from the ruling Justice and Development Party (JDP) and the Turkish media against him and the Hizmet Movement since December 17, 2013.

Historian al-Dhahabi (1274–1348) stated that if you were to tell Hammad ibn Abi Sulaiman (the teacher of Imam Azam Abu Hanifa) that "you are going to die tomorrow," there would be nothing he could add to what he was already doing.[52] Similarly, it may be said that if Gülen were told he is going to die tomorrow, there would be nothing he could add what he is already doing.

After all this, Gülen wants to leave the earth totally forgotten. He says, "I wish my grave not to be known. I wish to die in solitude, with nobody actually becoming aware of my death and hence nobody conducting my Funeral Prayer. I wish that nobody would remember me." In his wish, Gülen wants to follow the path of the *Salaf al-Saliheen*, many of whom died alone. However, they are not forgotten. Through their examples, they are in the hearts and minds of hundreds of millions of Muslims. Similarly, Gülen will not be forgotten. May God give him a long life, but when he closes his eyes forever, in my humble view, his spiritual sultanate will flourish even though he has never wished for that.

---

52 Al-Dhahabi, Biographies of Noble Scholars, 9/192–193, available at www.kalamullah.com/personality07.html. Retrieved 22.09.2016.

CHAPTER 2

THE LOST PARADISE:
GÜLEN ON THE ENVIRONMENT

The Lost Paradise: Gülen on the Environment

Fethullah Gülen's view of the environment has highly spiritual and physical dimensions. His understanding of natural beings and all things, as well as their connection to the Divine, is the major source of his works. He sees the existence of everything in the universe as a sign (*ayat*) of God. For Gülen, nature in its entirety is an exhibition of the wonderful arts of the Maker. Each creation is a piece of the puzzle of the universe and in harmony in the form of mutual relationships. Gülen views all aspects of the environment as gifts of God and says that preserving and developing it as much as possible to make a heavenly place is an obligation of humanity. He also argues that this is a primary duty of every Muslim.[53] According to Gülen, everything in the universe should be viewed with the *mahd-i ukhuwwat* (cradle brotherhood) principle.[54] Humans should seek ways to establish a good relationship with everything in the universe. In addition, contemplation of the environment will strengthen one's spiritual life. Gülen's approach to the environment can be categorised at the spiritual level of *ihsan* (being in constant awareness of the presence of God). To him, protection of the environment is one of the ways of ascension to find the "Lost Paradise."

In this chapter, first Gülen's philosophy of the environment will be analysed in the light of his works. Secondly, I will evaluate how his spiritual approach to nature is reflected in his life based on his close associates' and students' testimonials since his childhood. Finally, this chapter argues that his environmental perspective is highly spiritual, idealistic, and revivalist. It can be entirely applied only by those who are in the spiritual state of *ihsan*.[55]

The Creator created Adam and Eve in Paradise and then sent them to earth. Erol says that Gülen stresses the significance of the first creation, which was in Paradise (*Jannah*) and later descended to the earth.

---

53 Fethullah Gülen, *Fasıldan Fasıla* 3, 265.

54 Qur'an, 43:10.

55 *Ihsan* means perfection, excellence and doing things beautifully by being aware that God is constantly watching. It is based on a hadith which says that *ihsan* is "to worship God as if you see Him, and if you cannot achieve this state of devotion then you must consider that He is looking at you." (Bukhari, 50), *sunnah*.com/bukhari/2/43.

Jannah means "garden" and is the Arabic word for Paradise. Human beings long for their original place and try to imitate Paradise on earth.[56] Each individual is seen and accepted as a *khalifah,* or vicegerent of God on earth (Qur'an, 2:30). Therefore, while humans desire to return to the eternal Paradise, even if temporarily, naturally they would like to make the place they live in as beautiful as the imagined Paradise.

According to Gülen, reading the natural world with its rules will lead any individual to success in this world and the Hereafter. From the believer's perspective, the Qur'an continuously invites them to look into the system and the beauties of the universe.[57] To him, taking care of the environment is *wajib* (obligation), and it can lead to spiritual ascension. Furthermore, humans should be respectful of the environment and not seek primarily to adapt it to themselves.

2.1 Environment as the Maker's arts

Gülen asserts that the purpose of the creation of the universe is to exhibit the Divine Names,[58] as his spiritual master Said Nursi states. Nursi explains that every possessor of beauty and perfection wants to see and display its own beauty and perfection. Consequently, God wanted to lay out an exhibition to show His beauty and perfection in the cosmos.[59] This means of artful adornment for humankind to look upon, so that the cosmos comes to resemble a palace decorated with all forms of wondrous and subtle art, should also designate a teacher and a guide to the wonders of His creation.[60] The human is a mirror which reflects many Names of the Creator, similarly, animals reflect some Names of the Maker. They also invoke the Names of God in their own disposition.

Referring to the prominent tenth-century theologian Imam Maturi-

Retrieved 6.03.2017.

56 Mustafa K Erol, "Are we doing enough to save the environment?" Available at www. gulenmovement.us/are-we-doing-enough-to-save-the-environment.html. Retrieved 13.11.2016.

57 Erol, ibid.

58 Fethullah Gülen, *Prizma* 8 (Izmir: Nil Yayınları, 2011), 120.

59 Nursi's interpretation is based on the hadith qudsi: "I was a hidden beauty and I wanted to be known".

60 Said Nursi, *The Words*, trans. Şükran Vahide (Istanbul: Sözler Publications, 1996), 74.

di (853–944), Gülen states that since everything in the universe can lead to the recognition of the Creator, then it is precious. In addition, everything is seen as a sign of God who created it in a very intricate system. Erol says that Gülen's view of responsibility is firmly set in accountability and, in turn, is based on a theology of creation. God created the world and appointed humans to be the vicegerent (Qur'an, 2:30).[61] Therefore, human beings have responsibility to contemplate and explore the meaning of everything in depth. Gülen states that contemplation on the environment with enlightened reason and heart will lead the believer to view the excellence of the arts of God and in the end, this will lead to love and firmness of faith with spiritual joy.[62] Taking a metaphysical approach through the preservation of the environment is one of the ways of spiritual ascension if it is seen with the eyes of wisdom. Humans are in a position to comprehend and examine the mysteries of the laws of nature and study the environment like a book as part of the universe. Gülen states:

> The nature in its entirety is an exhibition of wonderful things, but we prefer to call it a "book." It is because we hear it like a book, read it like a book, just as if we were watching the gilded lines and decorations of a book in all colors, and we watch it in great admiration. Every morning we see it painted anew, decorated in front of us with its dazzling height and gaze at it losing ourselves in amazement and wonder.[63]

Gülen holds that everything in the universe, living and inanimate, worships God in its own manner and therefore has a spiritual dimension. He says that "whenever I look at the trees' branches, I see them as the hands of the worshipper turned up in supplication to God."[64] On the spiritual dimension of the environment, Gülen is influenced by Said Nursi, who argues that the Creator manifests twenty Divine Names on every single creation. The connections and harmony between these Names ne-

---

61 Erol, "Are we doing enough to save the environment?"

62 Fethullah Gülen, *Asrın Getirdiği Tereddütler* 2 (Izmir: Nil Yayınları, 2011), 74.

63 Doğu, Ergil, "Fethullah Gülen and the Gülen Movement in 100 questions", islamiccenter.org/environment-and-natural-living/ retrieved 9.12.2016.

64 Fethullah Gülen, *Çağ ve Nesil* 3 (Izmir: Nil Yayınları, 2011), 38.

cessitate a relationship between all creations.[65] For Nursi, everything in the universe is a manifestation of God's Names. Just as there is unity and harmony between God's Names, there is harmony between God's creations that reflects those Names.

Furthermore, according to Nursi, the universe has two faces. The first face, *mana-yi harfi*, looks to the Creator, while the second face, *mana-yi ismi*, looks to itself.[66] *Mana-yi harfi* is seeing creation and praising how beautifully it has been made by the Maker, while *mana-yi ismi* is seeing a creation and being amazed by its beauty in itself.[67] When applied to the environment, in the face of *mana-yi harfi*, it will manifest the Divine Names. From this perspective, the environment is to be appreciated as a magnificent and beautiful exhibition because it is reflecting the Divine Names.

Although ecology is not an Islamic discipline yet, the Qur'an and *Sunnah* regularly take the beauty of the world into account. According to Gülen, the aim is to make the world like a corridor which can lead to eternal Paradise. He refers to the Qur'anic verse: "And give good tidings to those who believe and do righteous deeds that they will have gardens [in Paradise] beneath which rivers flow. Whenever they are provided with a provision of fruit therefrom, they will say, 'This is what we were provided with before.' And it is given to them in likeness" (2:25). In relation to this verse Gülen says that by mentioning various dimensions of Paradise, the Qur'an sets a high benchmark for making the world like it. He continues that "if we have an unclean, dirty environment, how can the people of Paradise compare their place with this world. So, the Qur'an makes us envious and shows humans a very high standard for the environment. A beautiful environment is like a sample or copy of Paradise."[68] What makes Gülen unique in his perspective is that, unlike other scholars, he believes earth should resemble heaven. He states that "making this world like

---

65 Nursi, *The Words*, 656.

66 Ibrahim Özdemir, Bediüzzaman Nursi's Approach to the Environment (2006), www.nur.org/en/nurcenter/nurlibrary/Bediuzzaman_s_Approach_to_the_Environment_123. Retrieved 16.4.2009.

67 Nursi, *The Words*, 147.

68 Fethullah Gülen, "Mü'min Ufkunda Çevre," http://www.herkul.org/bamteli/mu-min-ufkunda-cevre. Retrieved 22.11.2016.

heaven is a human duty as *khalif* or vicegerent of God."[69]

In the face of *mana-yi ismi*, the environment is beautiful and re-sourceful on its own but its connections to humans are not recognised. The first one will view the environment as the arts of *al-Jamil,* the Most Beautiful, in the service of humanity. However, the second one will de-value it. For example, if one looks at a work of art on its own and does not come to the realisation that it is Van Gogh's, the art will have little value. Similarly, if one looks at creation knowing it to be the art made by God, it holds immeasurable value.[70]

By observing the spiritual dimension of the environment, Gülen says that "planting a tree is one of my wishes which I am so keen on to the degree of suffering for it. When I see the lands of my country without trees, I feel very sorry and I have difficulty to find an appropriate word to express my sorrow… Everyone must be encouraged to plant trees, and gradually this should become an ethical principle of society."[71] Like Nursi, Gülen believes that all things in the universe are connected to each other. He refers to the story of an ant in the Qur'an. Gülen argues that many lessons can be learned from the story of Prophet Solomon in conversation with an ant [as a miracle] in the Qur'an. According to the story, when Solomon with his army approached the valley of the ants, the queen ant said,

> O ants, enter your dwellings that you not be crushed by Solomon and his soldiers while they perceive not. So [Solomon] smiled, amused at her speech, and said, 'My Lord, enable me to be grateful for Your favour which You have bestowed upon me and upon my parents and to do righteousness of which You approve. And admit me by Your mercy into [the ranks of] Your righteous servants.'(Qur'an, 27:18–19)

Before looking at Gülen's understanding of this verse, it is important to know how it is interpreted by others. Qur'an exegete Ibn Ashur argues

---

69 Fethullah Gülen, "Mü'min Ufkunda Çevre," www.herkul.org/bamteli/mu-min-ufkunda-cevre. Retrieved 22.11.2016.

70 Salih Yücel and Selma Sivri, "Said Nursi's approach to the environment", *The Islamic Quarterly,* 55(1), (2010), 1–19.

71 Gülen, *Fasıldan Fasıla* 1, 375.

that these verses show that to be compassionate, one must give justice to all creation and not harm even an ant.[72] They are species like humans. Many lessons can be learned from them.[73] Nursi also supports the above views on lessons to be learned from ants and views them as God's blessed creations.[74] In addition, Nursi fed ants with breadcrumbs and did not allow his students to destroy their nests when they wanted to build a cottage.[75] In one instance, his younger brother Mehmed brought him some food. Nursi left the crumbs and smaller pieces to the ants and ate the rest. When he was asked why he did this, he replied, "I have observed that they have a social life and work together diligently and conscientiously, so I want to help them as a reward for their republicanism."[76]

Ismail Haqqi (1653–1725) states that it is one of the attributes of Prophet Solomon and his companions to avoid stepping on ants when they walk. This reflects the degree of respect the prophets and scholars had for all animals and insects.[77] Haqqi argues that Prophet Muhammad (pbuh) is more honourable in the sight of God than Prophet Solomon. So, the level of compassion in his treatment of animals and insects is much higher than that of Prophet Solomon. Prophet Muhammad, while travelling with his army, posted sentries to ensure that a female dog and her newborn puppies were not disturbed. Prophet Muhammad also (pbuh) prohibited killing four creatures: ants, bees, hoopoes, and sparrow-hawks.[78] The Prophet said that "the world is beautiful and verdant, and verily God, be He exalted, has made you His stewards in it, and He sees how you acquit yourselves."[79]

---

72 Ibn Ashur, At-Tahrir Wa Tanwir, altafsir.com. Retrieved 30.04.2017.

73 Muhammad Matwalli as-Sa'rawi, Khawatir al -Muhammaed Matwalli as-Sa'rawi, al-tafsir.com. Retrieved 30.04.2017.

74 Said Nursi, *The Letters*, trans. Şükran Vahide, (Istanbul: Sözler Publications, 2007), 373.

75 Nursi, *Tarihçe-i Hayat*, (Istanbul: n.d.), 36.

76 Necmettin Sahiner, *Son Şahitler* [The Last Witnesses], Online: www.nur.gen.tr. Retrieved 30.04.2017.

77 Ismail Haqqi, Ruhu'l Bayan, altafsir.com. Retrieved 25.04.2017.

78 Sunan Abu Dawud, Hadith 5267, *sunnah*.com/abudawud/43/495. Retrieved 10.04.2017.

79 Sahih Muslim.

There are many instances in Prophet Muhammad's life where he displayed empathy and mercy towards animals. When on a journey, the Prophet saw a bird circling above several Companions, beating its wings anxiously. He asked, "Who has hurt the feelings of this bird by taking its chicks?" He asked the Companions to return the chicks which they had taken from the nest.[80] The Prophet said, "There is none among the Muslims who plants a tree or sows seeds, and then a bird, or a person or an animal eats from it, but it is regarded as a charitable gift for him."[81] In another hadith, he says, "An ant bit one of the Prophets, and he ordered that the ant nest be burned. Then Allah revealed to him: 'One ant bit you, and you destroyed one of the nations that glorify Allah.'"[82]

In his commentary on the above verses (27:18–19), Gülen states that an ant's advice to Solomon was not only to be just towards humans and respect their rights but also to be just towards animals and not crush ants while he walked with his army in the valley.[83] He mentions a conversation of Prophet Muhammad (pbuh) with animals, trees and rocks as miracles to show the significant correlation between human beings and their surroundings. However, it is a human responsibility to discover this correlation in depth. Gülen continues, "If we could comprehend the peculiarity of the animal realms, then we would be able to learn many lessons and truths that can be helpful or beneficial for humanity."[84] Gülen's view is very similar to that of some great scholars in Islamic history. Animals were not just creatures running about on their own business, but beings that had many lessons to offer humankind. Ismail Haqqi holds that animals offer lessons that take the learner from ignorance to understanding and wisdom.[85] Abdulqadr al-Jilani (1077–1166) takes this even further, saying that truly and deeply contemplating animals and their abilities would lead to understanding the miraculous aspect of God's art, the perfection of His Power and Unlimited Knowledge, and finally, the

---

80　Sahih Muslim.

81　Bukhari, Hadith No: 2320, *sunnah*.com/bukhari/41/1. Retrieved 30.04 2017.

82　Nasai, Hadith No:4358, *sunnah*.com/nasai/42/96. Retrieved 30.04.2017.

83　Gülen, *Fasıldan Fasıla* 1, 238.

84　Ibid., 239.

85　Ismail Haqqi, Ruhu'l Bayan fi Tafsir al-Qur'an, www.altafsir.com. Retrieved 06.06.2015.

essence or core of wisdom.[86] As discussed previously, there are relationships between each creation with as many of God's Names as reflect on them.

Inspired by Nursi, Gülen believes that *Al-Quddus* (The All-Holy and All-Pure) is one of the Names of God that reflects in the universe. Due to the universe's impeccable cleansing system, it is implied that the natural structure of the ecosystem ensures all elements in nature are constantly being purified and self-cleansed. Nursi puts forth a God-centred definition of cleanliness through the Name of *Al-Quddus*.[87] Therefore, the cleanliness and purity that is found in the palace of the universe always comes from a wise cleansing and a careful purifying: "If there were no such cleansing and purification, all the animals who come to the earth would drown and die in one year because of its dirtiness. Even creatures of the seas and the earth that eat dead animals (such as eagles, wolves, and even ants) are working in this Divine factory to immediately clean up any ugliness apparent on earth."[88]

2.2 *Mahd-i ukhuwwat* or cradle brotherhood

According to Gülen, everything in the world should be viewed with the "*mahd-i ukhuwwat*" principle. *Mahd* refers to the cradle while *ukhuwwat* means brotherhood. This definition requires that humans should seek a way to establish a good relationship with everything in the world.[89] The cooperation between all created beings is a universal law. This cradle is a place where you cultivate and develop. It has a unique place in the heart of every human,[90] in addition to being the home of all creations. Therefore, it essential to look at the world from a conical perspective. This will provide an opportunity to attain a broader outlook on the environment. Furthermore, this will make it easier to view everything as a piece of the puzzle, as everything is an art of God and has great value.

---

86 Abdulqadr al-Jilani, *Tafsir al-Jilani*, www.altafsir.com. Retrieved 06.06.2015.

87 Yücel and Sivri, "Said Nursi's approach to the environment", 77–96.

88 Said Nursi, *The Flashes*, trans. Şükran Vahide, (Istanbul: Sözler Publications, 2002), 401.

89 Ünal, *Bir Portre Denemesi*, 365.

90 Yücel and Sivri, "Said Nursi's approach to the environment", 7

Mahd-i ukhuwwat can be defined in two ways. Gülen first views the world like a cradle, as mentioned in the Qur'an (43:10). Everything grows in the same cradle. By this expression, Gülen indicates that the world is a place where brotherhood and sisterhood can be established and relationships can be built with every creation. I have examined the interpretation of the above verse (43:10) in thirty Qur'anic exegeses (*tafsir*) written by the great classical and modern scholars. None of them interpreted the word *"mahd"* (cradle) as deeply as Gülen did. For him, there are bonds to being from the same country, same city, same school, and same neighbourhood. Similarly, seeing the world as a cradle and growing with everything there can lead to real friendship. Thus, a human being is in close embrace with nature and its contents, which leads to becoming inseparable companions. For example, for Gülen, soil can be seen as a host, since the human being is created from it and will return to it.[91] With such a developed understanding of environmental philosophy, a human will perceive the environment as a lovely festival exhibition, listen to the voices in it as a harmonic orchestra, and dwell in it as happy children.[92]

The second meaning of *mahd-i ukhuwwat* in Turkish culture, is that due to their sincere friendship, sometimes the parents of two children from separate families pronounce their babies in the cradle brothers or sisters. This is an indication of how the parents love each other like biological brothers and sisters. Consequently, it is expected that when these babies grow up, they will each view the other as brother or sister. This *mahd-i ukhuwwat* notion binds them, and both feel the necessity of leaning on and looking after each other, as well as being looked after by the parents.

In Gülen's thoughts, an ideal environment has a highly spiritual dimension along with a spiritual side after *mahd-i ukhuwwat* is well established. He imagines the world in the following way:

> With its natural environment unpolluted and in good order and harmony, its lovely towns and villages re-planned and re-designed, and its population

---

91 Fethullah Gülen, *Enginliği ile Bizim Dünyamız* (Izmir: Nil Yayınları, 2011), 78–79

92 Gülen, *Çağ ve Nesil* 8, 178.

equipped with such human values and virtues as belief, love, knowledge, mutual loyalty and high morals, this world would be a place fit for joyful, sincere-hearted people to dwell in; a place where rivers of love and other sublime feelings flow; where works of the finest artistry appear side by side with those of the sciences into which religion has breathed a new life; a place where families dwell whose members are attached to one another with love, respect and compassion. Those destined to live in this world will find it a Paradise-like place cleansed of all kinds of impurity and foulness, and purified of all kinds of misery and dissipation, where angelic souls fly around and all are for each and each is for all.[93]

Thus, he views the protection of nature as *wajib* (obligation)[94] upon every Muslim and a primary task.[95] By developing a theology of the environment, Gülen is theologising and spiritualising the social responsibility of mankind for the environment. Because everything comes from the "One," (God) and returns to the "One",[96] Gülen states that since Islam is a universal religion, it must encompass and protect the rights of all beings.[97] In his approach to the environment, whoever we come across and whatever we see on our way, all are loved because of the Beloved. To understand how he applies environmental ethics, it is necessary to analyse some of his close friends' and students' testimonials.

2.3 Testimonials from friends

Gülen reflects his environmental philosophy in his works as well as in his actions. Doğu Ergil was quite impressed with the environment of the retreat centre where Gülen has been residing since 1999. Ergil calls it a "natural Paradise," far from the noise of the city in a rural setting in the upper Pennsylvania region. While there were several small lodges, unrepaired for years, in the beginning, this natural place, decorated by the rich forest-like trees and bushes, is now completely renovated. The land-

---

93 Gülen, Horizon of Hope, www.fgulen.com/en/fethullah-Gülens-works/thought/towards-the-lost-paradise/24485-the-horizon-of-hope. Retrieved 14.11.2016.

94 Gülen, *Fasıldan Fasıla* 3, 221.

95 Ibid., 265.

96 Fethullah Gülen, *Fatiha Üzerine Mülahazalar* (Izmir: Nil Yayınları, 2011), 135.

97 Fethullah Gülen, *Prizma* 2 (Izmir: Nil Yayınları, 2011), 90.

scape of the premise is done properly, and some paths have been opened leading to the ravine at the lower part of the property. While the field resembles the campus of a school, without touching the natural appearance, it was made more beautiful.[98] The author witnessed the planning consultations a few times and saw how Gülen advised the landscape and gardening designers on maintaining the retreat centre.

Yusuf Pekmezci, who has known Gülen for almost fifty years, says, "In 1967 or 1968 Gülen organised retreat programs for about 150–200 high-school and university students. Once, he had an accident and crashed the car into a tree in the forest. It was necessary to cut down the big tree to pull out the vehicle. When I wanted to cut down the tree, Gülen said 'Did God create you to destroy the life of creations? No.' He was exhausted, and I asked him to return to the boys' camp. Gülen did not want to go because he thought that I would cut down the tree. I promised him that I would not and then he left. Instead of cutting down the tree, I broke the car into two pieces and then we were able to pull out the car without cutting down the tree. After a while, Gülen came back, and he saw the car. I told him you did not want me to cut down the tree, so I had to dismantle the vehicle. The car can be fixed. But he also saw the bark of the tree was stripped. He wrapped the trunk of the tree with muddy rags. And then for few weeks, we carried water to irrigate it."

Pekmezci says that Gülen never wants to harm the environment. Almost forty years later, Pekmezci visited the campsite and took a picture of the tree which Gülen did not want to be cut down to pull out the car and showed it to Gülen during his last visit in Pennsylvania.

Nevzat Türk, who has known Gülen since the early 1970s and lived with Gülen for three years, says that "whenever Gülen would see a trail of ants, he would walk to the other side of the path or the road. Gülen does not even want to step on an ant because he believes the creation of everything has many purposes and each creature has the right to exist."

Once when Gülen organised a retreat program for high-school and university students in the late 1960s, a student killed a snake in the

---

98 Doğu Ergil, "What is his perspective on the environment and natural living?", fgulen.com/en/Gülen-movement/fethullah-Gülen-and-the-Gülen-movement-in-100-questions/48368-what-is-his-perspective-on-the-environment-and-natural-living. Retrieved 13.11.2016.

bush. Gülen was very upset with the student and he did not speak to him for about a month. Nevzat Türk, who was a high school student at that time, recalls those days: "Gülen was upset because the snake was killed in the bush, not in the camp. Furthermore, the snake had not attacked or harmed any student."

Once a bee with a broken wing entered Gülen's room and it was ill. Gülen looked after the bee and gave it honey and sugared water. But the bee could not fly. Later, it died and Gülen wept for the bee as he threw the dead creature from his window.

Gülen has been an environmentalist since a young age. He does not like wasting even a piece of paper. His brother Kutbettin says, "I was in primary school in the early 1960s. Once, I wanted to do my home-work and I pulled two pages from my notebook. My brother was upset with me because I was wasting paper."

His brother Sıbgatullah says, "I went to see him in the early 1970s in Izmir. He was living in a small dormitory with poor high-school and university students. Gülen told me that there was a big rat which was entering the dormitory from the sewage pipe. I told him to let me take care of it. He asked me, 'What are you going to do?' I said, 'I am going to kill it.' He told me, 'God did not create you to kill creatures. Do you know any way to prevent the rat from entering the dormitory?' So, he did not allow me to kill it. Later, I found a solution. I did not kill it but rather I put a fitting in the hole the rat used to enter the building." Gülen saved the life of the rat and taught his students and his brother an unforgettable lesson about taking care of the environment.

Cevdet Türkyolu recalls, "Once, Gülen and few of us went to an uninhabited house of a friend in the forest on a mountain. There were three mice scurrying around in the house. I wanted to kill them but Gülen did not allow me. After three days, a cat appeared and the mice disappeared. Later, the cat left the house as well."

In not allowing a rat to be killed, Gülen is following in the footsteps of his spiritual master Said Nursi. In many instances, when Nursi stayed at a house and saw a mouse coming out of its hole, he would say, "Look! It wants something to eat!" and then proceed to put a piece of food by the hole, which the mouse would eventually eat. This became such a habit that people knew if he had any food, he was "bound to put a part of it for the mouse."[99] He would repeat this with cats and birds, leaving bread where they could reach it.[100] Once, when his student Tahsin Aydın saw Nursi giving food to a mouse, Nursi said to him, "This mouse is teaching me some lessons."[101]

Nursi's student Hasan Akyol was witness to another mouse incident in Emirdağ. Hasan saw a mouse enter his teacher's garment: "He woke up slowly and calmly. I was staring in awe. It didn't even occur to me to scare the mouse. Nursi did not say or do anything either. I saw the mouse go into the sleeve and go down to the elbow. He said, 'Hey, leave, O honourable animal!' It was as though the mouse was waiting for that order. It came out of the sleeve but did not get off his hand. I stood mesmerised. He said to me, 'O brother, put some bread on the floor, for this honourable creature wants bread.' Upon doing so, the mouse left Nursi's hand, ate the bread and left."[102]

Alaattin Kırkan recalls with tearful eyes how Gülen took care of the environment. Gülen and his friends organised a picnic for a spiritual and teaching purpose in the early 1970s. Kırkan said that hundreds of people attended: "It was a place in the forest but had no trash bins around. After the picnic, Gülen took a plastic bag and collected rubbish and then called to the people, 'Let's collect the rubbish and clean up the place.' He started collecting trash, and everyone began to do it as well. Among us there were some rich people, bureaucrats, public staff, elders, students, and all worked to make the place clean and tidy." Rich people and bureaucrats would not have done that by themselves, particularly at that time. This was due to the fact that most of them paid someone to do their cleaning at home. In their view or culture, cleaning or collecting rubbish was a servant's duty. For others, it could be an embarrassment to collect rubbish in the sight of rich people since they get used to asking others to do it.

At the picnics Gülen would give short speeches and lead the *Salat* or ritual Prayer performed in congregation. However, for Kırkan, the biggest lesson was to see the importance of being a role model. He says,

99 Necmettin Şahiner, *Son Şahitler*, 150. Retrieved 06.06.2015.

100 Ibid., 141.

101 Ibid., 10.

102 Ibid., 3.

"Gülen became a role model and he taught everyone to care about the environment on that day which I would never forget." After the picnic, Kırkan became fully aware of the significance of preserving the environment.

İrfan Yılmaz recalls that "Gülen would use a paper towel four times before disposing of it. He would use and then dry it four times." When Yılmaz spoke about it, his appearance demonstrated that he had received the best and most unforgettable lesson in his life about the environment from Gülen.

Osman Şimşek, one of his pupils, mentioned that there is a light fixture with multiple light bulbs in the study room where Gülen teaches. If he is not teaching but just sitting in the room, he turns off the unnecessary lights. Gülen is very delicate about consuming anything. He does not throw away even the cardboard packaging of new shirts. He uses it for his writing. Gülen also takes ablution with little water. Şimşek has witnessed Gülen's frugality on several occasions. To him, wasting anything equates to disrespecting the Maker. His habit of not wasting anything may be based on the well-known hadith about the Prophet: "The Messenger of Allah passed by Sa'd when he was performing ablution, and he said: 'What is this extravagance?' He said:

'Can there be any extravagance in ablution?' He said: 'Yes, even if you are on the bank of a flowing river.'"[103]

Gülen is very attached to the environment. He says, "Years ago a few of us had a rest under the shade of a tree on our way. Years later, if I passed by the same tree, I would visit it. If I forgot and those who travelled with me did not remind me to visit that tree, I would be disappointed with my friends."[104] There are many examples like this which are narrated by his friends. This shows his degree of attachment to nature.

After arriving in the United States for medical treatment, Gülen lived in a retreat centre in Pennsylvania. The garden was a wilderness and the retreat centre needed some maintenance. Some volunteers began the work by removing and cutting branches off the trees. When they cut the branch of a tree outside the window of Gülen's room, I saw Gülen close the curtain. I realised that cutting off branches made him unhappy

103   Ibn Majah, Hadith no 425, *sunnah*.com/urn/1254240. Retrieved 11.04.2017.

104   Ünal, *Bir Portre Denemesi*, 504.

because in one of his poems, he mentions how the falling of leaves from a tree makes him suffer. As a matter of fact, I observed his anguish later when he performed his Prayers in congregation. Usually, he would give a short talk or converse with people after each Prayer or have a cup of tea with them. However, he did not speak with anyone until the following day's Noon Prayer. During lunch, he asked why the branch was cut and he was still upset.

One of the Turkish Australians from Sydney told me that "seeing how Gülen cared for the environment changed me and my family's environmental approach entirely. Since we have been reading Gülen's books and listening to his sermons, we have become very hesitant to cut any tree or pull off a leaf. My wife and I have decided not to kill any insects at home unless they are harmful. We do not kill ants or cockroaches in the house, but we gently try to take them out. At times, we feed the ants in the backyard. When I walk, I try not to step on an ant as far as possible. If people saw how we act towards insects, they would think that we are crazy."

Most of the friends of Gülen mentioned above remembered the stories about Gülen with eyes filled with tears. All of them accepted that through the actions of Gülen, they have learned great lessons. His model behavior, including about the environment, has left a permanent impression on their hearts and minds. Also, they have never forgotten the knowledge which was conveyed through actions by Gülen.

2.4 Analysis

Analysing Gülen's works, his daily life and the testimonials of those who have known or been close to him since the early 1970s, I see that his actions precede his words about the environment as well. Although he has not written a book on the environment, each of his actions has left a permanent impression that has greater impact. In my humble understanding, Gülen's approach to the environment can be categorised at three levels, based on his works, actions and friends' testimonials.

First, the rational approach, which is primarily scientific in nature, for example, in observing the leaves, branches and fruits of a tree, provides reasonable evidence for the great beauty and value of the environment. The aim is to address ordinary people and persuade individuals to preserve the environment and benefit accordingly. Informing people through education, qualitative understanding and awareness is the first stepping stone. This can be observed in the media interviews with Gülen and in his works and is considered as a degree of *ilm al-yaqin* (the knowledge of certainty).[105]

The second degree is to approach by *qalb* (heart) without neglecting reasoning. This necessitates contemplating and observing how the Divine Names manifest on every creation. This results in a thorough realisation of the Creator through the creation. By acknowledging and accepting God and all of his attributes, a believer will comprehend the arts of God in every creature. This is a spiritual station which indicates being with the Maker while walking among the people.[106] At this stage, a believer views the entire world as a museum where the arts of *al-Jamil* (The Most Beautiful) are exhibited and on display. In this manner, the heart takes precedent over reason, action precedes words. There is a powerful impression of compassion towards the environment. Humans are sensitive to such imagery. At times this may not be rational. Actions such as spending significant time and money and putting one's at risk to protect an animal or to save a tree, or trying not step on an ant while walking may not be understood by ordinary people. Due to the higher degree of compassion, a person can give priority to their heart over reasoning. For example, some environmentalists spend many days to save the life of a whale or a few turtles. There are hundreds of such examples in Gülen's life with a few mentioned above. This degree can be classified as *ayn al-yaqin* (the eye of certainty).

The third degree is approaching the environment with the *aql* (reasoning), *qalb* (heart) and *ruh* (spirit) at the level of *ihsan*. This is the highest and most ideal level of environmental philosophy. Humans perceive with all their cells that the environment's spiritual dimension takes precedent over the physical aspect. The environment is not only seen by the eyes, but also loved by the heart and heavily felt by the spirit. This degree does not neglect reason and heart but combines reason, heart, and spirit in the service of the environment. Humans are not a creation outside the environment, however; they remain a part of the environment. At this level, besides being anxious or feeling apologetic, human hearts

---

105   Gülen, *Prizma* 2, 108.
106   Ibid., 109–110.

bleed and eyes shed tears for any environmental disaster. As mentioned in the testimonials of Gülen's friends and students above, shedding tears about not saving a bee, not talking to a student for a killing a snake, or crying about the cutting a branch of a tree are included in this highly idealistic and spiritualistic degree. Those who have this level of awareness will not harm or alter the physical environment as they desire. Rather they will adapt or integrate themselves as a piece of it. This can be seen by some as the attribute of a madman. As a matter of fact, initially, some of Gülen's friends could not understand this either, as shown by Yusuf Pekmezci's first reaction to destroying a car to save a tree.

It can be said that Gülen's understanding of the environment is highly spiritual and idealistic at the degree of *ihsan*. He is reintroducing the *Salaf al-Saliheen's* view of environment. Historically, all great scholars have a similar view of the environment such as Bahaud Din Naqshband (1318–1389), who spent three years in the service of animals for his own spiritual purification at the request of his spiritual master Amir Kulal (1277–1363). He would stand up when an animal passed by as a gesture of respect. Sometimes Rumi (1207–1273) would stay hungry but give his food to animals.[107] Ismail Haqqi holds that animals offer lessons that take the learner from ignorance to understanding and wisdom.[108] Abdulqadr al-Jilani (1077–1166) takes this even further, saying that truly and deeply contemplating animals and their abilities would lead to understanding the miraculous aspect of God's art, the perfection of His Power and Unlimited Knowledge, and finally, the essence or core of wisdom.[109] Said Nursi did not allow his students to build a hut where there was a nest of ants. He fed the mouse in the house instead of killing it. This can be seen in the life of all great scholars in Islamic history. They consider not harming animals and being helpful to them as a step in spiritual ascension and as a degree of piety. To all great scholars and schools of law, treating animals well was not merely a matter of compassion, but also an obligation which entails accountability in this world and the Hereafter. For Richard Foltz, in such an environment, in which animals were

---

107 Muhammad H. Kabbani (2004) *Classical Islam and the Naqshbandi Sufi Tradition.* Fenton, MI, Islamic Supreme Council of North America. pp. 182-183.

108 Ismail Haqqi, *Ruhu'l Bayan fi Tafsir al-Qur'an.* Retrieved 06.06.2015.

109 Abdulqadr al-Jilani, *Tafsir al-Jilani.* Retrieved 06.06.2015.

kindly treated in history, an average non-human animal would have preferred living among Muslims to living among Christians.[110] However, this compassion for animals has been neglected since colonialism, as Alan Mikhail argues.[111] Therefore, an animal would prefer to live in developed countries rather than in Muslim-dominated countries in our day. By applying highly idealistic environmental principles, Gülen wants to revive through his actions and works what has been neglected in the Muslim world since colonialism. His view of environment is tawhidic (God-centred) not egocentric or anthropocentric (human-centred).

People must always view their surroundings as an art and a great gift of God and treat the environment accordingly, as they are *khalifah* (vicegerent) on the earth. In educating people about the environment, Gülen sees the necessity of having many role models at the degree of *ihsan*. Particularly, this applies to those who lead the people in various positions and different fields. Gülen has not written a specific book about the environment but a few small articles and bits and pieces which are spread throughout in his works and sermons. However, with this little work, he has become more influential than many environmentalists. If we compare his writings with the works of an environment scholar, they do not seem much, but his actions are louder and more effective than those of any other contemporary environmentalist in the Muslim world.

Gülen has conveyed his message to the people about awareness of the environment mainly through his actions rather than his talks. Despite the fact that so much has been written or spoken about it, still, human beings are destroying the environment with their own hands. Due to technological development, human beings are gradually polluting space as well.[112]

Gülen views the universe as a mysterious book and everything in it is a part of the tree of creation.[113] As all the branches in a tree are con-

---

110   Richard Foltz, *Animals in Islamic Tradition and Muslim Cultures* (Oxford: One-world, 2006), 5.

111   Alan Mikhail, *The Animal in Ottoman Egypt*, pp. 68–83, published to OxfordScholarship Online, 2014: DOI: 10.1093/acprof:oso/9780199315277.001.0001.

112   Gülen, *Enginliği ile Bizim Dünyamız*, 315.

113   Fethullah Gülen, "Bir Aynadır Bütün Varlık", *Yağmur*, July, 2003.

nected to one another, similarly, all things in the universe are also connected to each other. It is a duty for all people to comprehend this un-
derlying connection. He calls this phenomenon *mavera-i yolculuk* which
means "spiritually travelling" to realise what is behind things and what
is the purpose of creation.[114] He argues that "as a traveler, the human
being can understand the purpose or purposes of each creation and sees
the wisdom behind it. When this degree is reached, everything will be
significantly valuable in the sights and deeply loveable by hearts. Gradually, from the smallest to the biggest, everything will be one of us or
part of us." Finally, the environment will be like the Gardens of Firdaws
(Paradise), where we walk with a deep spiritual pleasure.[115] Gülen wants
to see his environment as a "Natural Paradise." To him, this should be
a goal for every human. There is a strong relationship between human
beings and the environment, whether a person adapts themselves to the
environment or they emulate it. The degree of our actions valuing and
protecting the environment shows the level of a person's spiritual life.

Conclusion

In Gülen's environmental philosophy, everything in the universe is a
mirror reflecting the Truth, an eloquent tongue that speaks Him, a song
which glorifies God's Names and a witness of His Unity. Therefore, each
element can be a step towards a higher spiritual ascension. For individuals who look at the environment with *mana-yi harfi* as a mirror reflecting God's Names, their lives become an enjoyable spiritual life, and
the world is a corridor that leads to Paradise. In essence, destroying the
environment equates to devaluing God's arts and gifts and consequently
eliminating spirituality.

The portrayal of Paradise in the Qur'an and *Sunnah* shows a highly
ideal environment. The Qur'an says God "certainly created man in the
best of stature" (Qur'an, 95:4), so as the most beautiful creation, a human
has a responsibility to make the world an alluring place. For Gülen, human beings crave their original place and try to imitate the scenario of a
Paradise-like environment on earth.

His view is that one of the major duties of a Muslim is to take care

---

114   Fethullah Gülen, *Beyan* (Izmir: Nil Yayınları, 2011), 47.

115   Ibid., 135.

of our surroundings and to protect the ecological balance. To achieve an
optimal environment, it is necessary to mobilise the masses to protect
not only the physical aspects but also understand their deeply spiritual
side. If we do this, Gülen is highly optimistic about the environment, as
its beauty is planted and evident in human nature. When this inner dimension of human beauty is explored, nurtured and reflected outwards,
a wonderful and pleasant environment will become a reality both in this
world and in the Hereafter. Gülen, like Yunus Emre (1240–1320), indicates that everything must be loved because of the Creator.

In summary, the idea of protecting nature and conserving it has to
be appropriated by all individuals. Perhaps by doing so, humankind can
reach the "Lost Paradise" once again.[116]

---

116   Doğu Ergil, "What is his perspective on the environment and natural living". Re-
      trieved 13.11.2016.

CHAPTER 3

THE TEARS OF FETHULLAH GÜLEN

The Tears of Fethullah Gülen

Crying is part of human nature. As soon as the baby enters this world, his or her first action is to cry. The tears of a baby can be for future happiness or calamities. Suffering, weeping, crying and moaning for humanity is one of the major characteristics of all Prophets, saints, and great scholars. The Prophets, saints, and great scholars cry throughout their whole life at various levels for the wrong-doings, sins, crimes, injustices, oppression, and tyranny in the world. Their tears are like a cure for suffering, relieving depression and providing a peaceful way of resisting oppression and injustice. Sometimes shedding tears is a way of manifesting their helplessness. In that case, not just their eyes but also their hearts and souls cry. They do not only cry but they also make others shed tears. They view bursting into tears as one of the most acceptable *dua*s (supplications) in the sight of God. Then, the question arises, "Why do they weep, cry, and sigh?" To find out the answer, I focused on the Qur'anic verses related to the topic and the exegetical works of more than twenty great scholars, including Fethullah Gülen's interpretations. Then, I looked at *seerah* (biographies of the Prophet) and the biographies of the Companions, saints and scholars to understand the topic in depth.

Before analysing the reasons for Gülen's tears, it is necessary first to look at three Qur'anic verses which are directly related to this topic from the perspectives of various classical and modern major exegetical works. Secondly, I will briefly touch on the shedding of tears by the *Salaf al-Saliheen*. Thirdly, I will elaborate on how Gülen reads the tears of Prophets, Companions of the Prophet, and great scholars. Finally, I will investigate the crying, weeping and sighing of Gülen in the light of his works, sermons, public and private talks, close friends' testimonials, and my personal observations of him.

3.1 Tears in the Qur'an

The Qur'an honours the shedding of tears for many reasons with the exception of falseness or showing off. There are different reasons for shedding tears: out of a very deep knowledge about the Creator; out of love of the Beloved and fear of God; as a reflection of mercy, excitement, suffering and regret, physical pain and loss of loved ones. The last two topics are outside the scope of this study.

There are hundreds of examples of individuals or people who cry in the Holy Scriptures of monotheistic religions, especially in the Qur'an. We do not know if Prophet Adam, the father of humanity cried or not when he opened eyes to life. However, the sacred texts indicate that he cried when he was expelled from Paradise and sent to this world. Even though they are not authenticated, some sources report that Adam cried for forty or sixty years,[117] and then his repentance was accepted by God. It can be said that he cried for decades because he did not cry when he was created. He is not just the father of humanity but also the father of sorrow. Prophet Adam began his worldly life with sorrow: the fall from Paradise, Paradise lost, separation from God, and, Hereafter, the heavy responsibility of Prophethood. He sighed with sorrow throughout his life.[118]

For Ibn Arabi (1165–1240), it was necessary for Adam to cry in order to reach perfection.[119] The tears of Adam caused the mercy of God to descend from the heaven to earth and become the water of life for his soul. His tears were the seeds of happiness, a spiritual elevator of ascension, and a model of repentance for the sins of his offspring. Without tears, he would not have been able to relieve his separation from Paradise. He cried not just because of the *zalla* (error) which he and his wife committed, but also for the sins of his future offspring until the Day of Reckoning. He was the first ring in the chain of those who sigh. Thus, after him, Prophet Noah followed in Adam's footstep. Based on scholarly works, he cried longer than Adam.

Al-Alusi (1802–1854) asserts that Prophet Noah experienced great sorrow over his tribe's rejection of the faith and he wept heavily for his people. His constant crying led to his being called Noah, which means "the one who cries a lot." Noah's original name was Abd al-Ghaffar.[120]

---

117 Ibn Kathir, *History of the Prophets*, trans. Muhammad Mustapha Geme'ah (Riyad: Darus Salam, n.d), 13.

118 Fethullah Gülen, "Huzn" (Sadness or Sorrow), *Key Concepts in the Practice of Sufism*, www.fgulen.com/en. Retrieved 9.12.2016.

119 Ibn Arabi, Tafsir al-Qur'an, altafsir.com.

120 Cited in Elmalılı Muhammad Hamdi Yazır, *Kur'ani Kerim Tefsiri*, www.kuranikerim.com/telmalili/nuh.htm. Retrieved 5.10.2012.

Prophet Abraham did not just shed tears so often but also moaned without respite: "Indeed, Abraham was forbearing, grieving and [frequently] returning [to Allah]" (Qur'an 11: 75). The word *awwâh* (most tender-hearted) is used as an attribute of Abraham (Qur'an, 9:114, 11:75). According to al-Qurtubi (1214–1273), *awwâh* has fifteen different meanings. It means "very merciful, confident; completely sure, invoker of the Name of God a lot, making a deep sound of expressing pain, remembering the Names of God in solitary conditions with tears, deep sorrow, a deep reverence for God, showing clemency, weeping, sighing for his sins, and feeling sympathy for people who are suffering." *Awwâh* also means to feel very deep sorrow and pity towards all creation, including enemies and sinners.[121] This reflects in a state of extreme suffering, shedding tears, crying, and finally it transforms into a deep moaning. According to Fakhr al-Din al-Razi (1149–1209), *awwâh* is the spiritual station of Abraham. God honours Abraham with this honourable title.[122] He indicates that, when Abraham learned about the destruction of the tribe of Lot, he cried and sighed a lot for them. When angels mentioned that it was an order from God, Abraham still continued to pray for their salvation.[123] For Gülen, even though *awwâh* is the title of Abraham, whoever has this attribute, can be called *awwâh* as well.

Prophet David's (Dawud) tears left permanent marks on his face.[124] Prophet Jacob burst into tears after hearing that a wolf ate his son, Joseph. Eventually, he lost his sight after crying for many years.[125] Joseph cried when he was thrown into the well. After being rescued from the well and living in a luxurious mansion with enough food to enjoy, Joseph shed tears and his heart ached daily with longing for his parents and brother Benjamin.[126] He continued shedding tears in the jail for years and during his administrative position as controller of the granaries in the palace of the Egyptian king as well.[127] In a helpless state during his

---

121 Al-Qurtubi, Al-Jamiu Li Ahkami'l Qur'an, altafsir.com. Retrieved 17.04.2017.

122 Fakhruddin ar-Razi, Mafatih'ul Ghayb, altafsir.com. Retrieved 07.09.2016

123 Ar-Razi, ibid., altafsir.com. Retrieved 07.09.2016.

124 Fethullah Gülen, *Sonsuz Nur* 1 (Izmir: Nil Yayinlari, 2011), 479.

125 Ibn Kathir, *History of the Prophets*, 144–148.

126 Ibid., 75.

127 Ibid., 75.

sickness, Prophet Job (Ayyoub) turned to Allah, not to complain but to seek his mercy: "Verily! distress has seized me, and You are the Most Merciful of all those who show mercy" (Qur'an, 21:83–84).

Ibn Mubarak (726–797) stated that Wahb ibn Al-Ward narrated that Prophet Zachariah did not see his son John (Yahya) for three days. He found him weeping inside a grave which he had dug and in which he resided: "My son, I have been searching for you, and you are dwelling in this grave and weeping!" "O father, did you not tell me that between Paradise and hell is only a span, and it will not be crossed except by the tears of weepers?" He said to him: "Weep then, my son." Then both wept together. It is stated that Prophet Yahya cried so much that tears marked his cheeks.[128] Al-Ghazali adds that, when Prophet Yahya cried in prayer, the trees and plants used to weep with him. His father also used to cry so much at seeing his son's weeping that he sometimes fell into a swoon.[129]

On his return from Mount Sinai, Prophet Moses saw his people singing and dancing around the statue of the calf. Furious at their pagan rituals, he flung down the Tablet of the Law and he cried for them.[130] The Christian scriptures report that Prophet Jesus wept over knowing what would befall the inhabitants of the city because of their rejection of him (Luke 19:41). According to Isaiah (53:3), he would shed tears regularly during the years of his ministry.

There are about thirty-five verses in which tears are mentioned in the Qur'an. It is essential to explain three verses (19:58, 5:83, 12:16) which are directly related to the topic in the light of major Qur'anic exegeses:

> Those are some of the Prophets upon whom God bestowed His blessings (of Scripture, Prophethood, good judgement, and wisdom) from among the descendants of Adam and of those whom We carried (in the Ark) with Noah, and from among the descendants of Abraham and Israel (Jacob), and those whom We guided and chose. When the All-Merciful's Revelations were recited to them, they would fall down, prostrating and weeping. (Qur'an, 19:58)

---

128   Ibid., 171.

129   Al-Ghazzali, *Revival of Religious Learnings, Imam Ghazzali's Ihya Ulum-id-Din*, translated by Fazl-ul-Karim, V. IV p.139 ghazali.org/ihya/english/ihya-vol4-C3. htm. Retrieved 03.10.2016.

130   Ibn Kathir, *History of the Prophets*.

Ar-Razi states that this verse is about all the Prophets. Weeping during the act of prostration is the characteristic of all Prophets and those who believed in them.[131] Al-Qushayri (986–1074) adds that they do not prostrate physically only but also their inner (souls) prostrate with them.[132] Al-Baqillai (950–1013) asserts that during the prostration, the Prophets have *marifa* (gnostic knowledge) and are at the spiritual station of *muhabba* (love). They love to be with the Beloved. For them, nothing is sweeter or more enjoyable than prostrating and shedding tears.[133] Al-Qurtubi (1214–1273) says that when the believers read or recite the Qur'an, they weep and prostrate.[134] Additionally, al-Baqillai says that during the prostration, they are at the spiritual station of *ma'rifatullah* and *muhabbatullah*. Commenting on this verse, Ibn Arabi asserts that it is the crying of the heart. During the prostration, they feel and witness the Attributes of God, and there is a strong desire to be reunited with Him[135] Sayyid Qutb states that they are truly God-fearing and very sensitive to pleasing or displeasing God. This sensation is so strong that they cannot express their inner feelings in words. Their eyes are tearful and they fall, prostrating themselves before God, and weep.[136] Al-Sa'rawi (1911–1988) argues that the Qur'an does not address only the mind but also all parts of the body. This leads to the eyes filling with tears, the softening of the heart, and prostration.[137]

> When they hear what has been sent down to the Messenger, you see their eyes brimming over with tears because they know something of its truth (from their own Books); and they say, "Our Lord! We do believe (in Muhammad and the Qur'an); so inscribe us among the witnesses (of the truth in the company of his community)." (Qur'an, 5:83)

---

131   Ar-Razi, *Mafatih'ul Ghayb*, altafsir.com.

132   Al-Qushayri, *Lataif al-Isharat*, altafsir.com.

133   Al-Baqliyyu, *A'raisu'l Bayan*, altafsir.com.

134   Al-Qurtubi, *Al-Jamiu'l Ahkam*, altafsir.com. Retrieved 04.07.2016.

135   Ibn Arabi, *Tafsir al-Qur'an*, altafsir.com. Retrieved 04.07.2016.

136   Sayyid Qutb, *In the Shade of the Qur'an*, Vol. 11, p. 285, available at www.kalam-ullah.com/Books/InTheShadeOfTheQuranSayyidQutb/volume_11_surahs_16-20.pdf. Retrieved 03.10.2016.

137   Muhammad Matawalli Al-Sa'rawi, *Khawatir Muhammad Metwali Al-Sa'rawi*, altafsir.com. Retrieved 03.10.2016.

According to al-Tabari, this verse was revealed for a group of Christian clergy who were sent to Medina by Negus, the King of Abyssinia to obtain more information about the Prophet Muhammad (pbuh). When they listened to the Qur'an and witnessed his attributes and character, they wept and prostrated.[138] Al-Zamakhshari (1070–1143) asserts that the priests already knew the truth about the Prophet, but they prostrated to God after seeing Prophet Muhammad (pbuh) in Medina.[139] Ar-Razi states that when Jaffar ibn Abu Talib recited the chapter of Mary, King Negus and the priests who were present shed tears and then prostrated.[140] He adds that crying for fear of God is an attribute of all Prophets.[141] Al-Qurtubi states that weeping and making others cry is an attribute of scholars. They cry, but they do not faint, they supplicate and cry but not for getting human attention, they grieve but do not ask God to be allowed to die.[142]

Al-Baqillai interprets this verse as follows: It explains the attributes of sincere faithful people. They listen attentively to the invocation of the Names of God; their minds are totally satisfied with the evidence, and their hearts are sweetened. Their attributes are manifested in tears which are the product of *ma'rifatullah* and strong desire to be with God.[143] Ibrahim Haqqi adds that the Christian clergy accepted the truth after hearing it and hastening to be enlightened. Recitation of the Qur'an softened their hearts and filled their eyes with tears.[144] Also, Al-Baqillai says that this verse explains the sincere attributes and truthfulness at the degree of certainty of faith. They shed tears as their souls observe the Prophet. Their hearts are sweetened with *dhikr* (remembrance of God), they benefit from the ocean of knowledge and feel signs of *tawhid* (unity of God) in their consciousness. Their tears are aspiration. It is due to possessing in-depth knowledge (*ma'rifatullah*)of God. These attributes are reflected

138   Al-Tabari, al-Jamiu'l Bayan, altafsir.com. Retrieved 04.07.2016.

139   Al-Zamakhshari, al-Kashaf, altafsir.com. Retrieved 04.07.2016.

140   Ar-Razi, ibid., altafsir.com.

141   ibid.

142   Al-Qurtubi, ibid.,

143   Al-Baqillai, ibid., altafsir.com. Retrieved 04.07.2016.

144   Ismail Haqqi, ibid., altafsir.com. Retrieved 04.07.2016.

in their lives by shedding tears.[145] For al-Jilani (1077–1166), shedding tears means to reach a high spiritual station.[146] On commenting on this verse, Qutb states that they were so deeply touched when the Christian clergy listened to the Qur'an that tears sprang from their eyes in recognition of the truth they heard. In the first instance, they cannot express this appreciation in any way better than allowing their eyes to overflow with tears. No words are adequate to describe their feelings. Such a response, indicative of the profound effect, is a well-known human reaction.[147]

The Qur'an mentions the false tears (12:16) of Joseph's brothers. Those who shed false tears or cry for show are called the losers by al-Ghazali. To cry like an actor with false tears for show is very dangerous and kills one's spiritual life. As al-Ghazali says, the one who cries may lose, and the one who does not cry may lose as well. The tears are also a reflection of loyalty to someone's goals.[148] Tears are mentioned almost as many times as *zakat*, which is one of the five pillars of Islam. This shows how the Qur'an gives importance to crying and weeping for a variety of reasons. Additionally, tearful eyes can be due to the wonder of creation, and suffering for others is praised. It can be said that as *zakat* purifies the wealth, similarly tears for love or fear of God purify the heart and soul.

3.2 Tears in the *Sunnah*

The Prophet Muhammad (pbuh) would cry for the wonder of the creation during worship. He used to pray the *Tahajjud* and then would look at and contemplate the heavens and cry. Therefore, the Prophet sought refuge from eyes that do not shed tears as he took refuge from Satan.[149] Abdullah ibn Shikkheer said, "I attended the noble assembly of the Prophet Muhammad (pbuh). He was performing the ritual Prayer (*Salat*). Because of his crying, such a sound emitted from his chest, like

---

145 Al-Baqillai, ibid., altafsir.com.

146 Al-Jilani, ibid., altafsir.com.

147 Sayyid Qutb, ibid, Vol. 4, p. 186, www.kalamullah.com/Books/InTheShadeOf-heQuranSayyidQutb/volume_4_surah_5.pdf. Retrieved 03.10.2016.

148 Fethullah Gülen, *Kalbin Zümrüt Tepeleri*, 2, (Izmir: Nil Yayınları, 2011), 179.

149 Ibn Hajar, *Fathu'l-Bari*, 11/139. In Gülen, *Asrın Getirdiği Tereddütler* 4, 115–118

that of a boiling pot."[150] The Prophet would cry a lot and made his Companions cry as well. He would recite the Qur'an while shedding tears and strongly recommended reciting it with sorrow and weeping. According to Ibn Arabi, the Prophet views all humans as his children and relatives, and he even he saw them as being like the organs of his body.[151] So, he cries when any calamity or tragedy strikes them.

Gülen says that Prophet Muhammad (pbuh)) can be called a Prophet of grief and lamentation. One night he recited: "If You should punish them, indeed they are Your servants; but if You forgive them, indeed it is You who is the Exalted in Might, the Wise" (Qur'an, 5:18). And then he cried the whole night. When the Archangel Gabriel let him know that "God will not afflict you about your *ummah* on the day of judgement," he ceased crying.[152] Aisha said that "one night the Prophet asked my permission and he wanted to worship his Lord. He made his ablution and started praying the *Tahajjud*. He recited 'Indeed, in the creation of the heavens and the earth and the alternation of the night and the day are signs for those of understanding' (Qur'an, 3:190) and cried until the Morning Prayer." Gülen views fasting, the *Tahajjud*, enthusiasm and tears as being the foundation of one's spiritual life and strengthening of the faith. The status of performing the Prayer with tears does not just affect the person but also softens the hearts of others.[153] The Prophet says, "Humble yourself and cry. Inevitably, the heavens, earth, the sun and the moon and stars cry because of fear of God."[154]

The Qur'an narrates the stories of people who cry as exemplary. Al-Zamakhshari relates a story: Saleh al-Marwi saw the Prophet in his dream. He recited the Qur'an to the Prophet without shedding tears. The Prophet told him, "O Saleh, this is the Qur'an but where are the tears?"[155] For al-Jilani, those who shed tears (during the recitation) do so because of their desire to reach a higher spiritual

---

150   Shama'il Muhammadiyah, *sunnah*.com/urn/1803040. Retrieved 01.10.2016.

151   Ibn Arabi, ibid., altafsir.com. Retrieved 04.07.2016.

152   Al-Qurtubi, ibid., altafsir.com. Gülen, *Beyan*, 111.

153   Gülen, *Asrın Getirdiği Tereddütler* 4, 118.

154   Ismail Haqqi, ibid., altafsir.com. Retrieved 17.04.2016,

155   Zamakhshari, *Al-Kashaf*, altafsir.com.

rank.[156] Abdullah ibn Abbas (619–687) recommends supplicating, "O God make me cry during the recitation of the Qur'an" after each recitation. Most of the exegetes accept that this verse included all previous Prophets and their followers.

The Companions of the Prophet and righteous peoples also cry. Ali (r.a.) narrates that they spend the whole night in prayer and recite the verses of God. Their eyes shed tears, so much so that they wet their clothes.[157] Ar-Razi argues that it is a tradition of righteous people to express themselves during grief or sorrow like Mary, the mother of Jesus. On realising that she was pregnant with Jesus, she said, "Oh, I wish I had died before this and was in oblivion, forgotten" (Qur'an, 19:23). When Abu Bakr was the caliph, he saw a bird on a tree which was eating its fruit; he said, "Glad tidings to you, O bird. I wish I were the fruit which you eat." Umar took some chaff from the ground and said, "I wish I were chaff." On the day of the Battle of Jamal, Ali (r.a.) said, "I wish I had died before this day." All shed tears and wanted to be unknown or have no responsibility.[158] Abu Bakr was not allowed to pray in public in Mecca because when he recited the Qur'an and shed tears, those who listened would convert to Islam. Then, a thought occurred to Abu Bakr to build a small mosque in front of his house, and there he used to pray and recite the Qur'an. The women and children of the pagans began to gather around him in high numbers. They used to wonder at him and watch him. Abu Bakr was a man who used to weep very much, and he could not stop weeping during the recitation of the Qur'an.

Irbad Ibn Sariya was one of the poor Companions, and he is known for bursting into tears. Once, he wept because he did not have anything to donate and therefore he could not participate in the Tabuk expedition. A verse was revealed for his status and the Qur'an honours such tears (Qur'an 9:92).[159] Umar ibn Abdu'l-Aziz many times would cry or weep

156   Al-Jilani, ibid, altafsir.com. Retrieved 04.07.2016.

157   Al-Ghazali, *Revival of Religious Learnings, Ihya Ulum-id-Din*, trans. Fazl-ul-Karim, Vol. IV, 141, ghazali.org/ihya/english/ihya-vol4-C3.htm. Retrieved 03.10.2016.

158   Ar-Razi, ibid., altafsir.com. Retrieved 1.10.2016.

159   Abu Naim al-Isfahani, *Hilyetul Awliya (Allah Dostlari)*, 2 cev. Sait Aykut (Istanbul: Sule Yayınları, 2003), 79.

and sometimes even scream and faint after visiting the cemetery.[160] In the night, he would perform the *Tahajjud*, supplicate and cry until the *Fajr*, the Morning Prayer.[161] If a heart does not cry through the eyes, it has spiritual diseases, some Sufis argue. The Prophet and his Companions viewed shedding tears as part of the spiritual ascension in this world and the extinguisher of hellfire in the Hereafter.

3.3 Why humans cry

In this section, firstly, I will elaborate on the causes and spiritual value of shedding tears. Then, I will analyse how sorrow, grief, *ma'rifa* and love of God manifest as tears in the light of the works of great figures in the Islamic history because their works are products of a combination of the sacred suffering of their souls, the shedding of tears, the supplication of being helpless in status and gifted knowledge (*ilm mawhibah*). Finally, what has made Gülen cry from a young age will be studied by analysing his sermons, works, public and private talks, and the testimonials of his friends.

There could be physical, emotional, spiritual, religious, and other reasons for shedding tears. It is a fact that all Prophets, saints, and great scholars cried. According to Gülen, sadness and shedding tears are the status of the saints, groaning day and night are the shortest way to reach the Reality.[162] Also, the shedding of tears is the quickest and shortest way of acceptance of *dua* (supplication) in the sight of God because there is nothing that can purely manifest the enthusiasm of heart more than tears.[163] For al-Ghazali, shedding tears is considered by the great scholars and saints as an essential for purifying the hearts from spiritual diseases such as jealousy, hatred, rancour, animosity, and the like. He states that as a cloth polluted by foul acts can be cleaned with soap and warm water, so a soul polluted with passion and greed can be purified by the tears of the eyes and the fire of repentance.[164] Ismail Haqqi says *huzn* (sorrow)

---

160   al-Isfahani, ibid., 2, 235.

161   al-Isfahani, ibid., 2, 253.

162   Fethullah Gülen, "Bence Tam Ağlama Mevsimi", *Yağmur*, October, 2002.

163   Gülen, *Beyan*, 114.

164   Al-Ghazali, *Revival of Religious Learnings*, Vol. 4, p. 20, available at ghazali.org/ihya/english/ihya-vol4-C1.htm.

is the beauty of saints. The Prophets and *siddiqs* get pleasure from *huzn*. They are spiritually delighted with sorrow.[165] Abdulqadr al-Jilani, the founder of the Qadiri Sufi order says that if Allah loves a person, He will inspire sorrow in his heart. Through *huzn* the hearts will be purified.[166] Ibn Arabi states that such believers who have sorrow in their hearts are at the spiritual station of witnessing the signs and manifestation of the attributes of God in the universe. It is the weeping of the heart.[167]

It can be said that the lover of God cools down his/her heart by shedding tears, but the faithful one burns his inner self by bursting into tears inside himself. Tears are the mercy of the Most Merciful which bursts from the eyes. It is like a dew which combines the tongue, heart, and feelings of someone. For Gülen, the earrings of *huris* in heaven have almost no value compared with tears. Nothing is sweeter or more joyful than the tears of suffering for others.[168] Rumi asserts, "God takes a few drops of your tears, and gives you the Divine fount sweeter than sugar."[169] If it is not sweeter, how could Prophets, saints, and great scholars endure crying day and night? They cry for the separation from Him but also for a reunion with the Beloved. While they suffer from the pain of separation from the Beloved, their hearts are full of spiritual joy. Their souls are like birds which dwell in the heaven.

The tears sometimes are the product of *ma'rifatullah* (deeply knowing God), *muhabbatullah* (love of God) and *makhafatullah* (fear of God). The tears which do not come from the heart are deceitful. Crying and weeping for the sake of God is based on His love which sometimes is reflected in moaning. Suffering and crying for others is considered a form of worship and the tradition of all Prophets.

The great scholars cry when they are born, just like other humans. However, for them, shedding tears becomes part of their lives until they die. When they run out of tears, then their hearts and souls suffer and cry. Sometimes the eyes, heart, and soul cry together. They cry and weep

---

165   Ismail Haqqi, ibid., altafsir.com. Retrieved 5.9.2016.

166   Al-Jilani, ibid., altafsir.com. Retrieved 5.9.2016.

167   Ibn Arabi, ibid, altafsir.com.

168   Gülen, "Bence Tam Ağlama Mevsimi".

169   Rumi, Mathnawi, Book 6, www.sacred-texts.com/isl/masnavi/msn06.htm. Retrieved 29.09.2016.

so much they make others cry and weep as well. Seeing the perfection of the arts of God in the universe leads to the shedding of tears. The destiny of all great scholars is not being understood by their contemporaries and suffering beneath the hands of oppressive rulers. Instead of rebelling against oppression and tyranny, they reflect their civil disobedience through suffering and tears.

For Gülen, tears are shed from the eyes of sincere and tender-hearted people. Their suffering for humanity with the whole of the body is manifested as streaming tears.[170] He continues, "the Qur'an narrates the stories of people who cry as exemplary. Every teardrop is a witness of the compassionate heart and it is as valuable as the *khawthar* pool in Paradise.[171] Therefore, the Prophet seeks refuge from eyes that do not shed tears as he takes refuge from Satan."[172]

According to Gülen, shedding tears for his/her sin is a step in spiritual ascension.[173] Indeed, the shedding of tears is the quickest and shortest way of acceptance of *dua* (supplication) in the sight of God because there is nothing which can purely manifest the enthusiasm of the heart, except tears.[174] He says that disobedience to the commands of God, committing big sins and crimes is like an invitation to calamities and tribulations. Many tribes and nations are destroyed or have collapsed because of the transgression of their peoples. The devoted ones, however, who are tender-hearted and shed tears for their sins and others' transgressions, are like a lightning conductor protecting against sins.[175] As Prophet Muhammad (pbuh) says, "because of a person's tears, God saves the whole community."[176]

Gülen says that saints view tears as the water of life for the revival of a spiritually dead person and as the breath of Jesus which gave life

---

170   Gülen, *Asrın Getirdiği Tereddütler* 4, 113.

171   Ibid., 115.

172   Ibn Hajar al-Asqalani, *Fathu'l-Bari*, 11/139 in Gülen, *Asrın Getirdiği Tereddütler* 4, 115.

173   Gülen, *Beyan*, 113.

174   Ibid., 114.

175   Fethullah Gülen, İnancın Gölgesinde 1 (Izmir: Nil Yayınları, 2011), 74.

176   Tirmidhi

to the dead. He continues that tears guided Adam to be forgiven.[177] There is nothing falling on the earth that is more valuable than tears in the sight of God because all tears falling on the earth will eventually give life spiritually to others.[178] Tears which are shed from human eyes are the mercy of God.[179] In the sight of saints, tears are more valuable than the fountains of Paradise because each teardrop is like an elixir which can put out hellfire. Abraham invoked "*hasbi hasbi*" (God is sufficient) with tears in the catapult when he was cast into the fire, and this caused the fire to be cool and safe for him (Qur'an, 21:69).[180] Rumi says, "When the tears course down my cheeks, they are a proof of the beauty and grace of my Beloved."[181] According to Gülen, the saints, even if they unintentionally look at something *haram* (unlawful) only once, shed tears for the rest of their lives. Even at the point of death, they suffer for such sins and still they are critical of themselves for committing them.

Umar, the second caliph, despite his bravery and uncompromising nature, would cry with a broken-hearted person and made others cry with them as well.[182] Such a tender-hearted person is "one who fears God, sometimes sighs and sometimes weeps, especially when alone, in an attempt to extinguish the pain of being separate from Him as well as the fire of hell, which is the greatest distance between him and God."[183] A time comes when they express these pangs with sighs from the depth of the heart, and also when they put these feelings into invocations and tears in seclusion. Those with a self-accusing soul advance along the intermediate corridor between carnal appetites and

---

177 Gülen, *Beyan*, 116

178 Gülen, *Beyan* 118

179 Gülen, *Çağ ve Nesil* 1, 51

180 Gülen, *Çağ ve Nesil* 1, 52–53

181 Rumi, Book 4, www.sacred-texts.com/isl/masnavi/msn04.htm. Retrieved 29.09.2016.

182 Gülen, *Çağ ve Nesil* 1, 54.

183 Gülen, *Key Concepts in the Practice of Sufism* 1, available on www.fgulen.com/en/ fethullah-Gülen s-works/sufism/key-concepts-in-the-practice-of-sufism-1/24731- khawf-and-khashya-fear-and-reverence. Retrieved 07.09.2016.

sins, and spiritual peace.[184]

People who have not been able to make their inner worlds into a honeycomb of belief and knowledge and love of God are unaware of love and the meaning of tears. Such people live all their lives bereft of or wearied of pursuing excitement and emotions and can never feel the deep spiritual pleasure of pouring themselves out to God in a solitary corner with sighs and tears. Even though it has been witnessed that such crude souls weep, their weeping resembles the weeping of children whose toys have been taken from their hands. Weeping is, in fact, the voice or translation of purity of spirit and tender-heartedness. Human faculties are stirred up by this voice, and the slopes of the heart begin to green; spring arrives in the human world of emotions. How well expressed are the following words of Rumi:

> If clouds were not to weep, the grass would not smile;
> If infants were not to weep, the milk would not flow;
> You should know that unless there is weeping,
> The Lord of the lords does not give milk.[185]

Gülen says that some of God's friends say in the same strain, "Those who do not weep today will not be able to be saved from sighing and mourning tomorrow (in the Hereafter)."[186] This must have been said in accordance with the Prophetic supplication, "O God! I seek refuge in You from eyes that do not weep."[187] Sometimes suffering for others' guidance is revealed as shedding tears. When a person reaches the spiritual

184   Fethullah Gülen, *Key Concepts in the Practice of Sufism* 2, available on www.fgulen. com/en/fethullah-Gülen s-works/sufism/key-concepts-in-the-practice-of-sufism-2/25742-sayr-u-suluk-journeying-and-initiation. Retrieved 07.09.2016.

185   Fethullah Gülen, *Key Concepts in the Practice of Sufism* 4, available on www.fgulen. com/en/fethullah-gulens-works/sufism/key-concepts-in-the-practice-of-sufism-4/47815-putting-an-end-to-a-long-journey. Retrieved 15.04.2015.

186   Fethullah Gülen, "Taşlaşan Kalbler ve Gözyaşları," www.herkul.org/kirik-testi/taslasan-kalbler-ve-gozyaslari. Retrieved 25.04.2017.

187   Fethullah Gülen, *Key Concepts in the Practice of Sufism* 4, fgulen.com/en/fethullah-Gülens-works/sufism/key-concepts-in-the-practice-of-sufism-4/47815-putting-an-end-to-a-long-journey. Retrieved 07.09.2016.

level of complete nothingness and realises his/her defects or imperfection, this is reflected as tears in daily life. Sometimes a higher degree of compassion and mercy in an individual is transformed into tears. As Ibn Arabi mentions, a saint may cry, for descending from an angelic spiritual level to a normal human life causes him/her to cry. A saint may cry because she or he could not complete her or his mission as she or he wishes. Al-Alusi states that crying and weeping is an essential attribute of a real scholar. If a scholar does not weep, he or she cannot get the benefit of his or her knowledge.[188]

Through crying, hearts and minds are conquered, animosity reduced, conflicts ended, peace and social harmony established. It can be said that those who cry contribute or lead to social changes by their tears. The shared destiny of most of those who cry for others is not to be understood by their contemporaries. Their tears are valued after their death like the art works of eminent artists. They see bursting into tears as one of the most acceptable *dua*s (supplications) in the sight of God.

After studying and analysing the life of more than fifty of the most influential scholars in Islamic history, it can be said that their works are the product of suffering, crying and sighing. While their eyes well with tears, also their hearts bleed and the soul is joined to both through suffering. Gülen's life is very similar to these great scholars, specifically, Hasan al-Basri (642–728), who had marks of tears on his face because of crying; so too do Gülen's eyes remain swollen.

3.4 The tears of Gülen

Gülen is known as one of the most influential, most controversial, and also probably the most tearful, weeping and sighing scholars of our time. He has been known for his tearful eyes since his youth. He prayed to God, sighing like Abraham, crying like Jacob until people began to think he was a madman when he was a teenager. What makes him cry and what makes his audience cry?

Gülen, as mentioned in Chapter 1, grew up in a family in which his grandparents and parents shed tears mainly for spiritual reasons. His grandfather Şamil Ağa had tearful eyes. His grandmother, Munise

---

188 Al-Alusi, *Ruhu'l Ma'ani*. altafsir.com.

Khatun, was known as the lady who cried a lot when she invoked the Names of God. Gülen's parents, Ramiz Efendi and Refia, also had tearful eyes. As mentioned in the first chapter, when Imam Ramiz Efendi reached the age of sixty-four, he cried. The reason was that he felt that Prophet Muhammad (pbuh) lived sixty-three years and living more than him, made him burst into tears.

Gülen says, "My grandmother was like my parents who were very generous. There is no one like her. If she did not have a few guests at home daily, she would feel sorrow and shed tears. We would receive visitors from various backgrounds, including saintly people. My grandmother would love to offer everything that we have at home. She often would cry and weep for remembrance of God, sometimes so many times during day and night."[189] It seems Munise Khatun, the Gülen's grandmother, left a permanent mark on him regarding shedding tears. When both grandfather and grandmother passed away on the same night within one hour, when he was a teenager, Gülen cried a lot for them and asked God to be with them. Since then, tears have become a part of Gülen's daily life.

When Gülen studied the life of the *sahabah*, the Companions of the Prophet, their life stories would touch his heart, and he would burst into tears. In most of his sermons and public and private talks, Gülen's eyes brim with tears when he mentions the heroism of *sahabah*, the devotion of great saints and scholars, and their piety, asceticism, altruism and sincerity. When he was attending the study circle of Muhammed Lütfi Efendi, who had tearful eyes, Gülen witnessed and experienced tears for a deep love of God and the Prophet, for Lütfi Efendi so often would burst into tears when he mentioned God or Prophet Muhammad (pbuh). It can be said that the tears of Lütfi Efendi, and Gülen's parents and grandparents have left a permanent effect and rooted a very compassionate nature in the heart and soul of Gülen.

After Lütfi Efendi had passed away, Gülen began to attend the *Risale-i Nur* study circle in Erzurum with Said Nursi's students. One day, the students of Said Nursi received a letter in which Said Nursi sent his salaam (greetings) to Gülen. He was so excited about it that he shed tears. For Gülen, it was the happiest time for him. He went to Lale Pasha Mosque and spent the whole night offering supplication and begging God. He

---

189   Gülen, *Fasıldan Fasıla* 3, 73.

prayed, "O my God, dearest God, please include me spiritually in the Nur movement (which was established by Said Nursi). I would like to dedicate my whole life entirely to the service of the Qur'an and faith by being one of them." Then he shed tears and sighed until the Morning Prayer. "The whole night, I only asked this from my Lord," Gülen stated.

He prayed at a young age: "O God, I ask and beg You for shedding tears and making me cry to deserve your mercy and because of yearning not to be away from You. Make me cry and show Your clemency to my soul which is dark like the night. Make me moan because this is necessary to be forgiven for my insincere crying and weeping…O my God, make me *awwâh* (like Prophet Abraham), and to be like the Prophet Job."[190] Shedding tears, he continued, "O my God, make me cry a lot until people think that I am a mad person."[191] Gülen says that "in the morning, one of my close friends, Hatem Hodja, saw me in the mosque and shared his dream with me. In his dream, Said Nursi sent a letter to me. Now, I began to shed tears of happiness. I will never forget that moment in my life."

Gülen public image is of a learned scholar, a teary-eyed, saintly mystic and a highly passionate activist. He is famous within Turkey for his passionate and spiritual sermons bringing tens of thousands of listeners to tears along with him.[192]

The first time the author heard about Fethullah Gülen was at the age of thirteen at a Nur study circle[193] in Adıyaman, a city in the southeast of Turkey. A university student mentioned how Gülen was educating the students, showing his devotion, and performing the *Tahajjud* (night vigil Prayer) every night while weeping. Then, in 1975, I read his book "*Hitap Çiçekleri*" (Flowers of Speech). A year later, I was able to

---

190   Gülen, *Çağ ve Nesil* 1, 55.

191   Fethullah Gülen, *Sızıntı*, September, 1979.

192   Özalp, "Muhammad Fethullah Gülen", 37

193   Despite pressure from the secular government, Said Nursi's works would be studied in smaller study circles through Turkey. Between 1930 and 1960 there were more than 1,500 prosecutions of those who read Nursi's books and sometimes they were imprisoned. This could not stop the growth of the study circles in Turkey. Nevertheless, this oppression and persecution continued until the mid-1980s to a certain extent.

listen to one of his sermons on a tape cassette which was about youth and chivalry while shedding tears. Unfortunately, I was not able to meet him for almost two decades, despite my wishes. After moving to Australia, I continued to listen to his sermons on video recordings in the late 1980s. Later, whenever I listened to his tapes or video recordings, sometimes I could not stop myself from bursting into tears.

I have analysed over five hundred of Gülen's speeches and sermons. I asked questions of his close associates about the reasons for his crying. He weeps during the delivery of almost all his sermons and talks. His close associates told me that Gülen has been crying during the delivery of his speeches since the age of fifteen. When he came to Sydney in 1992, I had the opportunity to visit him for the first time. With tearful eyes, he talked to a small gathering in a house. I was very impressed at the level of his in-depth knowledge and humility. Although I was not able to attend his two sermons in Sydney and Melbourne, later I heard that he broke down in tears during the delivery.

In August 1997, I had another opportunity to visit him in New Jersey, and I stayed at the house where he lived for about twenty days. He would give short talks after performing the daily ritual Prayer (*Salat*) and sometimes after the breakfast, lunch and dinner as well. He would break into tears during each talk about spirituality. He also made others weep. His talks included the love of God, the Prophet, his Companions, great scholars and figures of Islam, serving religion, and various topics related to spirituality. He avoided talking about politics.

After he went to the United States for some medical treatment in 1999, I had the opportunity to visit him very many times, while I was working and studying in New York and Boston up until 2007. I witnessed that almost every time he talked, he shed tears. I can give hundreds of examples, but it would be outside the scope of this research. To understand why Gülen weeps so often, however, it is necessary to give a few examples based on testimonials from his close friends and some which I personally witnessed.

3.5 Testimonials from friends

Irmak and Mefkure TV channels in Turkey made a documentary called "*Geçmişten İzler*" (Marks of the Past) about the history of the Hizmet Movement in its early years. More than fifty people who played very important voluntary roles in the movement in the late 1960s and early 1970s were interviewed. Almost all shed tears when they recalled those years and especially Gülen's weeping, piety, altruism, hard work, commitment to serving the community, suffering for others, firmness in his faith, and so on. Gülen's tears had a deep effect on their minds, hearts, and souls. When recalling those days, they still felt like they were reliving those moments.

One of his students stated that once, Gülen, his eyes filled with tears, came out of his room with a scroll of paper. He wanted to burn the manuscript because he did not want to put it in the trash bin, and there was no recycle bin. We later realised that he had written an article about *Ahadiyyat* and *Wahdaniyyat* (Oneness and Unity of God) in a few days. Gülen did not see himself as worthy of writing such an article about God. Therefore, he thought that the article was not worthy and he wanted to destroy it. We asked him to rethink and revise it again instead of destroying it. He was very kind and accepted our request. He returned to his room still shedding tears.

Rıfat Sayar, who has known Gülen since the early 1970s, said that "*Erkekler ağlamaz*" (a Turkish proverb which means "men never cry") is like a macho culture. After attending his sermons, Sayar saw how Gülen and his congregation were crying while he was preaching about God, His Messenger and the Companions. He says, "Then, I changed my mind to 'men cry so much.' By shedding tears, we have deepened our faith in God, and we found our Lord." He said that "we would go to his sermon to shed tears, which in turn would strengthen our faith and motivate us to serve Islam." Sayar calls Gülen "*Yağmur Gözlü*" which means "rainy-eyed." He uses this because the tears of Gülen drop from his eyes like raindrops fall from heaven. Sayar said, "Whenever I pray behind him, I cannot stop my eyes flowing with tears." In his interview with Irmak TV in 2015, Ahmet Haskesen said, "Gülen has always cried in his talks or sermons and private study circle since I have known him."

Malik Ejder recalls the late 1970s: "One of my friends took me to Manisa for Gülen's sermon. When I wanted to enter the mosque, it was full of young people, a thing which I had never seen in my life. Gülen started preaching, and everyone was crying. I was shocked. No one was bashing, or torturing them. Why were they crying? I was told that they were crying because of the preaching about the Prophet and his Companions. Gülen was crying as well. I was so affected by those tears."

3.5.1 Crying over separation

Ahmet Haskesen tells a story. Osman Aykut, one of Said Nursi students who respected and loved Gülen because of his Islamic service, piety, and character. Aykut was Hizmet Movement volunteer in Turgutlu, one of those who took responsibility for setting up projects and fund raising for them. One day before he passed away, unexpectedly, he was so keen to talk to Gülen. So we called Cevdet Türkyolu who attends to Gülen's needs at the retreat centre in Pennsylvania. However, unexpectedly, Gülen picked up the phone. Aykut had hearing loss and did not realise that he was talking to Gülen. He repeatedly said that he would like to speak with Gülen. Finally, he realised that it was Gülen on the phone. He could not talk but started weeping and then sobbing; on the other end, Gülen was crying, and he could not talk to Aykut either. For about seven minutes both cried to each other without saying a single word. Then Aykut hung up the phone and the next day he passed away.

The son of Said Nursi's student Mustafa Birlik, Abdullah Ünal Birlik, recalls, "My father had a very high respect for Gülen. He visited our house many times from 1967. Gülen was like one of our family members. My dad would always visit him from the late 1960s. When my dad was very sick in the hospital, Gülen phoned him from the USA. He was not able to talk but he could utter just a few words. Then my father hung up the phone. He began crying for almost twenty to twenty-five minutes. Later, I was told that Gülen also cried for half an hour. My dad asked me to read Said Nursi's books and also to always be part of the Hizmet Movement as his last request. In addition, he told me to visit Gülen regularly."

3.5.2 Hours of crying

In Chapter 2, I have already described Gülen's grief and distress at seeing a tree branch cut off, and living creatures maltreated. He is known to weep for hours and grieve for days over the damage humans do to their surroundings, the environment, and to God's creatures—actions which might be seen as sins or bad deeds sometimes. His tears also flow freely when he sees good deeds have been or are likely to be thwarted.

In 1999, Hizmet participants in the United States planned to set up a school in one of the states. The foundation's board of education obtained permission from the Department of Education to open the school in early September 1999. They rented a building which needed renovating. The head of the foundation's board came to visit Gülen in mid-August. Gülen asked him if they would be able to open the school in September. He said that it was not possible as the renovation would not be completed by that time, and it might take another two to three months, although the contractor was supposed to have finished it by the end of August. Hearing that, Gülen became very sad, which could be read from his face. After a few words about the importance of education, Gülen asked him to go back and find a way to open the school for the fall season, otherwise, it would be delayed for one year. Gülen would normally give a short talk or have a conversation during the meal and after his daily Prayer, which was performed in congregation. That day he was very upset because of the news and he did not talk or converse with anyone for the whole day and night. The building in which he lived was not sound-proof, so any voice in the next room could be heard.

That night, I was sleeping in the second floor in a room very close above Gülen's room. Around one o'clock in the morning, I woke up to Gülen's supplication with sobbing. I listened to his crying unintentionally, and I could not stop my own tears. The sound of his sobbing was like that of someone who just had lost several of his children in a traffic accident and who was standing before their dead bodies. I listened for a while and then made my ablution for the *Tahajjud* Prayer. After performing it, I wanted to sleep, but Gülen was still offering supplications with sobbing. I tried to sleep but I could not. I felt very sorry for him, and my heartrate increased for a moment. I thought that I was going to have a heart attack. I could not stand because of feeling very sad and of his sobbing. I made the decision to change my room and sleep somewhere else. I woke up before dawn for the Morning Prayer and then performed it behind Gülen. Usually, after the Morning Prayer, two or three pages from Said Nursi's *Risale-i Nur* would be read in a study circle and sometimes Gülen would comment on them. This time, however, Gülen did not stay and went to his room. I was surprised and asked the person who attended to his needs why Gülen did not stay for the book reading.

He said that Gülen had not been able to sleep the whole night due to having received such sad news about the school. Indeed, I was shocked. I have never seen or heard of anyone who cried for hours because an educational institution was not going to open. I will never forget the experience and it was a lesson for me about the importance of education which I could not have learned by studying dozens of books and hundreds of articles. Fortunately, the school which had made Gülen cry for hours did open that fall. The board rented temporary buildings for two weeks and began teaching in them until the renovation of the building was completed.

3.5.3 Children's education above life itself

As a great advocate of education, Gülen always encourages his followers and anyone to open educational institutions, even a small one like a cultural centre. For Gülen, educating children means contributing to the society in which they live. Also, through a good education, the seed of good morality can be planted in their hearts and minds. This will lead to a prosperous and a healthy society.

A post-graduate student said that Gülen had strongly encouraged him and his friends in Long Island, New York, to open a cultural centre to educate children every time they visited him. Finally, he and his friends rented a place to open the cultural centre and the student visited Gülen again to let him know. Upon hearing this, Gülen became very happy. After performing Friday Prayer, Gülen invited the student to his room, where he opened the drawer of his study desk and showed him some money. Gülen told him to take the money for furnishing the cultural centre. Gülen added, "This money is for my medication, but the education of two children is more important than my life. Please, take it and spend it on furnishing the centre." As Gülen was saying these words, his eyes flowed with tears. The student wept as well. As Gülen had heart disease, was a diabetic, suffered from hypertension and another illness, he definitely would need that money for his medication. Yet, he viewed and preferred the education of two children as more important than his life. Initially, the student hesitated to take the money. How could he take the money which was needed for a great scholar's medication? But Gülen insisted he took it. So the student accepted it and spent it on purchasing tables, chairs, and other items for the cultural centre. When the student narrated this story to me, he also shed tears. Later, he learned that the money was Gülen's savings from the royalties of his publications for his livelihood and medications.

3.5.4 Mourning an officer

In early May in 2000, PKK terrorists shot down a helicopter and wounded its pilot, whom Gülen had known for a long time. Gülen's doctor read the news from an online media source. He let Gülen know about the attack and that the officer was in intensive care in Turkey. Gülen was very upset about the injured officer. After two or three days, the pilot passed away. Gülen's doctor was hesitant to tell him because he was aware that the news would have a very negative impact on Gülen's health. He consulted with a few of Gülen's close associates who were at present. They made the decision to let Gülen know when his hypertension and sugar levels were normal and under control. His doctor would check his blood pressure and sugar at least three times a day. After lunch, Gülen looked well, and his sugar level and blood pressure were normal.

It was a sunny day. Gülen went out of the building and sat at the back door where he could get some sunlight. He conversed with a few people who were around him. His doctor broke the news and told him that the officer could not be saved, and he had passed away in the hospital. Gülen started weeping, and he collapsed in a corner of the chair for a while. Then, he wanted to go to his room on the second floor but he could not as he had no energy to move. The people around him tried to help, but Gülen declined. He clung to the wall and slowly walked and, after taking few steps, he sat and wept for a while and then he was able to go to his room. Later, I asked the person who looked after him about Gülen's condition. He told me that Gülen had continued to cry for more than an hour in his room.

3.5.5 Shedding tears for the guests

From time to time, Gülen's old companions from Turkey, or another part of the world would visit him in the United States. When they met, the memories of beautiful or sad days of the past were topics of conversation for them. Some of these memories of the past caused Gülen to shed tears. Once, in 2006, a group of elders from the city of Kayseri came to visit Gülen. After staying a week, they wanted to leave at around 10 p.m. for their flight. Gülen was sick, and his private doctor told him that he needed to rest. However, Gülen wanted to see them off up to the gate of the retreat centre. This action is considered a *sunnah* (tradition) of the Prophet. The person who wanted to pick up the guests at 10 p.m. was late. Despite his sickness and weariness, Gülen did not want to rest. The guests also told him that he needed to rest. But Gülen would not. He started weeping, and he made the guests cry as well. Gülen continued to shed tears for a while. When the driver arrived, Gülen saw them off and returned to his room in tears. For how long he kept weeping, I could not ask. He keeps crying much longer than others over separations. Osman Gürbüz Özkara said that whenever Gülen sees someone off, tears flow from his eyes. Mehmet Eldem reported, "Once, after a visit, Gülen said, 'Whenever visitors come I feel happy, but when they leave I feel as if a part of my body is torn and that it goes with them.'"

Eldem continued, "Once a group of old friends of Gülen, including me, visited him in Pennsylvania. The aim was to persuade him to return to Turkey in 2003. We entered his room and sat down. Gülen welcomed us. Then we stopped talking for a while and kept silent. All of us hesitated to talk and invite him. Finally, Yusuf Pekmezci from Izmir said, 'The residents, your friends, and your students in Izmir have missed you a lot. They would love to see you [in Izmir].' All of us, including Gülen, began weeping for almost half an hour."

Haydar Eraslan, who has known Gülen since the 1970s, recalls, "I was taken by a friend to listen to Gülen's sermon on Friday. I could not find room inside the mosque. I thought that there were funeral services and that was why it was very crowded. Gülen was talking about the Prophet and his Companions. I looked to my right and then to my left: the people were crying. I thought again that it looked as if people were crying because of their deceased. After a while, I became so impressed by Gülen's preaching. The whole congregation was bursting into tears. Gülen was speaking in tears as well."

Osman Gürbüz Özkara recalls, "In 1997, two friends and I visited him in New Jersey. Gülen greeted us at the gate. He was excited to see us. Then he hugged Yusuf Pekmezci and cried for five minutes. Yusuf Pekmezci had many memories of him. He told us that when he hears the noise of a plane flying over the house, it makes him cry. He thinks that it is possible that he may catch a plane to go to Turkey. He was very homesick, and his eyes were full of tears."

3.6 Why Gülen cries

If the spirit (*ruh*) does not suffer, the heart does not cry, and only a crying heart will manifest as tears in the eyes. If someone does not spend time with Gülen, specifically when he talks and delivers sermons, it will be difficult to believe how he cries. Gülen's crying can be classified as two types, namely for positive and negative reasons. Crying for an increase in depth of knowledge of God, feeling the love of the Prophet, his Companions, and saints, experiencing numerous blessings of God, and observing the beautiful results of serving humanity can be considered positive. Shedding tears for others' suffering, bursting into tears as a reflection of a bleeding heart due to injustice and tyranny in the world can be regarded as the negative aspect. Gülen does not cry over trivial daily events, or political or financial or business failures.

He has been suffering and crying for many reasons since his early years. Based on Gülen's works, speeches, sermons, close associates' testimonials, my personal observation and humble understanding, his crying, weeping, and groaning has several causes.

First, contemplating, observing, and comprehending the significant arts of creation in depth and realising the wonders of the universe causes him to cry. Like an artist who understands the fineness of a piece of art and sees the details of the work more than ordinary people do, Gülen resembles other great scholars in Islamic history who grasp the wisdom of creation. To simplify it, such wisdom is like the observation of a shepherd, scientist, and saint looking at a tree. The first will see the tree under which he can rest in the shade and eat from its fruit. The scientist will observe its various parts, the roots, trunk, leaves, and fresh fruit, and how all of these function: "The roots of a tree serve to anchor it to the ground and gather water and nutrients to transfer to all parts of the tree. They are also used for reproduction, defense, survival, energy storage and many other purposes."[194] The wood gives structural strength to the trunk which supports the plant as it grows larger. Leaves are structured in such a way as to

---

194   Tony Russell and Catherine Cutler, *The World Encyclopedia of Trees* (NY: Lorenz Books, 2003), 14–15.

maximise exposure to light without shading each other. Also, the scientist can examine the nutrition of fruits and their health benefits.

A Prophet or saint will be able to see the wondrous art of God in every part of the tree and he may even hear the tree's glorification of God.[195] Such human beings can comprehend the correlation between the tree and everything in the universe and how the Divine Names are reflected on it. They can view with great pleasure the perfect order between soil, water, seed, roots, leaves, branches, and fruit.

Nursi who influenced Gülen defines this perspective as follows: "Looking upon each created thing as a piece of the puzzle of the universe, with the parts in harmony with each other[196] is a form of worship." He argues that "the reality of every being is based on one Name of God or many. Indeed, one group of the most learned of the saints stated that, even only on appearance, as many as twenty manifestations of the impressed of the Divine Names may be seen on a single living creature."[197] The connections and harmony between these Names necessitate a relationship between all creations.

Observing and loving such beauty of arts will lead to love of the Maker. Then, naturally, there will be a very strong desire to see the Creator. Since this is not possible in this temporary life, such a separation from the Beloved makes the spiritual elite cry. Gülen says that "the lovers of God cool down their hearts by shedding tears." Sometimes when Gülen talks about the wonders of the universe and arts of creation, he weeps. He says, "It is not possible for one who does not believe to have true knowledge of God; a breast devoid of knowledge of God cannot have Divine excitement, and a spirit bereft of such excitement cannot shed tears from love or yearning for or fear and awe of God."[198]

---

195 "The seven heavens and the earth and whatever is in them exalt Him. And there is not a thing except that it exalts [Allah] by His praise, but you do not understand their [way of] exalting." (Qur'an, 17:44)

196 Salih Yücel and Selma Sivri, "Said Nursi's approach to the environment: A spiritual view on the book of universe," *Quarterly Insights* (4) (2009), 77–96.

197 Nursi, *The Words*, 656.

198 Gülen, *Key Concepts in the Practice of Sufism* 4, fgulen.com/en/fethullah-Gülen s-works/sufism/key-concepts-in-the-practice-of-sufism-4/47815-putting-an-end-to-a-long-journey. Retrieved 07.09.16.

Second, it has been the destiny of all great scholars not to be understood by their contemporaries; even sometimes close associates have made them cry. Gülen is not understood either. He has mentioned this in a close circle many times and his students testify to this too. These scholars have had very high goals and almost all of them could not accomplish what they wanted for various reasons and obstacles. Therefore, they suffer and sigh for it. It was mentioned above, how Gülen cried for almost a whole night because of hearing that a school was not going to be opened as planned. According to his close associates, failure of any educational or other project makes Gülen sad, even sometimes sick and it causes him cry in public and private as well.

Although Gülen has no worldly ambitions, those who govern Turkey have feared him, due to his influence, since the late 1960s. They have worked very hard and developed many projects and plans to halt his activities. Sometimes these plans include slander, discrediting him or his activities, oppression, torture, imprisonment, assassination attempts, and all kinds of dirty political games. Yet, such scholars, including Gülen, are very devoted and bound to religious and ethical principles contrary to the Machiavellian political games of their enemies. For such scholars' strategies are easily known by their foes. Instead of playing political games, they stick to their ethical principles and do not compromise them. Thus, they suffer. Similarly, Gülen has not compromised his moral principles in the face of his enemies' plans. While his opponents or enemies have made many plans to destroy him and the Hizmet Movement, Gülen has always viewed them as potential good Muslims or *insan al-kamil*, perfect persons. Such approaches make conditions extremely difficult for him and the Hizmet Movement. The only option is to complain of his suffering and grief to God by shedding tears. There are hundreds of examples in Gülen's life. Thousands of times he has written or said to his followers that it is *"tam ağlama zamanı"* which means it is "just the right time for flowing tears" to seek God's aid because there is no other option for Gülen.

Third, Gülen cries out of love for the Prophets, particularly Prophet Muhammad (pbuh), his Companions and the great scholars in Islamic history. He delivered fifty-three sermons about the Prophet Muhammad from 1989 to 1990 in Valide Sultan Mosque in Istanbul. He did not deliver any of these sermons about the Prophet without bursting into tears. He also often shed tears when he taught about the Prophet and his Companions' ascetic life, suffering, devotion, altruism and so on. When he narrates any stories that made the Prophet and his Companions cry, it makes Gülen burst into tears in his study circle as well. In this he resembles Hasan al-Basri, Umar ibn Abdu'l-Aziz[199] and Abdulqadr al-Jilani, whose tears left permanent and visible marks on their faces.

Fourth, he cries because of injustice and tyranny in the world. Gülen says that "if, wherever there is a tragedy, there is immense pain, I too suffer from that pain."[200] He has made this statement many times, whenever a tragedy or disaster has happened, including the flood in the Philippines in 2016. Since he cannot avoid this and has no power to prevent disasters, he expresses himself by bursting tears instead of using the rhetorical language of politics or radicalism. According to the students of his study circle, hearing news of injustice, oppression, torture, and killing of innocent people or animals makes Gülen weep. This results in reducing sorrow, depression, and anger.[201] So, his disapproval or civil disobedience to oppression is reflected as tears in his eyes. It is not just shedding tears but also, sometimes, his heart and soul cry as well. In this state, he becomes extremely weary and has no energy to talk or even to move.

Fifth, in a pitiful state, Gülen cries for the wrongdoing of others. He does not want to hurt anyone nor for anyone to be hurt. As a result, his compassion or affection transforms him into a pitiful state and leads to his bursting into tears. He says that "while most people are in an impassive

---

199   For details of his crying and weeping, see: Al-Isfahani, *Hilyatu'l Awliya*, V 5 (Beirut: Daru'l Kitab al Ilmiyya, n.d), 253–323.

200   Fethullah Gülen, 390. Nağme: Filipinler İçin "Kimse Yok Mu." www.herkul.org/tag/ates-dustugu-yeri-yakar/.

201   Studies show that crying releases stress hormones or toxins from the body, and as a result, reduces tension. A good cry can also be a good way to kill bacteria. Tears contain the fluid lysozyme — also found in human milk, semen, mucus and saliva — that can kill 90 to 95 percent of all bacteria in just five to 10 minutes. It also can be self-soothing and elevate mood better than any antidepressant. For the benefits of crying, see Lizette Borreli, "Cry It Out: 6 Surprising Health Benefits Of Shedding A Few Tears," May 19, 2015, *Medical Daily*, www.medicaldaily.com/cry-it-out-6-surprising-health-benefits-shedding-few-tears-333952.

state, for some it is necessary to weep for humanity. If it were my task or if I could, I would constantly cry for twenty-four hours to soften others' hearts. Even I would cry like Jacob until I lose my sight."[202]

Sixth, every piece of God's favour or blessing, or the success of his followers in the service of humanity pleases and excites Gülen and causes him to cry. Although such a state does not last as long as his suffering for others, it still happens often. He considers tears of happiness as oxygen for his life.

Seventh, Gülen cries for the disloyalty and laziness of some his friends in the service of Islam. He says, "Many times, I have wept alone in my room because of the disloyalty of a friend whose loyalty I expected."[203] However, this crying is transformed not into hatred but pity for his disloyal friends. The supplication with suffering and shedding tears in solitude strengthens good deeds and will power.[204] According to Gülen, stone-hearted people do not cry. Neglecting the needs and suffering of others will gradually lead people to becoming stone-hearted. Commenting on the hadith in which the Prophet seeks refuge from heresy and in a similar way seeks refuge from the eyes that do not cry, Gülen states that the Prophet meant to say that not shedding tears is equal to heresy.[205]

Sometimes tears are the products of disloyalty to devotion. To him, his religion is conveyed through suffering, tears, altruism, sacrificing wealth, even sometimes self, for the sake of God. It is an important ethical principle of Gülen not to retaliate against those who betray him. He generally neglects his personal rights in responding to accusations, but if it involves Islam or the Hizmet Movement, then he replies according to philosophical principles or in a diplomatic way. Gülen would like any work to be done at the level of *ihsan*, which means as if God and His Messenger observe it and are pleased with it. This is highly idealistic for many, but Gülen always has high expectations and aims.

Eighth, Gülen sheds tears when sharing the pains and sufferings of the oppressed and victims of misfortune. He manifests his helplessness by crying or weeping. Rumi summarises this feeling of pity in the

---

202 Gülen, *Fasıldan Fasıla* 5, 46.

203 Gülen, *Kalbin Zümrüt Tepeleri*, 4, 147.

204 Fethullah Gülen, *Ruhumuzun Heykelini Dikerken*, (Izmir: Nil Yayınları, 2011), 116.

205 Ibn Hajar, *Fathu'l-Bari*, 11/139 in Gülen, *Asrın Getirdiği Tereddütler*, 115.

following lines:

> Wheresoever thou findest blood on the roads,
> Trace it, and 'tis tears of blood from my eyes.
> My words are thunder, and these sighs and tears
> Are drawn by it as rain from the clouds.
> I am distracted between speaking and weeping.
> Shall I weep, or shall I speak, or what shall I do?
> If I speak, my weeping ceases.[206]

Many great saints and scholars, instead of expressing themselves in words, do not speak but shed tears. They hope that through bursting into tears, many hearts may be softened and problems can be solved. Gülen says that it is likely that the problems which cannot be cracked by force or through wars may one day unexpectedly be resolved by supplications to God and shedding tears[207] because it is not a scholar's or a saint's duty to solve problems by force in Islamic jurisprudence. If necessary, using power is a state responsibility, not that of individuals. For Gülen, the Prophets and saints moan and shed tears for all humanity to protect them from crying because of the result of wrong doing.[208]

Alaattin Kırkan recalls that when Russia invaded Afghanistan in 1979, Gülen cried a lot and then fainted. When Israel attacked Jenin and killed hundreds of Palestinians, he fainted and was taken to the hospital with a suspected heart attack. According to his students and close associates, Gülen weeps when he watches sad news on television. Many instances like this have been reported of him.

Ninth, Gülen cries because of his and others' defects, shortcomings, and weaknesses. He views his previous deeds or actions as not having been done properly or as he wished. Even if the actions were done properly, he still thinks that they could have been done better. Gülen says, "The tears I have many times shed over the black lines [his writing], which I regard as my sins of thinking, are witnesses to this. I have many

---

206 Rumi, Mathnawi, Book 3, www.sacred-texts.com/isl/masnavi/msn03.htm. Retrieved 29.09.2016

207 Gülen, *Çağ ve Nesil* 8, 168.

208 Gülen, *Çağ ve Nesil* 9, 158.

times trembled with the consideration that I have not been able to present the elevated transcending truths in accordance with their essential reality or real nature, and have nearly decided to give up continuing to write about them."[209] According to al-Zamakhshari, all saints and righteous people cry even for their minor sins.[210]

Finally, like all other human beings, Gülen cries for the loss of any of his relatives or friends, and also for inevitable physical pain.

3.7 Criticism

There have been hundreds of comments in the Turkish media and many political Islamists, syndicate columnists and politicians that have argued that Gülen's tears are for showing off or fake, like an actor or actress who cries in the movies. For them, by shedding tears, Gülen is deceiving people. First of all, none of these accusers have been near Gülen. Second, they cannot provide any evidence for their argument except polemics aimed at discrediting him. It is not logical or possible for someone to deceive people with fake tears for almost sixty years. If Gülen's sermons are analysed carefully, it can be seen how he cries and weeps thousands of times in the mosques. Those who have been near him cry when they recall Gülen's tears during his sermons and public and private talks. I have also analysed the life of more than thirty great scholars who cried and who made their listeners cry. These scholars cried when they talked about the Prophet, his Companions, about life in the Hereafter, for their friends, during or after *dhikr* (remembrance of God), and when reciting the Qur'an or supplications. Similarly, Gülen also cries on the same issues.

3.8 Analysis

Weeping, crying, and sighing are important attributes of spiritual travellers who can be classified into three groups. The first group is those who have an in-depth knowledge at the degree of *ilm al-yaqin* (knowledge of the truth) and practice. From time to time they may weep or shed tears

---

209   Gülen, *Key Concepts in the Practice of Sufism* 4, www.fgulen.com/en/fethullah-gu-lens-works/sufism/key-concepts-in-the-practice-of-sufism-4/47815-putting-an-end-to-a-long-journey retrieved 22.12.2016

210   Zimakhshari, ibid., altafsir.com.

from their eyes only. They comprehend and digest knowledge mainly through reason. The second group is those whose eyes and hearts cry together. They are spiritually at the degree of *ayn al-yaqin* (witnessing the truth). At this stage, all items of their physical body and all the subtleties of the heart share their crying, besides comprehending and digesting knowledge through the mind and heart. They feel sorrow with their all subtleties. The third group combines the eyes, heart, and soul in weeping, crying and sometimes sighing. They are at the level of *haqq al-yaqin* (the truth of certitude) spiritually. This group is always on a spiritual journey, without slowing down, at a certain speed which depends on each individual's understanding and experiencing *ma'rifatullah* (deep knowledge of God), *muhabbatullah* (deep love God), *makhafatullah* (fear of God) and *dhawq ruhani* (spiritual joy). They are so attached to the place where they live and the spiritual level where they are that since their spiritual journey is a continuous one, leaving behind the physical place or the spiritual station makes them cry. They do as Rumi adjures and "[s]hed many tears of blood from eyes and heart,"[211] so their tears sometimes can be considered as the blood of the heart.

This group sometimes joins the cosmos in shedding tears or the cosmos shares their crying. Ismail Haqqi mentions a hadith which indicates that "the earth and heavens weep because of fear of God."[212] Nursi says that "the Prophet Muhammad (pbuh) supplicates with such a need, so sorrowfully, in such a loving, yearning, and beseeching fashion that he brings the whole cosmos to tears, leading them to join in his prayer."[213] Rumi reflects the cry of the creation as follows:

> And earth cries, "O keep me fixed and steadfast,
> Thou who hast placed me on the top of waters!"
> The obedience of stone and staff is shown to you,
> And informs you of that of other inanimate things.
> They cry, "We are all aware of God and obey Him."[214]

---

211   Rumi, *The Masnavi*, trans. E.H. Whinfield, [1898], at sacred-texts.com, book 1
      www.sacred-texts.com/isl/masnavi/msn01.htm. Retrieved 20.09.2016.

212   Ismail Haqqi, ibid., altafsir.com. Retrieved 04.07.2016.

213   Nursi, *The Words*, 248.

214   Rumi, *Mathnawi*, Book 4, www.sacred-texts.com/isl/masnavi/msn04.htm. Re-

This can be called "collective crying" for a higher purpose. Each of the groups mentioned above has sub-degrees as well. They comprehend, digest, feel, experience and live knowledge with total satisfaction of the mind, heart, and the soul without any doubt. Gülen also asks his students and followers to cry collectively to soften hearts. He believes the best supplication is the one which is done through actions and supported verbally with tears. Just as the state has soft power, for Gülen, the strength of a believer is supplication with sincere tears.

Great scholars and saints view themselves as the weakest and most powerless of creation like an infant child. As a baby expresses his/her powerlessness by crying, similarly saints also express their powerlessness and weakness though weeping. However, they do not request their needs from a human being but ask the One who has Infinite Mercy. As people attend to the needs of the baby, saints believe that shedding tears is an invitation to God's help. This is a tradition of all Prophets as mentioned in their stories. So, crying is a way of communicating with God for Prophets, saints, scholars and believers. It is also a natural way to heal humans spiritually, physiologically, and psychologically.

It can be argued that by crying, weeping, and suffering for others, Gülen is not inventing something new but reintroducing the way of *Salaf al-Saliheen*, the first three generations of Islam. As can be seen in the testimonials of his friends, the power of crying and suffering for others, has softened hearts, reconciled hearts and minds, motivated people for the common good and become a step in spiritual ascension. His tears have affected millions of people and mobilised them for educational purposes. The success of the Hizmet Movement was able to be achieved not by tens of billions of dollars but through sincere actions with tears, altruism, and devotion.

Conclusion

Shedding tears is a part of human nature. It is not harmful but has many physical and health benefits. A person can produce ten ounces of tears per day and thirty gallons per year.[215] Crying, weeping, and

---

trieved 29.09.2016.

215   Lizette Borreli, "Cry It Out: 6 Surprising Health Benefits Of Shedding A Few Tears,"

groaning are attributes of all Prophets, saints and great scholars for spiritual reasons more than physical ones. History does not record any Prophet, saint, or great scholars who did not shed tears. The wonders of creation, love of the Beloved, fear of the Creator, the pain of others, injustice, failure to achieve their goals, not being understood by contemporaries are the major reasons for their sorrow and tearful prayers.

It was at about the age of fifteen that Gülen faced his first experience of overcoming with sorrow the physical and spiritual tragedies in the Muslim world. He has become unable to hold back his tears during his sermons, talks, prayers and hence has become known as the weeping scholar, despite his last name meaning "the one who laughs." Despite all his tears, Gülen questioned the sincerity of his sorrow and crying and asked God for genuine and sincere tears. Based on my research, there is no scholar in the contemporary Muslim world known for crying as much as Gülen. Just as Hasan al-Basri's face was permanently marked from continued crying, so too do Gülen's eyes remain swollen. Each calamity that strikes the Muslim world seems to affect Gülen first. All his friends, students, and associates over the last fifty years confirm this characteristic of Gülen. He cries for the significance of creation, blessings, love of God, at injustice, and tyranny, other wrongdoing, and at calamities in the world. It can be said that tears are like walnut seeds. If they do not have proper soil, enough light, and water, their growth is too slow. Similarly, if their contemporaries do not understand the great mind of a scholar, then his/her ideas influence society slowly, but after the death, the value of tears is understood. As Rumi's father Bahauddin Walad says, their sultanates begin when their eyes are closed forever. It seems that Gülen is sharing the destiny of all the great scholars with tearful eyes in the history of Islam.

May 19, 2015 *medical daily*, www.medicaldaily.com/cry-it-out-6-surprising-health-benefits-shedding-few-tears-333952.

CHAPTER 4

GÜLEN AND *SAYYIDHOOD* LEADERSHIP

Gülen and *Sayyidhood* Leadership

ülen states that the world is in need of Islam and Islam is in need of *(tamthil)*, role models.[216] He believes people's ears are full but their eyes are hungry for role models in all areas of life,[217] including in leadership. To him, leadership through action comes before leadership through words. He argues that the Muslim world's crisis is due to the lack of qualified and altruistic leadership and education for the masses.[218] Zeki Sarıtoprak says that Gülen takes Said Nursi's theoretical foundations, puts them into practice in his own life,[219] and applies them to the Hizmet Movement's educational and leadership philosophy. With this view, Gülen devoted his life to the education and upbringing of youth. His dedication, practice, and preaching have inspired millions of people, primarily of Turkish background, to follow in his footsteps by serving humanity through education and spiritual leadership. Instead of calling this a servant-, guardian- or transformational-style leadership, as some scholars argue, I call it *"Sayyidhood"* leadership.

This chapter first argues that Gülen has reintroduced *Sayyidhood* leadership through *khadimhood* (servanthood) and *hijra* (migration for the cause of faith) and put it into practice in the Hizmet Movement over the past four decades. Second, it argues that Gülen has revived, reinterpreted and exemplified the hadith, *"Sayyidul qawm khadimihum"*—"The master of the people is the one who serves them," in the light of the Qur'an and the exemplary life of Prophet Muhammad (pbuh), the Companions, the major great scholars, saints and Islamic leaders, in accord with the modern age. Finally, it explores how he draws and acts upon the belief that a leader should never see himself as a leader, but as a servant of Muslims and all peoples regardless of their faith, colour, and ethnicity. This chapter takes the concept of *Sayyidhood* in the hadith as a theoreti-

---

216 All Turkish and Arabic sources are translated by the author.

217 Salih Yücel, "Spiritual Role Models in Fethullah Gülen's Educational Philosophy", *TAWARIKH: International Journal for Historical Studies*, 3(1), 2011, 65.

218 Gülen, *Çağ ve Nesil* 4, "Zamanın Altın Dilimi", 212.

219 Zeki Sarıtoprak, "Fethullah Gülen and His Theology of Social Responsibility", in Islamic Albayrak, ed., *Mastering Knowledge in Modern Times: Fethullah Gülen as an Islamic Scholar* (New Jersey: Blue Dome Press, 2011), 90.

cal framework, beginning with an analysis of the hadith's literary meaning and grammatical usage.

I analyse Gülen's *Sayyidhood* leadership philosophy through two notions: the way that Gülen uses the word *khadim* from the hadith cited above instead of "leadership"; and how major principles of *Sayyidhood* reflect in *khadimhood* in the Hizmet Movement as Gülen has applied these principles and influenced others to put them into practice.

It should be noted here that neither *sayyidhood* nor *khadimhood* are found in Gülen's works or speeches as terms to describe individuals or a form of practice within the Hizmet Movement. *Khadim*, or servant, is popularly used in Islamic tradition as a humble description for community leaders who have devoted themselves to a certain cause or organization. It is informally used among participants of the Movement for the same purpose to describe devoted individuals among them. Yet, it is not an official title or designation. Many descriptions of the ideal person in Gülen's books and speeches are directly or indirectly related to this hadith and thus I argue that Gülen's philosophy of service is derived from this hadith.

Beekun and Badawi classify Islamic leadership styles into two: guardian leader and servant leader.[220] Scholars describe Gülen variously as showing the style of a charismatic, transformational, servant or spiritual leader. Rather than seeing himself as a charismatic individual, he calls himself *Qitmir*,[221] the name of the Dog of *Ashab al-Kahf* (People of the Cave, also known as "the Seven Sleepers"). In calling himself *Qitmir*, Gülen follows the way of great scholars. He is applying a deeper meaning of humility in Islam and wants to show people that the source of all success and goodness is only God; it does not come from anyone else, as the Qur'an states: "What comes to you of good is from Allah" (4:79). In the light of this verse, a believer, particularly a pious and knowledgeable one, attributes his/her good deeds to the enabling God while accepting all responsibility for his/her misdeeds. So Gülen does this. Abd al-Rahman Jami (1414–1492) is the first scholar known to have called himself *Qitmir*, lamenting his separation from the Belov-

---

220 Rafiq I. Beekun and Jamal Badawi, *Leadership: An Islamic Perspective* (Beltsville, Maryland: Amana Publication, 1999), 14–15.

221 Fethullah Gülen, *Zamanın Altın Dilimi* (Izmir: T.O.V. Yayınları, 1997), 213.

ed, or humiliating himself by writing that he was as low as a dog.[222]

Lexilogos Arabic Dictionary defines *Qitmir* as a "white spot on a date-stone or the membrane of a date-seed."[223] Sometimes it is used for a person who does not own anything.[224] In the history of Islam, the Prophet, his Companions, numerous saints, purified and perfected scholars, and those honoured with nearness to God, have held that the signs of greatness in the great, are humility and modesty.[225] While recounting the Prophet's Ascension, the Qur'an refers to him as God's servant, as a sign of his humility and utmost modesty.[226] Abu Bakr Siddiq, the second caliph, viewed himself as bankrupt in righteousness.[227] Nur ad-Din Zangi (1118–1174) called himself a dog.[228] Imam Rabbani (1564–1624) viewed himself as less valuable than a donkey.[229] Al-Ghazali (1058–1111) states that "the more one is humble to himself, the more one is raised up to God."[230] Said Nursi mentions himself as a "sinful man."[231] There is a difference between humiliation and humility. Humility (*tawadu'*) is an honourable attribute in the sight of God and a spiritual and ethical principle in the Islamic tradition. For Nursi, giving up egotism and being humble is one of the preconditions for serving Islam. Nursi states that "you should know that

---

222 Farah Fatima Golparvaran Shadchehr, *Abd al-Rahman Jami: Naqshbandi Sufi, Persian Poet*, Unpublished Dissertation, The Ohio State University, 2008, p. 77, 105, available at etd.ohiolink.edu/rws_etd/document/get/osu1217869380/inline. Retrieved 15.04.2017.

223 www.almaany.com. Retrieved 11.4.2017.

224 Hand Wehr, A Dictionary of Modern Written *Arabic*, ed. J. Milton Cowan, Third Edition, (Ithaca, New York: Spoken Language Services Inc, 1976), 779.

225 Gülen, *Key Concepts in the Practice of Sufism*, www.fgulen.com/en/fethullah-gulens-works/sufism/key-concepts-in-the-practice-of-sufism-1/24742-tawadu-humility. Retrieved 12,04.2017.

226 Fethullah Gülen, *Sızıntı*, Dec 1993, Vol.15, Issue 179.

227 Fethullah Gülen, *Al-Qulubu Dari'ah* (Izmir: Define Yayınları, 2013), 21.

228 Amir Maluf, *The Crusaders Through Arab Eyes* (Manufactured in USA: Al-Saqi Books, 1984), 224.

229 Fethullah Gülen, *Yeni Ümit*, Vol. 32, 1996.

230 Imam al-Ghazali, *Ihya Ulum ad Din*, trans. Fazl 'ul Karim, III (Karachi: Daru'l Ishat, 1993), 253.

231 Nursi, *The Words*, 488.

this century the people of misguidance have mounted the ego and are galloping through the valleys of misguidance…The people of truth have to give up the ego if they are to serve the truth."[232] Thus, the former righteous and exacting religious scholars (*Salaf al-Saliheen*) were ego-free servants of the Qur'an. Gülen would like to revive this attribute through his actions, talks and works. If the works of *Salaf al-Saliheen* are considered a huge treasury and sufficient for every ill, a key is needed to open them for the benefit of this century. In my humble view, Nursi's magnum opus, *Risale-i Nur* and Gülen's interpretation of it and putting it into practice is a key to understanding the *Salaf al-Saliheen's* works for our time including leadership. For Gülen, a good leader is "as dignified as Mount Ararat and as modest as the Dead Sea."[233]

Çelik and Alan posit that Gülen has the style of a servant leader,[234] while Fontenot and Fontenot classify him as a transformational leader.[235] Çelik and Alan list ten characteristics of Gülen's servant-leadership philosophy: listening, empathy, healing, awareness, persuasion, conceptualisation, foresight, stewardship, commitment to the growth of people, and community building.[236] This chapter argues that it is more appropriate to use the term "*Sayyidhood* leadership" instead of servant, guardian or transformational for Gülen.

However, at the heart of Gülen's conceptualisation of *Sayyidhood*

---

232 Nursi, *The Letters*, 490.

233 Gülen, *Zamanın Altın Dilimi*, 213.

234 Gürkan Çelik and Yusuf Alan, "Fethullah Gülen as a servant leader." Paper presented at"Second International Conference on Islam in the Contemporary World: The Fethullah Gülen Movement in Thought and Practice" March 4-5, 2006, Southern Methodist University, Dallas, Texas, USA, fethullahgulenconference.org/dallas/read.php?p=fethullah-Gülen-as-servant-leader. Retrieved 17.09.2015.

235 Karen A. Fontenot and Michael J. Fontenot, Fethullah Gülen as a Transformational Leader: Exemplar for the "Golden Generation". Paper presented at "Islam in the Age of Global Challenges: Alternative Perspectives of the Gülen Movement" on November 14-15, 2008 at Georgetown University, Washington, www.fgulen.com/en/Gülen-movement/conference-papers/Gülen-conference-in-washington/26453-fethullah-Gülen-as-a-transformational-leader-exemplar-for-the-golden-generation. Retrieved 3.10.2015.

236 Çelik and Alan, "Fethullah Gülen as a servant leader."

lies the idea of *khadimhood* (servanthood). Servanthood is similar to a productive *insan-i kamil*, the perfect human, a concept promoted by Ibn Arabi (1165–1240).[237] In the Hizmet Movement, Gülen has revived, exemplified and institutionalized the notion of *Sayyidhood* leadership through education, humanitarian aid, and dialogue in the service of humanity regardless of faith, colour, and social conditions.

4.1 *Sayyid* in the Qur'an and *Sunnah*

The word *sayyid* is mentioned in two verses of the Qur'an (3:39; 12:25). A classical period exegete, al-Tabari, explains *sayyid* as a jurist who is pious, kind, the most honourable[238] of believers, and devoted to and most noble in religion, according to ar-Razi and al-Zamakhshari.[239] Al-Qushayri (986–1074) states that *Sayyid* is one who does not want any position, does not expect any rewards from any creation, and is free from any unlawful desires, making him the best of his people.[240] By this definition, the attributes of *Sayyidhood* are more important than a biological connection to the descendants of the Prophet.

The Prophet first used the *Sayyid* title for himself[241] and then gave it directly to his grandson Hasan (r.a).[242] In Islamic literature, it is an honorific denoting males accepted as descendants of Prophet Muhammad (pbuh).[243] *Sayyidhood* is the leadership style of the Prophet, the four Rightly Guided Caliphs, and righteous leaders. *Sayyidhood* lasted thirty

---

237 Ibn Arabi was a prominent Andalusian Sufi scholar. He was the first scholar to use the term *insan-i kamil*.

238 Al-Tabari, Jamiu'l Bayan altafsir.com. Retrieved 10.9.2015.

239 Al-Zamakhshari, Al-Kashaf, available at altafsir.com. Retrieved 1.9.2015; Fakhruddin ar-Razi, Mafatihu'l Ghayb, available at altafsir.com. Retrieved 1.9.2015.

240 Al-Qushayri, Lataifu'l Isharat, available at altafsir.com. Retrieved 1.9.2015.

241 Tirmidhi, Hadith no: 3615, *sunnah*.com/urn/634770. Retrieved 17.04.2017.

242 Bukhari, Fadâilü-ashâbi-Nabî, 22, Sunan Abu Dawud Hadtih no 4662, *sunnah*.com/abudawud/42/67. Retrieved 11.04.2017.

243 Ho, Engseng, *Graves of Tarim* (Los Angeles: University of California Press, Berkeley, 2006), 149; Morimoto Kazuo, "Introduction", in *Sayyids and Sharifs in Muslim Societies: The Living Links to the Prophet*, ed. Kazuo Morimoto (London: Routledge, 2012), 1–13.

years[244] during the caliphate period, including the term of Hasan (r.a), the Prophet's grandson. From the Umayyad dynasty, *asabiyya*[245] became the heart of Islamic leadership with some exceptions. Some great Islamic leaders applied *Sayyidhood* leadership in their life in varying degrees. This, however, is beyond the scope of this chapter.

The most prominent hadith on *Sayyidhood* leadership narrates an incident that occurred during the Medina period. The Prophet was serving water to his Companions when a Bedouin came in and shouted, "Who is the master of this people?" The Messenger answered in such a way that he introduced himself while expressing a strong principle of Islamic leadership and public administration in three words: "*Sayyidu'l qawm khadimuhum*"—"The master of the people is the one who serves them."[246]

To understand leadership in depth, it is necessary here to analyse the hadith from the grammatical, semantic, and contextual perspectives. Then, the focus will turn to how Gülen understands and applies this hadith in his daily life and implements *Sayyidhood* leadership in the service of humanity.

The term *sayyid*, used in the hadith, has twenty-seven meanings[247] including: chief, master, lord, sir or gentleman.[248] The term *al-qawm* translates as "the people" or "the tribe." It is with *harfi ta'rif* (*alif* and *lam*), which means the tribe or people that is known by the leader. Thus, *Sayyidhood* necessitates the knowledge and understanding of all aspects of the tribe and consultation with the people one serves. The *Sayyid* is also one of the best among the tribe or nation in the context of the hadith. *Khadim* comes from the root word

---

244   Abu Dawud, Hadith no 4647, *sunnah*.com/abudawud/42/52. Retrieved 22.04.2017

245   It means group solidarity. According to Ibn Khaldun it is social solidarity and sense of same goals. For detail information see Ibn Khaldun, The Muqaddimah, trans by Franz Rosenthal, chapter I and II, www.muslimphilosophy.com/ik/Muqaddimah/Chapter1/Toc_Ch_1.htm retrieved 10.14.2015.

246   Daylami Masnad, II, 324, Hindi, Kanz'ul-Ummal, v. 6, p. 710 in Fethullah Gülen, Messenger of God: Muhammad (New Jersey: The Light, 2005), 270.

247   *Sayyid* means "Leader or chief; (over)lord; boss; distinguished; eminent; emir; emperor; generous; high-ranking; king; leading personality; magnanimous; magnate; monarch; noble; noble(man); notable; peer; person of distinction; president; prince; principal; senior; sir; superior; supreme ruler. See Lexilogos Arabic Dictionary, www.almaany.com. Retrieved 3.10.2015.

248   Lexilogos Arabic Dictionary, www.almaany.com. Retrieved 3.10.2015.

khadama, service. Based on that word, we have the word *khidmah*, meaning to serve, be of service, provide work, or put into operation, while *khadim* means domestic servant, attendant, or waiter.[249] Detailed meanings include a person whose job is to provide a service in a public place, someone who does menial work or is employed as a designated person or government official, or a servant in a royal or noble household.

Gülen, inspired by Nursi, revives leadership through service (*khidma*) not just in theory but in practice. Nursi says, "We are hands working (*khadim*) on a dominical boat which will disembark the Community of Muhammad (pbuh) at the Realm of Peace, the shore of salvation."[250] For Nursi and Gülen, there is no position except servanthood in Islam. A nation's ruler is a public servant. As is known, those occupying all state positions are called "public servants" in the West. Ruling does not mean domination and despotism. Nursi considers service to people by a public servant, or any ruler to be the second article of the Islamic constitution.[251] To Gülen, leaders should never discriminate among their subjects; rather, they should strive to love them, prefer them over themselves, and act so that their people will love them.

Six major and distinguishing characteristics are associated with *Sayyidhood* in Gülen's leadership philosophy: *tamthil*, role modelling; *ma'rifa*, spiritual knowledge of God; *istighna*, not having worldly ambitions or expectations for reward or recognition; positive action; altruism; and *hijrah*, migration for a noble cause.

4.1.1 *Tamthil* or role modelling for social and self-renewal

Gülen reads the life of the Prophet as comprising of 90% *tamthil* or role modelling[252] for *da'wah*, and he believes that the finest representatives of Islam throughout Islamic history were the Prophet, his Companions, and then his descendants, or *Sayyids*.[253]

Looking at the above-mentioned hadith, it is seen how the Prophet

---

249   Hans Wehr, *A Dictionary of Modern Written Arabic*, ed. J. Milton Cowan, third edition (New York: Spoken Language Services, 1976), 229.

250   Nursi, *The Flashes*, 215.

251   Nursi, *Tarihçe-i Hayat*, 620.

252   Ünal, *Fethullah Gülen'le Amerika'da Bir Ay*, 217.

253   Gülen, *Asrın Getirdiği Tereddütler* 3, 22–23.

first serves his people before speaking about the importance of serving people. He responds to rudeness with a gentle smile before beginning to talk, perhaps as a way of defusing negative feelings and making his position clear. This is a characteristic of the Prophet, to practice before preaching and to wait a short time before speaking or responding. Therefore, his leadership through action comes before leadership through words.

When Gülen analyses the second half of the creed of Islam, "I bear witness that Muhammad (pbuh) is servant and Messenger of God," he points to the positioning of the word servant before the word Messenger. While most know the highest degree of human life to be that of a Messenger, the Prophet's servanthood comes first in the *shahadah*. Servanthood is manifested through *tamthil*, role modelling, while Messengerhood is about *tabligh*, preaching or inviting.[254] Gülen emphases education, investing in future generations and representation (*tamthil*) rather than the preaching (*tabligh*) of Islamic values.[255] *Tabligh* is to be carried out through *tamthil*, and where *tamthil* needs some explanation, then comes *tabligh*. This explanation fits with the hadith describing *Sayyidhood* leadership. A leader must win the hearts and minds of people first, and this is done by leading through example, as opposed to dictating commands. Gülen described an ideal believer as being like lightning first and thunder second, meaning a believer's actions are seen before his or her words.[256]

As previously noted, in describing Gülen, scholars have used the word "charismatic." But rather than seeing himself as a charismatic individual, he describes himself as a servant and moreover never considers himself a leader.[257] Instead of using the word "leadership," Gülen uses the term *khadim* from the hadith. He draws and acts upon the belief that a leader should never see himself as a leader, but as a servant of Muslims and all people. He has shown this in the form of a theoretical concept and as a practical principle within the Hizmet Movement. After analysing his life, works and talks, it can be said that he teaches first through his

---

254 Personal communication, September, 2007

255 Özalp, "Muhammad Fethullah Gülen", 43.

256 Personal communication, December 2006

257 Gülen, *Kırık Testi* 1, 104–105; *Sohbeti Canan, Kırık Testi* 2, 122.

actions, and then his words, making clear that those who direct people are responsible for serving people, and not those who pose as superiors. He views a strong spirituality as an indispensable attribute for a good leader.

His close friends and associates state that with the exception of 15–20 Prayers, Gülen has always prayed with the congregation, even during hospital stays. He is not known to miss his *Tahajjud* Prayers, a non-obligatory night Prayer that is conducted at a time when most people are in deep sleep. Most importantly, Gülen displays a deep devotion to God. Although he has never missed a Prayer since the age of five and every night he wakes up for nightly vigils, Gülen still thinks he does not truly fulfil his duty of servanthood before God. He dedicates a minimum of three to four (sometimes more) hours of his day and night to performing *dhikr*, supplication and Qur'anic recitation. His emotional state appears from time to time in the form of tears, especially when discussing the Prophet, his Companions and the state of Muslims. He is known to weep heavily and bears the signs of many days and sleepless nights in tears, with bags under his eyes.

He does not bend his principles for even the smallest requests in regard to *tamthil*, role modelling. Once, a photographer asked to take a photo of Gülen while holding a book, so it looked like he was reading. Gülen was displeased at the request and suggested that the picture should be taken during his daily reading time because even his photo should not be fake or insincere in any way.[258] In July 1997, the author went to the mosque with Gülen for Friday Prayers. Due to double parking, we were unable to move our car. A young acquaintance suggested that Gülen and his friends join him in his vehicle and leave together to avoid waiting. During the drive, Gülen asked the young man if the car belonged to him. The young man replied that it belonged to the company he worked for. Upon reaching his home, Gülen wrote a letter of apology to the company, asking for forgiveness because of getting in the car without the consent of the owner of the company, and arranged for gifts to be delivered with a message. He followed the examples of the Prophets, who had to be loyal to their principles down the smallest detail, especially in

---

258 *Milliyet*, Mehmet Gündem, 8–29 January 2005, www.fgulen.com/tr/turk-basi-ninda-fethullah-Gülen/fethullah-Gülenle-gazete-roportajlari/milliyette-meh-met-gundemle. Retrieved 20.09.2015.

order to be real spiritual leaders.

Gülen has published over seventy books, some of which have been translated into over forty languages and have become bestsellers. He gives ninety percent of his earnings from these books to charities, mainly scholarships, while setting aside ten percent to see to the needs of his many guests.[259] He has a pension in Turkey but arranged for that pension to be used by a family in need. He does not possess anything of worldly value. He has his books and a few clothes. Without applying the peak of *tamthil*, Gülen would not have been able to influence millions, according to his close associates. Gülen's *tamthil* philosophy and its practice will be analysed in the next chapter.

4.1.2 *Ma'rifa* or knowledge of God

Based on the hadith, people who serve others must be their *sayyids* or chiefs or the chiefs must be like *sayyids*, who must be knowledgeable and have the capacity to enlighten the heart and mind. For enlightening hearts and minds necessitates having *ma'rifa*. Gülen defines *ma'rifa* as follows:

> *Ma'rifa* literally denotes skill or talent, a special capacity belonging to certain people, means and knowing by means of something. According to travellers on the path of God, it is the station where knowing is united with the one who knows, where knowing becomes second nature, and where each state reveals what or who is known. Some have defined *ma'rifa* as the appearance and development of knowledge of God in one's conscience, or knowing God by one's conscience. In other words, one has attained self-realisation and has realised his or her humanity with all of its intrinsic values and dimensions.[260]

Ma'rifa is a step after the faith for reaching the degree of *muhabba* (love) in *Sayyidhood* leadership. A leader who is equipped with *ma'rifa* will be able to love his people and it will be reflected in serving at the degree of ascetic love that is considered a form of *ibada* (worship). For attaining *ma'rifa*, the first step is to be well versed in Islamic sciences.

---

259   Yücel, "Fethullah Gülen: Spiritual Leader in a Global Islamic Context".

260   Gülen, *Key Concepts in the Practice of Sufism* 1, available at www.fgulen.com/en-fethullah-Gülens-works/sufism/key-concepts-in-the-practice-of-sufism-1/24757-marifa-spiritual-knowledge-of-god. Retrieved 18.10.2015.

Gülen is recognized as an erudite scholar with an authority on a broad spectrum of disciplines, including all *usul*, methodology subjects, *aqida, usul al-tafsir, usul al-hadith, usul al-fiqh* and *fiqh* of four *madhhabs* (schools of Law), *tasawwuf, seerah* (the life of the Prophet and his Companions), Islamic philosophy, logic and psychology. In addition to being a *hafidh* of the Qur'an, he is also known for his mastery over *hadiths* and their chain of narration. He is well versed in the biographies of most of the *tabiun*, who saw the Companions of the Prophet, and all other eminent traditional scholars such as the imams of the four *madhhabs*, major *hadith, tafsir, kalam* and *tasawwuf* scholars, and all great leaders and rulers in the Islamic history. Additionally, as Yavuz and Esposito state, it is not rare that he gives references in his speeches and essays to the works of some of the leading figures of the Western thought, like Kant, Shakespeare, Victor Hugo, Dostoyevsky, Sartre, and Kafka, to reinforce his reinterpretations of Islam to meet contemporary needs.[261]

As Ali Bulaç states, such a degree of knowledge and expertise in the methodology of all Islamic disciplines, as well as his understanding of modernity and the modern world, place Gülen in the category of *dhul janahayn*[262] in the light of Said Nursi's works.[263] Bulaç continues:

> He is neither reformist nor modernist and does not use a secular language as some contemporary Muslim scholars do. However, he is a link in the chain of revivalists. His methodology of using the language is similar to Imam al-Sarakhsi (d.1096), al-Shatibi (d.1388) and other great scholars during the Golden Age of Islamic civilisations.[264]

Some leading Islamic scholars in the Arab world support Bulaç's view in their works.[265]

---

261 Hakan Yavuz and John L. Esposito, *Turkish Islam and the Secular State: the Gülen Movement* (Syracuse: Syracuse University Press, 2003), 185.

262 A scholar who is very good at religious and worldly sciences.

263 Ali Bulaç, Foreword for *Ölümsüzlük İksiri* by Fethullah Gülen, (Izmir: Kaynak Yayınları, 2011), 13.

264 Ibid.

265 For detail, see Farid el-Ensari, *Avdetü'l-Fursan*; Muhammad Babaammî, *Fethullah Gülen Meşruu'l-hizme*; Süleyman Aşratî, *el-İnbiasu'l-hadari fi fikri Fethullah Gülen,*

4.1.3 *Istighna* or absence of expectation

According to verses of the Qur'an, one of the essential characteristics of Prophets is *istighna*.[266] The verse "I ask you for no wage; my wage is only due from God" (10:70) or a similar form occurs twelve times. Three times it refers to Prophet Noah, who conveyed the message of God for close to a millennium. Suitably, the first time the *istighna* verse appears, it is about Noah. Both these verses show the significance of *istighna*. This notion will be analysed in detail in Chapter 7. It is necessary, however, to explain it briefly in this section.

Gülen views believers, especially those who teach, as having an obligation to serve humanity without expecting rewards, material or otherwise, because the world is an "abode of service," not the place of pleasure, reward, and requital.[267] He uses "*mabda-muntaha*," which means the day when a human comes into this world with nothing and the day he or she dies without taking anything. In a comparable way, the day a leader takes position or office and the day she or he leaves office must be the same financially.

Istighna is a characteristic of the companions of all Prophets, saints (*awliya*) and great leaders in Islamic history. Well-known examples include the four Rightly Guided Caliphs, Umar ibn Abdu'l-Aziz (682–720), Salah ad-Din Ayyubi (1138–1193), Imam al-Ghazali (1058–1111) and Mawlana Jalal ad-Din Rumi (1207–1273). These leaders led a simple life, gave away or shared what they received as gifts or spoils of war, and did not leave any inheritance. Among Saladin's possessions at the time of his death, there was one piece of gold and forty pieces of silver.[268] He had

---

Handasatü'l-hadara tajalliyatu'l-umran fi fikri Fethullah Gülen; Fuad al-Banna, *Abkariyyetü'l-Fethullah Gülen bayna Qavaribi'l-hikmeti ve Shevatii'l-hizmeti*; Maryam Ayat Ahmed, *Nidau'r-ruh rihletün fi alemi'l-fürsan*; Muhammad Jakeeb, *Eşvaku,-nahda ve'l-inbias Qıraat fi meşrui'l-üstad Fethullah Gülen*; Abdulhalim Üveys, *Fethullah Gülen Raidü'n-nahdati'r-raşideti fi Türkiye'l-Muasıra*.

266 *Istighna* is to serve the cause of Islam by all means without any expectations for reward, whether material, social, or otherwise. See Salih Yücel and İsmail Albayrak, *The Art of Coexistence: Pioneering Role of Fethullah Gülen and the Hizmet Movement* (New Jersey: Tughra Books, 2014), 131-147.

267 Nursi, *The Flashes*, 23.

268 Bahā' al-Dīn Ibn Shaddād, *The Rare and Excellent History of Saladin* (London: Ash-

given away his great wealth to his poor subjects, leaving almost nothing to pay for his funeral. Gülen follows this principle and donates almost all his income and his entire pension to those in need.

When serving as the head of the Qur'anic boarding school in his late twenties, Gülen resided in a small timber shed in the garden of the institution.[269] Gülen did not eat the food prepared for student and staff, but if he did eat of the prepared food, he paid for it although he was not required to do so. He paid for the water he used to perform ablution at the mosque. He would even leave money as payment for the food he ate at his siblings' homes. While staying at Hizmet or public institutions, he always pays rent, often more than required. He has been paying rent for his room at the retreat centre where he has been secluded since the first day he started living there in 1999. These actions are based on his principles: the principle of not partaking from public property or assets that belong to others, the principle of avoiding indebtedness, and the principle of seeing oneself as a servant. By acting strictly, Gülen wants to educate his students and future leaders through role modelling.

The way to educate leaders and build their character is not solely through courses in religion, leadership or ethics, but mainly through the setting of good examples, known as *tamthil*, or role modelling. The word *khadim* in the hadith indicates a continuous action, and it means that a leader must always serve his people without discriminating against anyone. For Gülen, serving God is incomplete without serving humanity, crucially forming a link between a traditional understanding of religious piety (*taqwa*) and social action.[270] He has reintroduced the "serve all" principle of Sufism. The great Sufi Master Ali Hujwīrī (990–1077) said that a person should view everyone as his or her master and be ready to serve.[271] Muhammed Çetin says that for Gülen servanthood to God is by means of serving, first of all, humanity. Gülen says, "This service is our right; conveying it to others is our responsibility."[272]

---

gate,2002), 19.

269   Özalp, "Muhammad Fethullah Gülen", 36.

270   Özalp, "Muhammad Fethullah Gülen", 39.

271   Jean-Luis Michon, "The Spiritual Practices of Sufism", cited in *Islamic Spirituality Foundations*, ed. Seyyed Hossein Nasr (New York: Crossroad, 1987), 271–272.

272   Muhammed Çetin, *The Gülen Movement: Civic Service without Borders* (New York:

According to Gülen, *khadimhood* is to disregard one's desires and strive for others' well-being without showing off or seeking attention. The *khadim* does not become proud or boastful because his or her duty is to serve the people and he or she sees every person as a master. The salary or wages she or he receives should be just enough to see to her or his basic needs. A *khadim* cannot become wealthy because of his wages and must be in a situation similar to that of his or her poor citizens or constituents. Gülen does not even use the word salary for these *khadim*s in the Hizmet Movement. Instead, he refers to it as a scholarship, enough just to meet regular needs. Gülen himself and his close associates and most of the *khadim*s in the movement do not possess any wealth, not even a house. One of the major principles which Gülen inspired in the representatives and local leaders of the Hizmet Movement is not doing trade or business because they must allocate all of their time to serving others. By strictly following this principle, Gülen is reintroducing what Umar ibn Abdu'l-Aziz did in the second century of Islam. He forbade his governing bureaucrats to do trade or business.[273] Gülen ends by saying that a sincere *khadim* can be said to be spiritually a part of *Ahl al-Bayt*, the family of the Prophet Muhammad (pbuh).[274] This is because they have no worldly ambitions.

When it comes to the application of this principle within the Hizmet Movement, I researched a local example. I surveyed teachers at Sirius (formerly Isik) College in Melbourne and found out that the minimum volunteer hours worked per week (including weekends and holidays) was ten and the maximum was thirty-five. On average, each teacher spends 17.76 hours per week volunteering for the school and school community. They donate between 5% and 15% of their income for educational purposes annually.[275] The *khadim*s in the movement are expected to live like the lower class or average members of their community.

Blue Dome, 2010), 82.

273 Al-Isfahani, *Hilyatu'l Evliya*, trans. Sadik Aykut at al., *Allah Dostları*, Vol. 2 (Istanbul: Şule Yayınları, 2003), 273–284.

274 Gülen, *Asrın Getirdiği Tereddütler* 3, 22–23.

275 For detail, see Yücel, "Spiritual Role Models in Fethullah Gülen's Educational Philosophy".

Another fundamental principle of *khadimhood* is not seeking personal promotion, position or office, particularly political positions. Gülen holds that those close to him should never take this path or enter politics. Even if all global political leaders offer it, they should turn away from the offer without even a glance. Gülen admits that some people may not understand why a person should not aspire to leadership or political power, especially if he or she has good intentions, but he asserts that ultimate happiness comes from pleasing God. This is done through constant striving to exalt the Name of God and understanding of God. "This is my last will and advice for my friends,"[276] he concludes. However, he has met politicians from time to time and a few Hizmet-affiliated people became members of the Turkish Parliament in 2011 election. This is the only such case in the Hizmet Movement's history regarding politics. In my view, the aim was for direct communication with the government and not for any other purposes.

4.1.4 Positive action

According to Gülen, the prophets are embodiments of positive action.[277] Positive action dictates a focus on what needs to be done rather than reacting to others. It means engrossing oneself in the constructive actions of building and repairing, rather than engaging in destructive behaviour.[278] There is a strong correlation between positive action and *Sayyidhood* leadership. Those who act positively are pro-active rather than reactionary. They prefer peace instead of conflict as much as they can. Acting positively is one of the major principles of Gülen and the Hizmet Movement.

As mentioned in Chapter 1, when Gülen was born his first name, which contains the word "Allah" was not accepted by the registrar due to the aggressive secularists' prevailing policies. Throughout his life, he has dealt with discrimination, numerous slanders, persecution, and insults, and he has faced oppression since 1960. Gülen's character since 1960

---

276 Mehmet Gündem, *Milliyet*, 8–29 January 2005 www.fgulen.com/tr/turk-basinin-da-fethullah-Gülen/fethullah-Gülenle-gazete-roportajlari/milliyette-mehmet-gun-demle/8328-milliyet-vasiyeti-idareye-talip-olunmamasi. Retrieved 20.09.2015.

277 Fethullah Gülen, "Ve Gaybın Son Habercisi," *Kendi Dünyamıza Doğru*, (Istanbul, 2003), 3–5.

278 Özalp, "Muhammad Fethullah Gülen", 39.

has been observed and recorded by his associates, students, friends, and foes. He escaped from death at the last minute during the 1960 military coup led by aggressive secularists. During the 1971 military intervention he was imprisoned for six months and in the 1980 coup, was placed on the wanted list, alongside communist terrorists responsible for mass murders, for allegedly wanting to bring *sharia* law to Turkey. He had to keep a low profile away from the public scene for six years. In 1986, the courts removed him from the wanted list and granted a pardon. Since then, almost all Turkish governments have viewed him as a threat in different degrees.

Just like many other religious or faith-based groups, the Hizmet Movement is no stranger to suffering assaults. As Hans Küng argues, in the early Turkish Republican era, the government engaged in an ambitious and Jacobin secularisation program that essentially sidelined Islam from all aspects of life and oppressed religious leaders.[279] Such aggressive secularisation continued until the constitutional referendum in 2010 to a certain extent. Despite all oppression, tyranny and suffering, Gülen did not revolt or preach for revolt. There was political tension which could cause conflicts or even spark a civil war between Jacobin secularists and some religious groups over freedom of religion and religious practices, particularly women's wearing headscarf in the governmental and educational institutions between 1980 and 2010. Gülen and the Hizmet Movement played a significant role in reducing this tension through promoting diplomacy and dialogue.

In my humble view, there are six major reasons that Gülen and his followers act positively against aggressive secularists and political Islamists:

> ‣ The strategy of the Prophet Muhammad (pbuh) and the other Prophets mentioned in the Qur'an was to form friendships and alliances instead of creating enemies or cementing hatred. So, Gülen followed the same strategy.
> ‣ Gülen views securing safety and stability in a country as the duty and obligation of all Muslims, as his spiritual master Said Nursi argued.[280]
> ‣ He sees every individual, including those who are anti-religion as potential

---

279   Hans Küng, *Islam: Past, Present and Future* (Oxford: Oneworld, 2007), 434.

280   Yakup Arslan, "Contents and Principles of Risale-i Nur Service according to the Works in The Third Said Period of Bediüzzaman Said Nursi", *Köprü*, 2010 p. 112.

believers or future friends.

> Gülen believes Islam means peace and it can flourish in a peaceful society. Where violence wreaks havoc, it is not possible to convey the truth and principles of faith.

> If patience is not shown against oppression and injustice, and the response is a negative action such as violence, it can lead to breaching innocent people's rights and even conflict. This will cause more oppression and provoke further enmity.

> Responding to injustice and oppression negatively will only harm the enforcers, not the people who decide and order the injustice.

Positive action means to focus more on major problems rather than prioritising minor ones and trying to solve them in a civilised way instead of blaming external causes. By doing that Gülen is applying Ibn Arabi's "*al-insan al-kamil*" or "perfect human" model in the service of faith and humanity. He brings faith, Islam, and human beings together and develops a productive and beneficial role model.[281]

The military toppled Necmettin Erbakan's administration in 1997. Two years later in 1999, Gülen went to the United States for medical treatment. Under the control of the staunchly secular military, the courts decreed that Gülen was conspiring to gain control of the state and intending to bring Saudi-style *sharia* law to Turkey, thereby causing chaos and division in the nation. All charges against Gülen were dismissed and decreed by the Supreme Court of Turkey in 2008. After examining Gülen's writings, speeches and having spoken to hundreds of Gülen's followers, Helen Rose Ebaugh concluded, "I see no evidence that he intends to take over the Turkish state and replace the secular government with an Islamic state."[282]

Doğan Koç has examined more than 500 defamatory articles, books, op-eds, and newspaper articles to show that these defamations are not random and that they appear according to their respective audiences.[283] Aland Mitzell and Paul Williams argue that Gülen is restoring

---

281 Bilal Sambur, Musbet hareket forumu www.risalehaber.com/said-nursi-ve-musbet-hareket-panelinden-notlar-15923yy.htm. Retrieved 03.08.2014.

282 Helen Rose Ebaugh, *The Gülen Movement: A Sociological Analysis of a Civic Movement Rooted in Moderate Islam* (London: Springer, 2010), 116.

283 For detail, see Doğan Koç, *Strategic Defamation of Fethullah Gülen: English vs. Turk-*

the Ottoman Empire. "Today, the Ottoman Empire is back," said one de-
tractor who saw Gülen as an "Ottoman proponent" threatening the West
and seemingly working to reverse everything Atatürk did.[284] Neo-con-
servative Michael Rubin, argued that the caliphate, formally dissolved by
Atatürk in 1924, had been restored by Gülen.[285] Since 1999, Maoist communists in Turkey have held Gülen to be an English agent; the ultra-nationalists have accused him of being an agent of the CIA and Mossad.

Some radical political Islamists claim that Gülen has a secret agreement with the Pope. His interfaith activities and moderate form of Islam
are veiled attempts to destroy Islam and slowly Christianise all Muslims.
Some went as far as saying that Gülen is employed by the Vatican[286] as
a secret Catholic cardinal, pointing to the meeting with Pope John Paul
II and ongoing dialogue initiatives with Christians as proof. They have
called him a crypto-Christian, Armenian, Mossad agent, CIA agent, and
American puppet.

Despite accusations, persecution, and imprisonment in the last
forty-five years, Gülen has acted positively and has not given up striving
against ignorance, poverty, and disunity which he believes to be the three
major enemies of humanity. He has inspired people to establish several
thousand educational, humanitarian, health, cultural and dialogue institutions throughout the world in the last forty-three years. Hundreds of
thousands of Hizmet-affiliated people have established these institutions
by donating money and sacrificing their time in volunteering. The contribution of these institutions to education and social harmony is welcomed
by over 170 countries in the world. However, such a large and influential
transnational movement has been seen as a threat by Jacobin secularists
and political Islamists at different levels in Turkey.

Since December 2013, countless accusations have been made against
Gülen. He has been labelled an assassin, a fake Prophet, an infidel and
traitor, while a legal campaign has been launched accusing him of con-

---

ish (Lanham, Maryland: University Press of America, 2012).

284　Koç, *Strategic Defamation of Fethullah Gülen*, 21.

285　Michael Rubin, "Turkey's Turning Point", *National Review Online*, April 14, 2008,
　　　www.nationalreview.com/article/224182/turkeys-turning-point-michael-rubin.
　　　Retrieved 17.09.2015.

286　Koç, *Strategic Defamation of Fethullah Gülen*, 21.

spiring against the government. As a result, over 3,000 Hizmet institutions including thirteen universities, around 800 primary, secondary and high schools, 750 tutoring centres, about a thousand dormitories, 16 hospitals, and childcare centres, as well as free tutoring centres in the highly volatile regions in eastern and south-eastern Turkey, have been shut down by the political Islamist government. Some mosques and Qur'an courses which were run by the Hizmet Movement, were forced to close their doors for good as they were accused of educating Israeli agents.

Regardless of his situation and conduct, and whether conditions are favourable or not, Gülen has remained on the side of maintaining peace and security and lowering tensions. Despite discrimination, incarceration and slander, and despite growing praise and an increase in his followers, Gülen has not changed his stance.

His responses have been made according to philosophical, ethical, and legal principles. He has responded to the accusations and charges through a lawyer or legal processes. Gülen is critical of wrong attributes but does not explicitly mention the names of those involved. He cites the outright lies in his sermons without giving the names of those who are openly spreading them. He has not responded to most of what has been said against him. Despite the campaign against him, he has not set aside even a single day for the legal proceedings or responses, as he has a mission to fulfil. Without fail, he aims to raise young people who will continue to serve humanity. Despite having heart problems, hypertension, and diabetes, he devotes every day to educating his students.

With mountains of accusations and slander against him, he is following Said Nursi, who faced similar treatment in his life.[287] On religion, leadership, and politics, he follows Said Nursi's principles. To Nursi, religion must not be used for any other reason except religion. Using it for political reasons is tantamount to killing religion.[288]

---

287 Nursi faced countless assassination attempts, was poisoned no less than 18 times, exiled several times, and suffered in countless ways over thirty years. Members of some religious and spiritual orders were unhappy and perhaps envious of him while others wanted to kill him, but when Nursi was on his deathbed, he forgave them for their injustices toward him as an individual. He conveyed this to his students clearly and strongly emphasized in word and on paper that no one was to avenge him.

288 Said Nursi, *Sunuhat*, 336, www.erisale.com/index.jsp?locale=tr#content.tr.15.336.

For the injustices which he has suffered and for the personal harm he has endured, Gülen continuously offers forgiveness and asks members of the movement to forgive as well. He said, "Yes, I have two hands as well, but even if I had one hundred hands, I would never consider using them for any other purpose except conveying the Divine words."[289]

His ardent desire for peace, even if it means seemingly unfavourable conditions for Muslims, is not simply an idealistic position. He believes that Islam has flourished in peaceful societies throughout history. As the well-known saying goes, the first casualty of war is truth. Nursi also stated that where there is conflict or heated arguments, the truth cannot be presented or heard.[290] The word for faith in Arabic, *iman*, comes from the root *a-m-n*, the same root as *ameen*, trustworthy and safe. Islam came from *As-Salaam*, another Name for God, through *Jibreel* (Gabriel) al-Amin to Muhammad al-Amin. This means a leader needs to work for safety, security and peace. According to Imam Azam Abu Hanifa, the land of Islam means where there is peace and security, or that where the people live in peace and security; it is the land of Islam.[291] By prioritising peace and security against verbal aggression, insult, oppression and tyranny, Gülen follows Imam Azam's principle of the land of Islam because he does not want to cause or be used to cause any political, religious and social tension which can lead to a conflict. Where there is no peace, there is no progress through education, economy, and social life. For the sake of peace, a leader should be open to any criticism and use appropriate language not radical speech.

This means the leader should be kind to those who are critical and rude to him and he must welcome any criticism or inappropriate action and respond to it politely with wisdom. Only then will a leader properly follow Prophet Muhammad's (pbuh) example. That was the style of leadership of the Prophet and the four Rightly Guided Caliphs. In such way, there is no leadership but only servitude when looking at the description above. When one does not pose as a superior leader or claim to be a leader, then he will gain respect from those whom he serves.

Retrieved 22.04.2017.

289   Fethullah Gülen, "Başkanlık Kimin Hakkı," www.herkul.org/kirik-testi/baskan-lik-kimin-hakki/. Retrieved 8.3.2015.

290   Said Nursi, *Asari Bediyye* (Istanbul: Envar Nesriyat,2012), 107, 680.

291   Al-Kasani, *Bada'i al-Sana'i*, Vol. 7 (Beirut: Daru'l Kitab al-Arabi, 1974), 131.

Through his example, the Prophet displayed gentle persuasion, a necessary quality of *Sayyidhood* in Gülen's leadership philosophy. It is an arduous task at times to refrain from conflict, especially when one is directly harmed. His predecessor Nursi said, "For conquering the civilized is through persuasion, not through force, as though they were savages who understand nothing."[292] This is not just a principle for the easy times. Gülen has taken this on as a guiding value in all his steps and espoused this principle through his actions. The Hizmet Movement takes this principle seriously and does not deviate from this Prophetic *Sunnah*.

One characteristic of *Sayyidhood* is gentle persuasion, just as the Prophet responded to the Bedouin and refrained from inciting conflict. The Prophet's strategy was to make friends out of enemies.[293] Also, Gülen puts forward common points rather than differences with others. With regard to understanding Gülen's leadership and how he strives for peace, I analysed some testimonials of his friends and my personal connections with his close associates.

Yusuf Pekmezci, who has known and been close to Gülen since 1967, recalls, "I was a board member of the Kestanepazarı Qur'anic Boarding School, where Gülen was teaching. Turkey was politically divided into leftists and rightists (nationalists). Also, there was conflict especially between the youth of the two camps. Once, I went to the historical part of Izmir with twenty young people. Our aim was to fight against leftists whom we considered to be communists. The communists had a gathering and were surrounded by the police for their safety. Suddenly, I saw Gülen standing next to me. He asked me what I was doing there. I told him that I was there to fight against leftists. He asked me not to fight and return home as soon as possible." Pekmezci concludes, "Gülen has always been against conflicts." In one of his statements, Gülen prefers to live one thousand years under tyranny instead of living one day in chaos. With this view, Gülen follows al-Ghazali who said, "A hundred years of injustice is better than a day of chaos."[294] For internal conflicts always harm society and coun-

---

292 Said Nursi, *Damascus Sermon*, 'Hutbe-i Şâmiye' trans. Şükran Vahide, second revised and expanded edition (Istanbul: Sözler Neşriyat, 1996), 79.

293 Gülen, *The Messenger of God*, 251–252.

294 Mimat Hafez Barazangi, M. Zaman Raquibuz and Omar Afzal, *Islamic Identity and the Struggle for Justice*, (Gainsville: University of Florida Press, 1996), 25.

try. Despite all oppression, persecution, imprisonment and exile, Gülen's peaceful actions are evidence of Pekmezci's view of him.

When I asked his close associates Abdullah Aymaz and Mehmet Ali Şengül about Gülen's approach during political conflicts between left-wing and right-wing groups, both mentioned that Gülen does not like conflicts at all, especially internal ones. Therefore, he never allowed his followers to demonstrate in the streets because there is a substantial risk of conflict during a demonstration, especially when democracy does not exist. Both said that later they realised that the same power in the deep state (Turkish intelligence service or military intelligence service) was organising the conflict between the left-wing and right-wing groups. Due to the conflict between them from 1970 to, almost five thousand young people were killed in Turkey, mostly university students.

4.1.5 *Ithar* or altruism

The term *al-qawm* in the hadith can refer to a tribe or nation which can include Muslims, Christians, atheists and believers, saints and sinners. A leader must serve each equally. When it came to issues of justice, everyone was equal in the eyes of the Prophet.[295] The word *khadim* is in the form of '*ism fa-eel*' in Arabic grammar, pointing to a continuous action, and meaning that a leader must always serve his people without discriminating against anyone. According to Gülen, the *khadim* has an obligation to serve without any expectation.[296]

Gülen saw a need to redefine the concept of "us" and "others" within the framework of serving others. "Us" refers to those who serve and "others" are those who need to be served. This includes all people, not just Muslims or those who have a physical need.[297] According to him, human beings can be classified as *ummati icabet* which means those who have accepted Islam and *ummati davet*, those who need to be invited to Islam. Thus, the leader will serve both *ummas* with equality regardless of their religious status.

For such leaders, he states that "they see themselves responsible

---

295 Tirmidhi, Shamail, p. 59–60 in M. Asım Köksal, *İslam Tarihi*, available at www. canibim.com/islamtarihi.php. Retrieved 26.08.2015.

296 Nursi, *The Flashes*, 23.

297 Jill B. Carroll, *A Dialogue of Civilizations* (New Jersey: The Light and the Gülen Institute, 2007), 38.

before anybody else, and answerable for any work left undone."[298] Gülen views the *khadim*s as being like angels. The *khadim*s, who persevere to enlighten others, work for the happiness of others and extend a helping hand, have such a developed and kind spirit that they are like the guardian angels of the communities in which they live.[299] *Khadim*s say "we" before "I" and choose the common good over personal needs. Striving to enlighten every part of the world with a Companion-like quality, they disregard their desires and dedicate themselves to others' happiness, all without ostentation or expectations of reward.[300] For Gülen, a leader or *khadim* combines a full sense of responsibility with sincerity and altruism.[301] A leader overcomes insurmountable obstacles, sacrificing comfort and worldly pleasures, but when it comes to reward, "s/he walks away without ever looking back [without any expectation]."[302]

4.1.6 *Hijra* for service

Gülen says that every individual is a traveller and therefore, in some sense, a migrant. Journeying starts in the world of spirits, continues through the stations of the mother's womb, childhood, youth, old age and to grave, and from there to an entirely new world which is eternal. He argues that migration is an indispensable action for revivalism (*tajdid*) and it has two stages. In the first stage, one with a cause develops character, overflows with belief, is inflamed with love, surpassing one's self and grows into a passionate slave of truth. One struggles, in this stage, against the temptations of the carnal self to build an authentic and spiritual character. This is called "the major or greater struggle"—*al-jihad al-akbar*. Then the traveller rises, in the second stage, to radiate the lights of belief to the world around. This stage is, in fact, the door to

---

298　Fethullah Gülen, "People of Service," www.fgulen.com/en/fethullah-Gülens-works/thought/pearls-of-wisdom/24949-people-of-service. Retrieved 12.9.2017.

299　Fethullah Gülen, "Ideal Spirits," www.fgulen.com/en/fethullah-Gülens-works/thought/pearls-of-wisdom/25914-ideal-spirits. Retrieved 19.09.2012.

300　Fethullah Gülen, "Toward a Global Civilization of Love and Tolerance." (New Jersey: The Light, Inc, 2004), 107.

301　Özalp, "Muhammad Fethullah Gülen", 36.

302　Gülen, *Zamanın Altın Dilimi*, 212.

migration.[303]

Gülen states that almost all great saints, scholars, and rulers made a *hijra* for their noble cause to a new land in Islamic history. However, there is no *hijra* after the conquest of Mecca[304] as mentioned in the hadith. But as Ibn Hajar (1372–1449) states, *hijra* would be required again only whenever the conditions so demanded.[305] Sufis view *hijra* as spiritual travelling which is from the land of human beings to the presence of Allah.[306] Ibn Khaldun calls *hijra* a vehicle for travelling from this to the other world.[307] Imam Rabbani says that *Ashab al-Kahf* (the Seven Sleepers) are valued and well-known because of their *hijra*. Indeed, when the enemy attacks, even a small movement of cavaliers is highly valuable.[308]

In Gülen's works, *hijra* combines both physical and spiritual in the service of Islam and humanity. To him, while physical *hijra* is done, the spiritual one must not be neglected. Both are not separate, but they complete each other. Islamic civilisation is a product of not just physical but also spiritual *hijra*. Contrary to many classical and modern scholars, Gülen encourages his followers to immigrate to non-Muslim countries. He views *hijra* as part of Islamic civilisation like other civilisations. According to al-Ghazali, "*hijra* dislodges the things hidden in the inward of a human."[309] By *hijra*, a person can develop himself or herself mentally, spiritually, and educationally. Eventually, it will lead from egotism to collective spirituality, which is an important principle of the foundation of

---

303   Fethullah   Gülen,   "Sacred   Immigration,"   www.fgulen.com/en/fethullah-gu-
       lens-works/thought/towards-the-lost-paradise/24488-sacred-emigration.   Retrieved
       14.11.2016.

304   Bukhari, 3899, *sunnah*.com/bukhari/63/125. Retrieved 16.2017.

305   Khalid Masud, "The obligation to migrate: the doctrine if hijrah in Islamic law", in
       Muslim Travellers: Pilgrimage, Migration, and the Religious Imagination, ed. Dale F.
       Eickelman and James Piscatori (London, Routledge 1990), 33.

306   Ibid., 36.

307   Ibn Khaldun, The Muqaddimah, trans. Franz Rosenthal (London: Routledge and
       Kegan Paul in association with Secker and Warburg, 1967), 160.

308   Imam Rabbani, *Mektubat*, Tr. Hüseyin Hilmi Işık (Hakikat Kitabevi, 2014), 103.

309   Al-Ghazālī, *Revival of the Religious Sciences*, On Conduct in Travel, trans. Leonard
       Librande (Cambridge: Islamic Texts Society, 2015), 30.

civilisation. Sociologists hold that most civilisations were established by individuals and groups who migrated there. English historian, Arnold Toynbee (1889–1975) states that twenty-seven civilisations were established by those who migrated to other lands.[310] Because those who migrate for the common good and education or a religious purpose are less attached to the world, they gradually gain the higher skill of a collective personality and become more productive.

According to David Tittensor, Gülen has reintroduced the "*rihla* tradition (seeking and teaching knowledge)"[311] in a modern context. The teachers in the movement are following in the *rihla* tradition of their forebears, striking out to other countries in the Name of their God and Prophet and act as pioneers for their fellow Muslims.[312]

Unlike the Tabligh Jamaat, in which men must go on *khuruj* (a trip to teach Muslims with weak practice) three days a month and forty days a year (and women somewhat less),[313] those who have a role within the Hizmet Movement commit to *hijrah* for the rest of their lives. Gülen emphasises the idea that whichever country a person goes to, he or she must go there with the intention of never returning, but also being prepared to leave that new place at any time when the need arises. Many in the movement move elsewhere after serving several years at a certain institution or place in the name of *hijra*. Gülen's modern notion of *hijra* has institutionalised an essential characteristic of ninety percent of the Companions' lives. Khalid Masud argues that *hijra* established a bond of relationship between Muslims (the Companions of the Prophet), and

---

310 Fethullah Gülen, "Mukaddes Göç," *Sızıntı*, October, 1985, 3–4.

311 Both the Qur'an and the hadith direct the believer to undertake rihla (travel) in the world that God created in order to better understand the Creator. The terms *rihla* and *'ilm* inspired a literary genre, *al-rihla fı talab al-'ilm* (travel in search of knowledge), in medieval Islam (David Tittensor, "Islam's Modern Day Ibn Battutas: Gülen Teachers Journeying Towards the Divine", *British Journal of Middle Eastern Studies*, 42:2, (2015), 163-178. DOI:10.1080/13530194.2014.993864.

312 Ibid.

313 Barbara Metcalf, "Islam and Women, the case of the tablighi jama'at", SEHR, Vol. 5, Issue 1: Contested Polities, 1996, web.stanford.edu/group/SHR/5-1/text/metcalf. html. Retrieved 7.10.2015.

particularly with the *Ansar,* the helpers.[314] Similarly, it can be argued that *hijra* in the Hizmet Movement has minimised internal disunity and rivalry, and established unity among the affiliates. For the one who commits to *hijra,* he or she gains a fresh start, a new place to apply and gain valuable professional and personal experiences and freedom from the material world. When a person has committed to lifelong *hijra*, he or she loosens the grip on the world and avoids buying property or possessions that cannot be carried.

4.2 Training for service

The way of education and training *khadim*s and building their character is not just to offer courses in religion, leadership or ethics, but rather to set good examples or role modelling.[315] His *tamthil* precedes his *tabligh*, or his action comes before his words in leadership as well. According to the testimonials of his students in the early 1970s, Gülen would cook for the students, do their laundry and, after they went to bed, check on them to make sure they had not thrown off their blankets on cold nights. He would spend half his salary on the poor students, practicing his principle of living for others. Despite his age and health condition, he continues to fastidiously clean his room and look after his own needs.

In his younger years, he would work as intensely as the workers in the construction and cleaning of the dormitory, according to testimonials from his students. For Gülen, a leader must work harder than everyone else, be of more service than everyone else, and worship more than everyone else.[316] Those who lead the way must set a good example for their followers. Just as they are imitated in their virtues and good morals, so do their wrong and improper actions and attitudes leave indelible marks upon those who follow them.[317] Therefore, for Gülen

---

314   Masud, "The obligation to migrate", 32.

315   Karen Fontenot, and Michael Fontenot, "Fethullah Gülen as a Transformational Leader," available at www.fgulen.com/en/gulen-movement/conference-papers/gulen-conference-in-washington/26453-fethullah-gulen-as-a-transformational-leader-exemplar-for-the-golden-generation. Retrieved 21.12.2016.

316   Personal communication, September 2006

317   Gülen, "Essentials of the way," www.fgulen.com/en/fethullah-Gülens-works/

there is no *hakim* (ruler or manager) but the *khadim*, the servant, in the Hizmet Movement. Osman Şimşek asserts that Gülen is delighted when he sees those in charge are not giving orders but doing work by themselves together with others. This can be even cleaning, cooking, making tea, helping others, and so on.[318] Those who devote their lives to service must refrain from seeking leadership positions or assigning them to themselves, but when it is granted to them, they must fulfil it with the utmost enthusiasm.

Being a leader in the Hizmet Movement begins with being a mentor. This does not even require adulthood. A middle-school student can be a mentor for a primary-school student, a high-school student for a middle-school student and a university student for a high-school student. The mentor's role is to impress upon the younger person the values of contributing and sacrificing for the greater good and working for the betterment of humanity. Also, the mentor consults with experienced individuals or a committee when making decisions. The younger mentee is often invited to the annual fundraisers to pledge even a small amount of what may amount to pocket money to educational programs. The mentor also encourages the younger one to read while dedicating himself or herself to learning as well. Throughout this time, the mentor is to lead by example when it comes to religion, not only by practicing the minimum religious requirements, but also the extra deeds such as non-obligatory fasting and the *Tahajjud* (night vigil) Prayers.

The mentor and mentee take part in retreat programs several times a year. At these retreats, participants spend much time reading, reflecting, praying, invoking God's Names, and developing the habit of doing additional forms of worship such as the *Tahajjud*. In the time spent together, the mentee learns a great deal from the mentor, not only regarding religious life but in terms of individual and community life. By the time of graduating from university, the mentee would ideally be ready to serve humanity as a young leader.

Leadership is given in stages. First, a person is granted responsibility for a group or project. As they gain experience, they develop the ability to solve problems and make necessary sacrifices of rank. Based

---

thought/pearls-of-wisdom/24554-essentials-of-the-way. Retrieved 19.09.2015.

318   Şimşek, *İbretlik Hatıralar*, 129.

on successful application of the above-mentioned leadership principles and sincerity, a person's responsibility and rank rises in the movement. A leader solves problems not only through personal insight, but through accessing the collective wisdom of a well-formed committee and acting in accordance with consultation (*shura*) principles.

It can be said that the educating and training process is a rigorous academic learning of *medrese* that is combined with deep spirituality as in *tekke* (Sufi lodge), and discipline as in *kışla* (barracks) according to the needs of the modern era. The *khadim* learns Islamic knowledge via mentors and study circles, strengthens his or her spirituality through *nafila Salat* (optional Prayers) such as the *Tahajjud*, recitation of the Qur'an, invocation, and fasting on Mondays and Thursdays. By serving others, the *khadim* becomes disciplined and altruistic under the supervision of a mentor. With these qualities, he or she is ready to serve in any part of the world.

4.3 Testimonials from friends

Gülen's close associate Abdullah Aymaz states that "although we were studying at religious high school (*İmam Hatip Lisesi*) in Izmir, we would only fast during the month of Ramadan and pray five times at the Kestanepazarı Qur'anic Course." After the arrival of Gülen, the students began to perform the *Tahajjud* and fast on Mondays and Thursdays every week: "He taught us to be like Companions of the Prophet because Gülen considered them to be a walking Qur'an. Therefore, it is necessary to be like them. He told us so many times that 'it is necessary to act according to the philosophy of *seerah* (the Prophetic biography). If you do that God will bless your work.'"

Yusuf Pekmezci has been a volunteer for the Hizmet Movement since 1966. He stated that Gülen did any kind of work. He cleaned the toilets of the dormitory and school. He worked voluntarily as a labourer during the construction of the schools and dormitories. He did the cleaning, cooking, dish washing, and any other kind of work which was needed. Pekmezci added that Gülen does not give any orders. He does it by himself, and then people see and do it as well.

Gülen's brother Sıbgatullah recalled tearfully: "It was the mid-1970s, Gülen called all of his brothers, sisters and aunts for an important meeting in Erzurum. After giving a short speech about Islam, he stated,

'I have devoted myself in the way of Allah. First, you must not expect any material benefit or worldly ambition from myself. Second, you may face insults, persecution, oppression, tyranny even sentencing because of me. Be prepared for this. If you are not going to or cannot, then, now you can say that we don't have any brother who is named Fethullah." In Turkish culture, that means, "We do not validate any of his actions but also, we are against him and we totally disassociate ourselves from him." Sıbgat-ullah continued, "We told him whatever we face, we are ready to take it. Thus, he made a covenant with all his brothers and sisters."

Sıbgatullah states that Gülen does not worry for himself. He always feels very sorry for those who have dedicated themselves to serving Islam when they face any difficulties or calamities. Their well-being is his prior-ity. [If anything goes wrong,] he worries deeply about the people around him. Sıbgatullah says that "since we promised, none of his brothers, sis-ters or close relatives have had any political or worldly ambition. Although some of us were offered positions [by local politicians], we declined. None of us even accept even to be *muhtar* [an elected person to run a village in Turkey]." Alaattin Öksüz a businessman from Erzurum, who has known Gülen since the early 1970s, recalls with tears after meeting with Gülen "what I learned from him is that someone cannot serve Islam if he or she does not care about *Hizmet* as much as caring about his business."

Gülen's brother, Kutbettin, recalls: "After the 1980 military coup, my brother was on the wanted list. His picture was hung on many display boards and walls as a wanted man along with communists who killed many people. There was a psychological war in the media against the Hizmet Movement. Although he was a wanted man and hid as a fugitive, he visited most of the cities and met with local leaders of the movement in secret to boost their morale. He was unafraid and did not avoid partic-ipating in some activities in a close circle or small groups."

Haji Ahmet Gündüz, another close associate, says that "this na-tion lost its true leadership. Therefore, an individual should approach the people by sharing and caring about their problems so that they can open their hearts. Then you will be able to guide them. This is what we see and learned from Gülen."

Mehmet Eldem says, "Gülen very actively follows up if he gives someone a task. He will so often ask about the progress of the given task. If there is an obstacle or need, he will try to solve it or provide advice to figure it out. Therefore, everyone working with him must work harder and harder. Of course, such fellowship leads to success."

Communication is a key factor for success. Gülen has excellent communication skills, which reflects in his public and private talks. He is very eloquent in his speeches and does not pause when he talks. Although over the age of eighty, he still rarely pauses in his speeches. Şakir Ersoy remembers his early days of involvement with the Hizmet Movement: "Although Gülen was very busy in the early 1970s, whenever I called, I was able to get him. I was surprised at such availability. Only once did he say: 'I will call you back half an hour later.' Gülen was available seven days a week and twenty-four hours a day."

İrfan Yılmaz recalls with tearful eyes: "Gülen is very open-minded. He often consults with others and values all ideas with which he agrees or disagrees. So many times, I was able to attend board of trustees' meetings or *Sızıntı* Magazine editorial meetings. Gülen often chose others' proposals or suggestions, rather than sticking to his own views. He was writing the editorial for the monthly magazine and would ask us to edit his piece. He would welcome any changes. Naturally, every writer in *Sızıntı* Magazine loves his or her own articles. Having seen Gülen's example, all the contributors of *Sızıntı* Magazine would welcome any changes in their work before publishing. By doing this, we were able to work collectively as a team, and it affected us to be altruistic instead of egoistic. Gülen taught us how to deal with many problems and the ways of success through his well-disciplined and exemplary lifestyle. On the one hand, he is very generous but on the other, Gülen is so contented and does not waste anything."

Alaattin Kırkan recalls that there was Şaban, whom we called Uncle Şaban. Once he asked someone to take him to Eid Prayer. This person had never prayed in his life and was a heavy drinker. It is a tradition to go to mosque early for Eid Prayer. Before Eid Prayer, Gülen was preaching. He was crying a lot during the sermon. Not only he, but also everyone in the mosque was crying, including Uncle Şaban. He performed the Eid Prayer for the first time and felt spiritually uplifted. After that, this person repented, quit alcohol, became a very pious person, and dedicated his life to serving humanity.

Fethi Ün, a solicitor recollects: "In the early 1970s, there were eight students' houses for high schools and one for the university students.

We were told that another house for the university students was going to be opened. All of us gathered for the opening ceremony. Gülen prayed and he thanked God with tears. At that time, most of the students, specifically university ones, were leftists and denied God. Despite all this negativity, Gülen was delighted to educate thirty to forty students and was never pessimistic. Some political parties offered him the chance to be a candidate in parliamentary elections, but Gülen declined. He preferred to be an educator instead of being a member of parliament. Gülen declined such offers many times. Not being involved directly in politics is an important principle of Gülen's philosophy."

Fethi Ün remembers the mid-1980s: "Gülen was preaching in one of the mosques, but his sermon could be heard in more than forty mosques in Izmir through an intercom system. Secularists and anti-Islam newspapers were accusing Gülen of aiming to introduce *sharia* to secular Turkey. As a lawyer, I was Gülen's proxy for defending him and suing those newspapers. There was one journalist who had been writing against Gülen for more than twenty years.[319] He claimed that Gülen was a cult leader who aimed to destroy the secular regime. Yet again, this journalist published news based on false accusations. When Gülen saw the news, he said, 'Look, Fethi Bey, he has written again.' I thought Gülen felt sorry for himself, but then he said: 'Is this journalist going to die without faith?' I realised that he felt sorry for him not for himself. I was surprised at the level of his compassion even towards a journalist who has been writing against him for two decades. Normally, a person should be angry at such news and would hate such a journalist."

Nevzat Türk remembers the three-year period he stayed with Gülen in Izmir in the early 1970s. Türk said when they went to sleep late at night, Gülen would be deep in his prayer session. When they woke up at four in the morning, they would still find Gülen in deep prayer. This pattern would be repeated every night.[320]

Mehmet Özalp attended a sermon by Gülen only once in his lifetime. He recalls that he was very impressed by the sermon, which Gülen delivered in Sydney, Australia, in 1992. The most memorable aspect was

---

319 This journalist continued to write against Gülen for over thirty years but then he apologized. Name withheld because I was not able to get his permission.

320 Özalp, "Muhammad Fethullah Gülen", 38.

when Gülen sobbed, "If I am not to serve God and humanity any longer, I pray to God not to let me down from this pulpit alive."[321]

The first quality of his leadership is a high level of personal integrity and dedication to his cause. As one of his close students, Mehmet Şeker, puts it, "He never writes what he does not practice."[322]

4.4 Analysis

In Islamic history, the debate over who should lead the Muslims has been raging since the Prophet Muhammad (pbuh) died and then caused division after the assassination of the third caliph, Uthman (r.a.) (576–656), and during later periods of time. Although the debates did not die down, they decreased significantly within some Muslim populations. Leadership was viewed as a competition to do good and to serve the needs of the people for the sake of God, although it was considered as a burden difficult to bear.

The decline of Islamic civilisation and the effects of colonialism, along with various internal and external factors, stirred the debate again about who should lead Muslims. Naturally, most people sought out leaders who could undertake the heavy burden and duty of governing people and solving society's problems. Many leaders who arose were sources of hope for Muslims. However, many hopes for a better future ended in abject failure. Few people have addressed the topic of how the historical examples of the Prophet's leadership and the example of the Companions could be applied in a modern context. The discussion revolved around the theory of leadership but could not be put into practice. However, there have been very few examples of such leadership locally.

Portraying Prophet Muhammad (pbuh) as a role model is common to all Islamic revivalist leaders. Özalp argues that the key difference with Gülen is that he applies the ideal model of the Prophet to current times and has developed the theology of social responsibility. Gülen particularly directs the attention of youth to higher aims and values in the modern world, where they may be easily distracted by icons of popular culture.[323]

It can be argued that Gülen's understanding of Islamic leader-

---

321   Ibid.

322   Ibid.

323   Ibid., 40.

ship is inclusive, uniting rather than dividing, and highly idealistic. To him, the actions of the leader must precede his words just as lightning precedes thunder. In his philosophy, a leader should talk less but work more. Sometimes not words, but only actions speak. He focuses more on the internal factors to make society spiritually and socially healthy rather than blaming others. It can be said that an ideal leader in Gülen's view is the one who solves all his or her problems and passes successfully all tests such as enduring hardship and demonstrating altruism, compassion, dedication and no worldly ambition. For anyone who has not gone through these tests can be a problem for society instead of helping people and solving their problems.

For Gülen, a leader should be open to any criticism and even welcome it, but the response to criticism or accusation should be on philosophical principles and constructive. Abdullah Aymaz recalls, after sharp criticism and accusations from secularists against Gülen and the Hizmet Movement after the death of President Turgut Özal (1927–1993), in 1994 Aymaz and his colleagues complained to him about these smear campaigns. Gülen responded, "It is not their fault. We have not explained ourselves to them sufficiently. We must engage them in dialogue."[324] Such critical thought will reduce tension and conflict and will inspire peace and social harmony internally and externally.

In Gülen's philosophy, the leader should promote common respect and minimise differences. Instead of "divide and rule," his outlook is to serve, focus on the common good and to come together on universal principles. He does not view truth as lying in powerful leadership but the power of a leader as lying the truth and justice.

Leadership is not something to fight over but a sacred duty to serve people after being given it. Instead of the literal understanding of the meaning of *Salaf al-Saliheen* leadership that some Muslims have, Gülen revives its meaning according to our era. Even though he very occasionally differs with the *Salaf al-Saliheen* by mentioning his opinion on some issues, he always uses the language of respect and honour for them.[325] Unlike some reformist interpretations, his views do not contradict the

---

324   Mehmet Özalp, "Muhammad Fethullah Gülen", 43.

325   Besir Gozubenli, "Hoca Efendinin eserlerinde fikih usulun onemi ve fanksiyonelligi", in *Bir Alim Portresi Etrafinda*, ed. Hamza Aktan (Istanbul: Nil Yayınları, 2014), 31.

sacred texts, the Qur'an and hadiths. In leadership, Gülen combines *aql* (reason), *qalb* (heart), and *ruh* (*spirit*), from the inner and the outer, in the service of people because if one is missing, then *Sayyidhood* leadership is incomplete. It can be said that, just as al-Ghazali injected spirituality into the dry body of theology, Gülen has injected spirituality into the dogmatic rules of contemporary Islamic leadership. In today's Muslim world, this kind of complete leadership is mostly missing. Leaders are accountable to God, people and environment. To have a strong sense of accountability, there needs to be a combination of *aql* (reason), *qalb* (heart) and *ruh* (spirit). For Gülen, the real power of leadership is in sincerity and truth, not in despotism. With this true approach, a leader will gradually gain an angelic quality and will minimise human weaknesses. Gülen lists seven qualities of effective leaders:

> Realism: the leader's messages and demands should be in tune with reality and human nature.
> Knowledge of each follower: this includes character, abilities, shortcomings, and ambitions.
> Absolute belief in their message, especially before preaching and leading.
> Courage, perseverance, strong willpower and resolve: even in the worst of conditions, a leader should not lose hope or stop persevering in his or her mission.
> Awareness of responsibilities, the work to be done and input of effort accordingly.
> Far-sighted and goal-centred: this includes the ability to look into the past, present and future and see the potential.
> The ability to adapt and develop: leaders can be determined but flexible.[326]

After analysing his works, Gülen's leadership philosophy can be summarised as being more proactive than reactionary. For any problem, he takes a step to solve it and it does not matter how big or complicated the problem is. For Gülen, the best leader must grievously suffer for his fellow humans, listen to those who are suffering, propose solutions to their problems and help them.

Conclusion

Regarding *Sayyidhood*, Gülen reviewed, reinterpreted and exemplified the

---

326   Gülen, *Prophet Muhammad*, 251–252.

"*Sayyid-ul qawm khadimihum*" hadith in the light of the Qur'an and exemplary life of the Prophet, Companions, great scholars, saints and Islamic leaders in accordance with the modern age. He injected love of serving others for no reward, altruism, and compassion in hearts. For him, this love, *istighna, ithar* and compassion are preconditions for successful leadership and he systematised this type of leadership in the Hizmet Movement.

Unlike some leaders, Gülen does not make big claims. He started with a small Qur'an course and gradually moved up to students' houses and dormitories over several years. Once there were a reasonable number of supporters of his cause of education, he set out to establish schools and tutoring centres. Later came the establishment of publishing companies, universities, hospitals, relief organisations, dialogue institutions, media groups and Islamic banking. Currently, these institutions, primarily schools, are to be found in 170 countries.[327] These schools have gained solid reputations as good schools academically and as good environments due to the exemplary teachers. Even though many, if not most, of these schools only provide religious education according to the national curriculum, they offer Muslim role models.

Since the mid-1960s, the Hizmet Movement, under the spiritual leadership of Gülen (who does not accept this leadership), has continued to grow and develop. He has been and is still seen as a threat by the Turkish government. Being a highly influential religious scholar means to be seen as a threat in undemocratic or semi-democratic countries in the Muslim world. There are two major reasons. First, these influential scholars do not approve rulers' corruption, injustice and tyranny. The second is that they are not silent but critical of their wrongdoings and unlawful actions. Despite the attacks, the lawsuits and slander, Gülen has charted the ship through dangerous waters time and time again, encouraging people to steer clear of politics and hubris and emphasising positive action as opposed to reaction. Even in his most challenging and trying moments, not once did Gülen abandon the cause of education. He has taken Nursi's three universal enemies of humankind and devoted his life to fighting against ignorance, poverty, and disunity. His life's actions are focused on this and this alone.

This chapter finds that Gülen is reintroducing *Sayyidhood* leader-

---

327　All institutions in Turkey were confiscated by the government after the failed military coup of July 2016.

ship, not just in theory but in practice. Through *Sayyidhood* leadership, Gülen has combined guardian, servant and transformational leadership successfully, and built group solidarity and minimised internal conflicts in the Hizmet Movement by reintroducing lifelong *hijra* and the application of *istighna, ithar* and *fana fil-khidmah*[328] principles which are being neglected by Muslims at large. According to Gülen, leadership is an Islamic goal which mentioned in the Qur'an (25:74),[329] and it can be achieved through Islamic means and methods only. It is incumbent on a Muslim to pursue Islamic goals and adopt an Islamic way in attaining his or her goals.[330]

Gülen's can be seen as a revitaliser of *Sayyidhood* leadership as it suits the current global situation and needs of Muslims. He has brought a new understanding of *tabligh*, which is known as inviting people to Islam. Gülen holds that what makes a leader is having the essence and heart of leadership (being the sultan of hearts), not eloquent or lively words. A leader must rank first in his or her knowledge, piety, righteousness, generosity, spirituality, altruism, and conduct himself or herself accordingly. A leader is one who leads by example and then wins over hearts and motivates people as opposed to one who dictates commands. Although he never claims any leadership, Gülen is well respected and seen as a leader by millions of people. His leadership can be summarised as being one who seeks the happiness of others, and through great suffering has overcome numerous calamities during his whole life. His leadership, however, is not

---

328 In Sufism, the notion of annihilation means the breaking down of the ego. This concept applies to annihilation in the sheikh, then in the Prophet, and then in God. Gülen uses fana fil-khidmah which means annihilation in the service of people. It connects to the notion of submission to God and losing oneself within the goodness of the Divine. For further information, see, Fethullah Gülen, "Fena Fillah," *Sızıntı*, Mayıs, sayı 376, 2010, www.sizinti.com.tr/konular/ayrinti/fena-fill-ah-2-mayis-2010.html. Retrieved 1.9.2015.

329 "And who say: 'Our Lord! Grant us that our spouses and offspring may be a means of happiness for us, and enable us to lead others in piety (to become a means of the promotion of piety and virtue).'"

330 Fethullah Gülen, *Sızıntı*, January, 1993, Vol. 3, Issue 19, fgulen.com/en/fethullah-Gülens-works/thought/towards-the-lost-paradise/24463-towards-the-world-of-righteous-servants. Retrieved 19.09.2015

understood by his contemporaries, specifically politicians in Turkey.

It is the destiny of many great scholars throughout history to be misunderstood or underestimated or seen as a threat. Gülen's words and actions have captured the hearts and minds of many who are now dispersed in 170 countries, not for worldly gain or power, but for the common good. Just as Imam Azam Abu Hanifa (699–767), Imam Malik (711–795) Imam Shafi'i (767–820), and Ahmad ibn Hanbal (780–855) each established a school of law for jurisprudence, and Abdulqadr al-Jilani (d.1166) and Baha ud-Din Naqshband (1318–1389) established Sufi *tariqa* (pathways) that have been taken up by Muslims for centuries, so too has Gülen set out a model of *Sayyidhood* leadership according to the needs of modern times through the Hizmet Movement which will be taken up by more Muslims in the future.

CHAPTER 5

RENEWAL THROUGH *TAMTHIL*
TO SERVE ISLAM AND HUMANITY

Renewal through *Tamthil* to Serve Islam and Humanity

ethullah Gülen states that the world is in need of Islam and Islam is in need of *tamthil*, representation or role modelling.[331] He believes people's ears are full but their eyes are hungry for role models in all aspects of life, including in educational institutions. In Gülen's vision, *tamthil* comes before *tabligh* (conveying the message, teaching). To him, action should precede words as lightning precedes thunder. In this case, the second sentence of the *shahadah* or testimony of faith will manifest itself in *tamthil*. Analysing the wisdom of the *shahadah*, Gülen says that "the word *abd*, or servant, comes before the word *Rasul*, or Messenger. *Abd* means to practice as a servant. This means that *tamthil*, representing or role modelling, comes before conveying the message"[332] or teaching. For Gülen, to change misconceptions about Islam, it is essential that the universal *tamthil* of religion be observed by the majority of Muslims. It is necessary, particularly for those who serve Islam and are in leadership positions, to strive harder to establish a pleasing universal *tamthil* for overcoming crises and misconceptions.

Since Islam is a universal religion, for Gülen, *tamthil* must be universal. The Prophet represented a universal Islam.[333] Later, the Companions and great figures in Islamic history followed in his footsteps. *Tamthil* is also the most inclusive universal language. In this chapter, first, Gülen's views regarding a universal *tamthil* and how he applies it in his daily life will be covered in depth. Second, the eleven criteria of *tamthil*, which Gülen calls *Hasani ruh*, will be analysed in the light of his work. Third, some testimonials from his close associates and friends who have been near to or have known Gülen since 1967 will be discussed. Fourth, the institutionalisation of *tamthil* will be touched on. Finally, my personal observations on the topic will be briefly included.

5.1 Universal *tamthil*

Prophet Muhammad (pbuh) represented a universal *tamthil* of Islam at the peak of complete perfection as the Messenger of God because he

---

331   *Tamthil* means role modelling or representation as required, in Turkish.

332   Personal communication, July 17, 2007

333   Gülen, *Fasıldan Fasıla* 5, 91.

was sent "as a mercy to the worlds" (Qur'an, 21:107). In the Qur'an, it is stated that "there has certainly been for you in the Messenger of Allah an excellent pattern for anyone whose hope is in Allah and the Last Day and [who] remembers Allah often" (33:21). The Prophet had two aspects of his mission which are *tabligh* and *tamthil*. Gülen states that conveying the truths is *tabligh* and fulfilling his perfect role modelling with the purest sincerity can be considered *tamthil*.[334] Gülen reads the life of the Prophet as comprising nine *tamthil* (representations) out of ten[335] and believes that the finest representatives of Islam were the Prophet, his Companions, and then his descendants[336] throughout Islamic history. Those who serve religion are charged with following the Prophets in disseminating the truth.[337]

Gülen continues that the Prophet's *tamthil* aspect always precedes his *tabligh* dimension. The Prophet's *tamthil* includes every aspect of his life and is at the degree of the peak of *al-insan al-kamil*, the perfect human. This is essential for all prophets who represent the truths at the highest level because the issues related to faith can be elucidated through *tamthil*. In fact, acceptance of the truth by the people depends on the degree of *tamthil*, or it will be hypocrisy, as Gülen argues.[338] If the *tamthil* is done only in words, it will be ineffective. When it is performed in words and actions, it becomes effective. *Tamthil* will be most effective if it encompasses word, action, and soul.

Gülen believes that the sublime attributes that all prophets possess are accepted as good attributes in every period and era, and by all people.[339] These attributes are *sidq* (truthfulness), *tabligh* (communication), *amānah* (trustworthiness), *fatānah* (Prophetic intellect), *ismah* (infallibility), and freedom from physical and mental defects. According to all Sunni Muslim scholars, these attributes are represented in the best way by Prophet Muhammad (pbuh), other prophets and *sahabah*, the Com-

---

334 Gülen, *Fasıldan Fasıla* 4, 156.

335 Ünal, *Fethullah Gülen'le Amerika'da Bir Ay*.

336 Gülen, *Asrın Getirdiği Tereddütler* 3, 22–23.

337 Nursi, *The Letters*, 31.

338 Gülen, *Fasıldan Fasıla* 4, 156.

339 Süleyman Sertkaya, *The Sirah Genre: An Evaluation of Fethullah Gülen's Approach*, unpublished dissertation, Australian Catholic University, 2016.

panions of the Prophet and then the second and third generation of early Muslims. For Gülen, those who convey the message have to represent (*tamthil*) Islam at the degree of the Companions. Otherwise, ultimate success in their works related to *tabligh* is unthinkable.[340] For a believer, the level of *tamthil* is inversely proportional to the degree of practicing these five attributes. For Gülen, the best *tamthil* is representing Islam at the degree of *ihsan*, which is to be conscious that God is always observing. *Tamthil* includes representing not just by action but also with reason, heart, and soul. In short, doing everything in a most beautiful way and according to *sharia at-takwiniyyah* (the natural law which God created) is considered *tamthil*.

Gülen states that *tamthil* is the most significant character of a responsible generation which will lead to true faith, wisdom, righteousness, and peace. As a bird requires two wings for flight, similarly words will affect the depth of the heart and mind with both *tamthil* and *tabligh*.[341]

According to Gülen, *tabligh* can be done in two ways. The first is passive; that means conveying a message through sincere actions, not talk. This can be considered *tamthil*. The second one is active *tabligh*, which means through talking.[342] *Tamthil* leads to curiosity in a person's mind and then the person asks questions in order to learn. The passive *tabligh* is to reflect the human dimension of Islam through a transaction with others. This is more effective than active *tabligh* because it builds trust. Also, if *tamthil* is not done properly, the truth will be devalued in people's eyes and eventually it will disappear from the hearts and minds of society. Gülen argues that many lofty ideas and truths have not been valued and have died out due to misrepresentation.[343] Therefore, speaking must elucidate actions.

Tamthil does not just apply to religious or ethical issues but to all fields, including politics, sciences, justice, human rights, dignity, and the environment, and so on. For Gülen, those who have any type of leadership position must be more vigilant about *tamthil*. If they neglect any type and their duty (including the spiritual) for one hour, then the followers,

---

340　Gülen, *İrşad Ekseni* (Istanbul: Nil Yayınları,2006), 214.

341　Gülen, *Çağ ve Nesil* 7, 17.

342　Gülen, *Fasıldan Fasıla* 5, 103.

343　Gülen, *Fasıldan Fasıla* 1, 151.

congregation, or citizens will be negligent for the entire day because there is a strong relation between rulers and their subjects in *tamthil*. *Tamthil* can be done individually, as a group, nation, or *umma*, that is, as the whole Muslim community. The value of a system or thought in the sight of God is based on the degree of *tamthil* of individuals, groups, and the nation. Through *tamthil*, groups or movements spiritually grow and collectively can reach the degree of the Spiritual Pole (*Qutb*)[344] of the time. For Gülen, attaining such a degree is based on the following conditions:

> There should be strong relations between all individuals of the group or movement
> All must have high goals and the same or very similar attitudes
> All must be devoted to all types of worship (obligatory and supererogatory).[345] For a right and successful *tamthil*, it is necessary to take all precautions by conforming with the rules of nature which God has created.[346] Even if all things are done properly, in the end, it must be kept in mind that a perfect *tamthil* is by the grace of God. Therefore, individuals or groups must not see *tamthil* as their skill but embrace it as a blessing of God.[347]

The *tamthil* will be more effective in a peaceful society because, during conflicts, the truths are first killed and they cannot be heard. Therefore, Islam spread very quickly throughout the Arabian Peninsula after the Prophet signed the *Hudaybiyya* Peace Treaty with the Meccan polytheists. A Muslim is a representative of peace on earth and is "the one from whose hand and tongue other Muslims are *safe*" as the Prophet mentions.[348] In that case, it is absolutely wrong to do anything which can harm peace and safety. For Gülen, one important characteristic of *tamthil* is to be peaceful and uniting instead of dividing, and focusing on similarities between humans rather than differences. A Muslim should not hesitate to sacrifice his or her dignity,

---

344 Qutb is the one who leads the saintly hierarchy of time. He is *insan al-kamil*, the perfect human being, or the Universal Man. There is only one Qutb per century according to Sufi scholars.

345 Gülen, *Fasıldan Fasıla* 1, 210–211.

346 Gülen, *Fasıldan Fasıla* 1, 131.

347 Gülen, *Fasıldan Fasıla* 2, 106.

348 Bukhari and Muslim, *sunnah*.com/riyadussaliheen/1/211. Retrieved 16.04.2017.

position, or financial benefit for the sake of peace and social harmony, as the Companions did, because the strength of Islam is dependent on Muslims' uprightness, integrity, and acting peacefully. Otherwise, the *tamthil* is incomplete.

Most significantly, through stories of the Companions, Gülen aims to establish a similar community to provide the critical mass needed to stimulate change in society. A community imbued with the attributes of the Companions, not just with a single leader, could provide leadership for a whole society. No matter how competent, communities cannot achieve transformation on their own.[349] Gülen says, "I have been reading the biography of the Companions since my childhood. I thought that being like them was a utopia and that it was not possible to have such lifestyle. However, later, I changed my mind because I have witnessed some people who are like the Companions, not in their rank of spiritually, but by resembling them in actions. I saw that some of them established brotherhood similar to the Companions,"[350] who reflected the character of the Prophet in their hearts and actions in a perfect way. He continues, "They also represented Islam in a perfect way by a complete imitation of the Imam of the Imams (Prophet Muhammad, the head of all prophets). They practiced his message with their hearts and souls and then enlightened all humanity with God's grace."[351] The Companions of the Prophet conveyed the message of Islam in three continents in a short period through the universal language of *tamthil* first. Wherever the Companions went, they did not conquer only lands but also hearts and minds.[352] Despite all this success, they viewed themselves as ordinary people and were never proud of being Companions. Also, they were self-critical and open to criticism. Anyone could stand up and be critical of the four Rightly Guided Caliphs while they were preaching or giving sermons in the mosque.

For Gülen, those who are responsible for *tabligh* duty, must do self-criticism and self-supervision of their actions and whether they are done for the pleasure of God or not, instead of being proud of their influence, or acceptance by people and having many followers. This is one of the

---

349   Özalp, "Muhammad Fethullah Gülen", 42.

350   Gülen, *Asrın Getirdiği Tereddütler* 3, 62.

351   Gülen, *Asrın Getirdiği Tereddütler* 2, 87.

352   Gülen, *Fasıldan Fasıla* 4, 153.

most significant principles of the *tabligh*.[353] They must be very generous and altruistic and willing to sacrifice whatever they have for the sake of God.[354] Even though they live among people, their hearts must remember God.[355] Gülen asserts that when deeds talk, there is not much need of words.[356]

When referring to *tamthil*, Gülen uses the term *Hasani ruh*, "the Spirit of Hasan," the grandson (625–669) of the Prophet Muhammad (pbuh) in his works. Gülen summarises *tamthil* at the degree of *ihsan* in the expression "*Hasani ruh*" in his works. Hasan's exemplary spirituality symbolises a beloved leader who sacrifices for the peace, security, and the welfare of his people, while striving to prevent conflict and bloodshed in the Muslim world. In Gülen's works, *Hasani ruh* refers to being altruistic, trustworthy, peaceful, and devoted to the service of humanity. There is unanimous agreement among the Muslim scholars that Prophet Muhammad (pbuh) is the pinnacle of humanity in regard to *tamthil* and his Companions come after him. The majority of scholars and Muslims are agreed that Imam Azam, Imam Malik, Ahmad ibn Hanbal, Imam Shafi'i are the best jurists in jurisprudence, Imam Ashari and Imam Maturidi are outstanding theologians in theology. Abdulqadr al-Jilani and Muhammad Baha ud-Din Naqshbandi are leading figures in Sufism. All of them are the finest in their fields of expertise in *tamthil*.

5.2 *Hasani ruh* and *tamthil*

In Gülen's works, "*Hasani ruh*" the Spirit of Hasan is used literally and metaphorically. Hasan (r.a) is from *Ahl al-Bayt,* the Family of Prophet Muhammad (pbuh). Gülen refers to Hasan (r.a) when exemplifying spirituality because he is the embodiment of the values needed today. One of his values is choosing "we" over "I" or preferring the communal benefit over his leadership. This is clearly seen in Hasan's choice to decline the highest political and spiritual position in Islam of caliph in order to prevent bloodshed.[357] The Muslim community was politically

353   Gülen, *Asrın Getirdiği Tereddütler* 3, 183.

354   Ibid., 188.

355   Gülen, *Asrın Getirdiği Tereddütler* 4, 186.

356   Gülen, *Çağ ve Nesil* 8, 104.

357   Yaqubi 2:226, Zahabi 2: 260 in Adnan Demircan, "Hz Hasan ve Halifeliği", *Harran İlahiyat Fakültesi Dergisi*, Vol. 2, (1995), 94–106.

divided into two groups. If either leader had insisted upon leadership, it would have caused further conflict. Although he had the majority of the community on his side, Hasan (r.a) did not want to endanger people's lives and risk the community's stability by accepting that widespread support. [358] Choosing the greater communal benefit over all kinds of personal benefits is a vital rule in Gülen's philosophy of *tamthil*. Being peaceful and striving for peace is another vital feature of *tamthil*.

Gülen himself has been oppressed and persecuted since the early 1960s. One of Gülen's oldest friends, Hasan Üzümcü, calls him, "a man without rest and not allowed to rest throughout his life" due to oppression by the military, police, intelligence service and government, as mentioned in the previous chapters. He has faced all kinds of discrimination, stereotyping, prosecutions, threats, and injustice. A few times secularists have tried to assassinate him. There has been almost no single day when he was not persecuted since the early 1970s. Despite all of that, Gülen did not rebel or ask his followers to do so. He has also mentioned very many times that he forgives those who wronged him for breaching his personal rights.

Gülen's works, sermons, and public talks have been reflected in his life. He has experienced all types of hardship similar to all great scholars in the history of Islam, specifically *Ahl al-Bayt*, the family of the Prophet and his descendants. Historically, most of them have been seen as a threat by rulers due to their commitment to religious and spiritual principles, education, devotion to worship, and their influence on people like that of Hasan (r.a).

According to Gülen, *Hasani ruh* is a metaphor for those who completely represent Islam at the level of *ihsan*. Whoever has such degree of *ihsan* in *tamthil*, "he or she, even if they are not from the Prophet's lineage, can be considered to be part of his spiritual lineage," he argues.[359] They carry the same characteristics as *Ahl al-Bayt*. They turn their backs

---

358   Hasan (r.a) said, "I hate to be caliph if it means people will be killed. I gave up the caliphate so that the blood of the community of Muhammad (i.e. Muslims) does not spill." Even though Hasan took part in the Battle of Siffin, he did not engage in direct combat. (Abu Nuaym al Isfahani, *Hilyatu'l-Awliya wa Tabaqatu'l-Asfiya* 2. 37 and Ibn Manzur Vol. II, 35 cited in Demircan, "Hz Hasan ve Halifeliği".

359   Gülen, *Asrın Getirdiği Tereddütler* 3, 22–23.

on the world, serve their people, refrain from causing harm, live to help all humans and animals. They live as trustworthy, altruistic, and devoted believers[360] for whom spiritual progress is measured in terms of or determined by others' happiness in this world and the Hereafter.[361] According to Gülen, those who are in a leadership position have to abandon the world before the world abandons them. This is necessary for *tamthil*. They must not possess even a house and only have an income or salary which is just sufficient for survival. The second caliph Umar (r.a) demolished the grand house of a governor.[362] Gülen himself and most of his close associates do not own a house. This is highly idealistic, and only a small group of people can apply it in daily life. It is necessary, however, for an ideal degree of *tamthil*.

In my humble understanding, in Gülen's works, there are eleven major and distinguishing characteristics which are associated with the bearers of *Hasani ruh*. Each characteristic reflects an aspect of *tamthil or* role modelling. For Gülen, if a believer neglects one characteristic in both spirituality and action, then the truth that he or she represents will lose its value.[363] Even if a believer speaks eloquently or uses the most beautiful words to express the truth, it will decay or be ineffective in time.[364] To obtain these eleven characteristics, it is essential to have in-depth knowledge (*ma'rifa*). For Gülen, it is necessary for the *muballigh* (the one who conveys the message of Islam) to know the knowledge of the heart, which is an Islamic discipline, and he or she must also know secular sciences, which enlighten the reasoning (*aql*), at an encyclopaedic level. Besides the knowledge of heart and mind, the "*muballigh* must strengthen his/her spirituality in depth with genuineness and sincerity."[365] The future of the umma is dependent on a generation which combines knowledge of the heart and mind with both successfully reflected in their lives. For gaining knowledge, reading is essential, as commanded by God in the first revelation (Qur'an, 96:1) to the Prophet. According to

---

360   Ibid., 23.

361   Gülen, *Key Concepts in the Practice of Sufism* 2, 235.

362   Gülen, *Fasıldan Fasıla* 3, 163.

363   Gülen, *Fasıldan Fasıla* 1, 151.

364   Gülen, *Fasıldan Fasıla* 2, 156.

365   Gülen, *Asrın Getirdiği Tereddütler* 3, 181.

his friends, Gülen reads five to six hours daily. He is well versed in many sciences besides the religious sciences. Thus, his *tamthil* also has an intellectual dimension beside a spiritual one. *Hasani ruh* characteristics cannot be gained without reading and studying.

The first characteristic of those with *Hasani ruh* is that they seek to win people over, not politically, but spiritually. Displaying another trait common to the majority of *Ahl al-Bayt*, they refrain from politics and focus on enlightening minds and widening hearts. During the periods of instability in the Muslim world, they become indispensable in serving the Muslim community. Said Nursi who was one of the most influential contemporary scholars and Gülen's spiritual leader, referred to the Prophet's cousin Ali (r.a.), father of Hasan, as the "King of Sainthood." He was a blessed person, worthy of the highest position, not merely of political rule. He became a spiritual ruler whose status surpassed that of the political caliphate, a Universal Master, whose spiritual rule will continue even until the end of the world.[366] This title can be extended to Ali's sons, Hasan and Hussein (626–680) as well.

Despite many opportunities since the early 1970s, Gülen has avoided being involved in politics due to this characteristic of *tamthil*. Several times, political parties offered him the opportunity to be on the candidate list for elections to the Turkish Parliament, but Gülen declined as mentioned in the previous chapter. He preferred to be an educator instead of being a politician. Not being involved in politics is an important principle of Gülen's philosophy. He was severely criticised many times by Islamic-oriented political parties because he abstained from politics and for his criticism about using religion for political purposes. He has taken on Nursi's principle of avoiding politics. Nursi said, "I seek refuge with God from Satan and politics."[367] This is due to religious scholars representing all Muslims, not just those who vote for a religious political party. Politics devalues the truths of Islam in people's minds. However, Gülen does not entirely disconnect himself from rulers and politicians. Just as al-Ghazali advised and sometimes warned rulers by sending letters to

---

366   Nursi, *The Letters*, 75.

367   Said Nursi, *The Rays*, trans. Şükran Vahide (Istanbul: Sözler Publications, 2002), 395.

them, Gülen also tries to keep good relations with all the main groups or political parties in Turkey. From time to time, Gülen gives advice directly or indirectly to leaders and rulers in a diplomatic way.

The second characteristic that *Hasani ruh* evokes is the desire to establish relationships based on trust and a common ground, which is essential for *tamthil*. Those who represent Islam properly can get along with everyone, including the pharaohs of society, by accepting that even the most difficult person has a positive trait. God commanded Moses and Aaron to talk to Pharaoh politely (Qur'an, 20:44). This characteristic is necessary because a Muslim should be helpful to all individuals[368] with the exception of those who are unjustly aggressive in attacking others.

The third characteristic of *Hasani ruh* is to serve others without any expectation. Gülen argues there is a need to redefine the concept of "us" and "others" in the framework of serving others. "Us" refers to those who serve, while "others" refer to those who need to be served, which includes all people, not just Muslims, or those who have a material need. Through this new definition Gülen shows the importance of a positive perception between Muslims and non-Muslims.[369] Because it is easier to learn when a person sees a live example,[370] this characteristic can be achieved through service to others, which Gülen views as *ibada* or worship. By doing this, Gülen is reintroducing the philosophy of Ali Hujwīrī (990–1077) who said, "see everyone as your master for reaching the truth."[371] So the love of serving others is the foundation of Gülen's philosophy as a principle of *tamthil*.

Gülen often refers to a saying of one of his spiritual masters that humility is a principle of serving others. For example, Muhammed Lütfi Efendi said, "Everybody else is good but I am bad; everybody else is wheat, but I am chaff, the inhabitants of the heavens will kiss him or her

---

368   "The best people are those most beneficial to [other] people." Prophet Muhammad (pbuh)

369   Carroll, *A Dialogue of Civilizations*, 38.

370   Valerievna, Izbullaeva Gulchehra, "The Theory and Application of Utilizing Jalal-Ad-Din Rumi's Spiritual and Moral Views", *Creative Education* 5, no. 18 (10, 2014): 1678-1683 search.proquest.com/docview/1620433634?accountid=10344.

371   Jean-Louis Michon, "The Spiritual Practices of Sufism", in *Islamic Spirituality Foundations*, ed. Sayyed Hossein Nasr (New York: Crossroad, 1987), 271.

on the head."[372] To that Gülen adds that service requires: "seeing oneself as devoid of all virtues necessarily originating in oneself, treating others humbly and respectfully, seeing oneself as the worst of humanity (unless being honored by a special Divine treatment)… Do not boast of yourself in a way to see yourself as greater than others. As creatures are equal in being distant from being worshiped, so also are they equal in that they are all created."[373]

According to this line of thought, Gülen views believers, especially those who teach, as having an obligation to serve humanity without expecting rewards, material or otherwise, because the world is an "abode of service, not the place of pleasure, reward, and requital."[374] Spiritual representatives need to lead a life of "pietistic activism." This should be based on a "rejection of the world" but not the "flight from this world" found in escapist mysticism.[375] This is an aspect of the *istighna* described in Chapter 4 and means sacrificing one's resources, including time, money, abilities, and networks to serve humanity, and desiring Allah's pleasure alone. Wanting financial return and hoping for a political, religious, spiritual or social position is contrary to *istighna*. Desiring respect for the acts done or a particular title such as *efendi, ustad, alim,* master, or *pir* will weaken the sincerity of service.[376] Even expecting not to fall into difficulties, experience loss and suffering, nor receive criticism is against the principles of *istighna*. *Istighna* will also be explained in detail in Chapter 7.

Gülen takes this further when stating that the leaders of spiritual representatives should lead a very simple life.[377] The time will come when profit and self-interest will cause division among the community of be-

---

372 Fethullah Gülen, "Humility", in *Key Concepts in the Practice of Sufism* 1, www.fgu-len.com/en/fethullah-gulens-works/sufism/key-concepts-in-the-practice-of-su-fism-1/24742-tawadu-humility. Retrieved 21.11.2016.

373 Ibid.. Retrieved 22.04.2017.

374 Nursi, *The Flashes*, 23

375 Elizabeth E. Özdalga. "Worldly Asceticism in Islamic Casting: Fethullah Gülen's Inspired Piety and Activism", Critique: Critical Middle Eastern Studies, Vol. 17 (Fall 2003), 83–104.

376 Gülen, *İrşad Ekseni*, 67.

377 Gülen, *Fasıldan Fasıla* 3, 163.

lievers. At that point, the altruistic bearers of *Hasani ruh* will decline worldly benefits, thus preventing conflict among believers,[378] just as Hasan did.

The fourth characteristic of *Hasani ruh* is being trustworthy. *Amānah* or trustworthiness is one of five major significant attributes of all Prophets. Since *tamthil* necessitates following the Prophet Muhammad (pbuh), this must be a high aim for those who represent Islam. The Prophet defines the believer as one whom other believers do not fear will harm them.[379] Based on that principle, Gülen concludes, "Our greatest capital is our credibility (i.e. reputation). This must never be lost (i.e. misused)."[380] In order to protect one's reputation, a person must be trustworthy, must believe in the value of being trustworthy, and accept trustworthiness as a pillar for *tamthil*.[381] To advance one's credibility in the eyes of the entire community,[382] a person must serve to benefit others. Gülen holds that "the ideal people burn like candles despite themselves, and they illuminate others."[383]

The fifth characteristic requires spiritual representatives to focus on a person's inner dimension, not only on appearance to gain the ethical aspect of *tamthil*.[384] For Gülen, believers' piety can be seen in dealings with others[385] and their concern for the well-being of others rather than their own.[386] He says that a common fallacy in the Muslim world is to believe that change is manifested through appearance only and that modernity means wearing a suit and tie, while piety means having a beard

---

378   Fethullah Gülen, *Prizma* 1, (Istanbul: Nil Yayınları, 2011), 217-218

379   The Prophet was asked, "Who is the most excellent among the Muslims?" He said, "One from whose tongue and hands the other Muslims are secure." Hadith by Bukhari and Muslim.

380   Personal communication, January 2006

381   Gülen, *Sonsuz Nur* 1, 318.

382   Gülen, *Prizma* 1, 318.

383   Gülen, *Ölçü ve Yoldaki Işıklar*, 108.

384   For related verses look at Chapter 2: 177, 3:134, 5:93, 4:149, 13:22,25:72.

385   Gülen, *Ölçü ve Yoldaki Işıklar*, 133

386   Ibid., 122.

or wearing a turban.[387] Some Muslims take this appearance as a condition of piety. Having a beard is following in the tradition of Prophet Muhammad (pbuh), but for Gülen, piety cannot be measured by appearance only. It is more about applying ethical principles in dealing with others.

The sixth characteristic is being altruistic in all matters, whether it is physical, spiritual, financial, or otherwise. Hasan (r.a) twice gave his entire wealth to help the poor, and three times he gave half his wealth for the same purpose,[388] alongside giving up his right to be caliph. To embody *tamthil*, a believer must be the one who gives, not the one who receives. Believers are those who give their time, money, knowledge, and sacrifice their pride, position, and daily needs.[389] In addition to that, embodying *tamthil* is not about individual effort alone. It requires the development of problem-solving projects for the benefit of the community and even the natural world.[390] Muslims understand that they have responsibilities not only to themselves but also to the communities of which they are a part.[391] This is another important principle of Gülen's philosophy of *tamthil*.

For Gülen, there is no limit to helping others. For this to be possible, a believer must have a sincere intention, and give without desiring reward, and should serve all humanity, not only those of his or her own race or nation.[392] A Muslim must give his or her time, energy, knowledge, skills, and other things for the well-being of the local community, Muslim community (*ummah*) and humanity.

The seventh characteristic of *Hasani ruh* is using gentle persuasion and refraining from inciting conflict. This characteristic is drawn from Said Nursi's works. Nursi states, "For conquering the civilized people is

---

387   Ibid., 241; Gülen, *Fasıldan Fasıla* 3, 64.

388   Demircan, "Hz Hasan ve Halifeliği", 94–106.

389   Gülen, *Asrın Getirdiği Tereddütler* 2, 85–87.

390   Gülen, *Fasıldan Fasıla* 5, 153.

391   Muhammed Çetin, "Is the Gülen Movement a Civil Society Initiative?" *Today's Zaman*, Sunday, 19 April 2009.

392   Gülen, *Ölçü ve Yoldaki Işıklar*, 118.

through persuasion, not through force as though they were savages who understand nothing."[393] For successful *tamthil*, Gülen asserts that a believer is obliged to have a gentle manner, a compassionate nature, a soft heart, and consideration and kind words for others.[394]

The eighth characteristic of *Hasani ruh* for a believer is to weave friendships with everyone on the common ground of everyday life and work to increase the commonalities in a way that does not call for a compromise in religion or values.[395] Instead of stirring meaningless controversy and engaging in acts or talks related to enmity, Gülen believes that a believer must live according to his or her values, love his or her way of service, and busy him- or herself[396] with building friendships and continuing service projects that promote friendship. Moreover, a believer should not think that his or her way is the *only* right way, but, according to Nursi, he or she may say, "My way is right and the best."[397] For Gülen, believers should also encourage or assist others who work for the good of humanity.[398]

To better understand how to build common ground and not see one way as the only way, it is necessary to look at Gülen's definition of Islam. He does not draw a line between Muslim and non-Muslim but views the word "Islam" as having three meanings, one within the other like three circles.

The core meaning defines Islam as the religion that stipulates how people should conduct their lives. The second meaning is that Islam refers to the actions and attributes of individuals independent of their religious persuasion. Gülen gives the example of a non-Muslim who may possess a believer's attribute of honesty and a believer or a Muslim with the non-believer's attribute of dishonesty. The third meaning that encompasses the meaning of Islam is the "laws of creation" (*şeriat-ı kawniyye*) according to which the universe conducts itself. These laws are

---

393   Said Nursi, *Damascus Sermon, (Hutbe-i Şâmiye)*, 79.

394   Gülen, *Prizma* 1, 40.

395   Gülen, *Fasıldan Fasıla* 3, 76.

396   Gülen, *Ölçü ve Yoldaki Işıklar*, 200.

397   Nursi, *The Letters*, 22.

398   Gülen, *Fasıldan Fasıla* 1, 68.

similar to the rules of religion because both are ordained by God, but dissimilar because humans have free will to follow the religious laws, whereas the universe does not.[399]

The ninth characteristic is doing the deed at the degree of *itqan*. Gülen says whoever does anything, must do it at the level of *itqan* which means to have the best and right knowledge and then put it into practice in the best way. As mentioned in the Qur'an "And say, Do [as you will], for Allah will see your deeds, and [so, will] His Messenger and the believers" (9:105). This is a command to do everything in the best way as it is going to be presented to God and the Prophet. "...[It is] the work of Allah, who perfected all things..." (Qur'an, 27:88) Commenting on this verse Ismail Haqqi states that "He makes everything in the most beautiful shape and for the most beautiful goals."[400] This is called *itqan*. Also, the Prophet says that "God loves those who do their deeds at the degree of *itqan*"[401] In another hadith "May God have mercy upon the one who does all his action in *itqan* which is the most proficient [as Allah and his massager observe]."[402] For Najmaddin al-Kubra (d.1223), the acceptance of a deed is based on the degree of doing in *itqan*.[403]

The tenth characteristic of people with *Hasani ruh* is that they forgive everyone who did injustice to them. Despite suffering for more than a decade because of their jealousy and mistreatment by his brothers, Prophet Joseph forgave them (Qur'an, 12:91). Similarly, after almost twenty years of persecution and the tyranny of polytheists, after conquering Mecca without bloodshed, Prophet Muhammad (pbuh) said, "No blame will there be upon you today. Allah will forgive you, and He is the Most

399 Çelik, G, Kirk, K, Alan, Y. "Gülen's Paradigm on Peaceful Coexistence: Theoretical Insights and Some Practical Perspectives." Paper presented at the conference "Muslim World in Transition: Contributions of the Gülen Movement" at SOAS University of London, House of Lords and London School of Economics on 25–27 October, 2007, en.fgulen.com/conference-papers/peaceful-coexistence/2512-Gülens-paradigm-on-peaceful-coexistence-theoretical-insights-and-some-practical-perspectives.

400 Ismail Haqqi, *Ruhu'l Bayan*, altafsir.com. Retrieved 28.04.2017.

401 Şimşek, *İbretlik Hatıralar*, 142–143.

402 Al-Qurtubi, *al-Jami li Ahkam al-Qur'an*, altafsir.com. Retrieved 28.04.2017.

403 Najmaddin al-Kubra, *Ta'wilat*, altafsir.com. Retrieved 27.4.2017.

Merciful of the merciful. Go and you are all free."[404] This was unimaginable in the culture of tribalism of that time anywhere in the world.[405]

The final characteristic of *Hasani ruh* is humility and avoiding fame or publicity so as not to be known or popular in the sight of people. For Gülen, people should not talk about their personal virtues, but, he says, "let your actions speak." Gülen dislikes being praised. According to his close associates, he refrains from fame or pride and publicity about himself. In early 2001, his close associates Abdullah Aymaz and İsmail Büyükçelebi, with a few other leading people in the Hizmet Movement, wanted to introduce Gülen by organising a conference in the United States of America because he might otherwise be misunderstood due stereotyping or misinformation from the secularists' media in Turkey. Gülen initially declined, when they consulted with him. After one year or so, other close associates approached Gülen about such a conference but he declined again. Finally, he was told that it is not for him but that the conference would be important for Islam and Muslims. Otherwise, there would be a great risk that he would be misunderstood.[406] The conference would be an academic conference and his philosophy would be critically examined as well. Gülen reluctantly accepted. Then, a few conferences were organised about him and the Hizmet Movement in the United States of America and, later, in some other countries. The second notable quality of his extreme humility is loyalty to his associates and followers. Gülen abhors public acclaim and sees himself as "a human being among other humans."[407] As mentioned earlier, Gülen never calls himself a leader or scholar but *Qitmir,* the dog of the *Ashab al-Kahf* (the Seven Sleepers). He also wants to be forgotten when he dies.

5.3 Testimonials from friends

To understand Gülen's degree of *tamthil,* role modelling it is essential to consult to those who have been near him since 1965. I also, analysed over 500 of his sermons and talks about how he views regarding *tamthil.*

404 Ibn Ishak in Mustafa A. Köksal, *İslam Tarihi,* 6 (Istanbul: Köksal Yayıncılık, 2002), 396–397.

405 Şimşek, *İbretlik Hatıralar,* 142–143.

406 Personal communication, 2002

407 Mehmet Özalp, "Muhammad Fethullah Gülen", 37.

There are hundreds of examples, but I will give a couple of testimonials of his close associates and mention a few of my personal observations. It can be said that Gülen does not only preach or talk but he lives in his soul before talks.

Kutbettin Gülen recalls: "My elder brother Fethullah has been under the scrutiny and oppression of the Turkish state since the age of eighteen. Many times, he has been mistreated and insulted by the law enforcement but Gülen never mentioned these to anyone. In 1963, after a semi-military coup, he was arrested. My father went to see him; he was arrested as well. A few days later, however, my dad was released." If Gülen tells how he is treated badly to his followers, it may cause tension and even conflicts which Gülen never desired.

In June 1999, the secularists and Turkish Military leaders had a mass media campaign against Gülen. They fabricated many news stories about him over two months. The *Türkiye* newspaper (which is considered an Islamic newspaper aligned with the secularists) fully participated in the anti-Gülen campaign. When a student of Gülen wanted to report what the *Türkiye* newspaper wrote about him, he did not allow him. Gülen said that "I don't want to have any grudge in my heart towards them when I meet with this group. If you read what they wrote, as a human, it can plant a grudge in my heart. Maybe they had to do this because of the military pressure."[408] I was very surprised by Gülen's positive thinking and action towards that group. Gülen states that "I don't want to die with having any grudge in my heart towards any human, especially towards Muslims."[409] About two months after the mass campaign against Gülen, he wrote: "I forgave all of those who attack me through media. However, if they attack to my religion, I have no right to forgive because it belongs to God."[410]

When Gülen was studying at a Madrasa in Erzurum at the young age of fifteen, he borrowed some money from someone. However, the person left Erzurum without leaving his address. It was not much money, but Gülen tried to find him. Years later, he was able to locate him

---

408   Personal communication, June 20, 1999.

409   Ünal, *Bir Portre Denemesi*, 502.

410   Fethullah Gülen, Editorial, *Sızıntı*, October 1999.

and returned his money with some gifts.[411]

Alaattin Kırkan, who has been near Gülen since the early 1970s recalls the righteousness of Gülen. He says: once; Gülen asked someone in the room "What is the time" He replied that it is 3 p.m. Gülen unintentionally looked at his watch and saw that it was 2:57 pm. Then, Gülen said that "we must tell the time exactly as it. Otherwise, we are not telling the truth. Without being aware, it can be a lie. We must tell the truth even we inform the time to any person."

Again, Kırkan recollects: We were sitting in a big hall with a group of individuals including Gülen. Someone called one of the people on the phone, and he wanted to speak to Gülen. The person, who received the call, said to the person who called: 'one second.' Then he brought the phone to Gülen. After he had spoken to him, Gülen said to us "we must always tell the truth. Sometimes without being aware, we don't. By responding a call and saying, 'one second' is not right, because it is impossible to bring the phone in one second. By doing that, we are annoying the one who calls. Also, we are not speaking the truth. It is better to say one minute or two minutes instead of one second."

Kırkan narrates another story. Once, we were travelling with a group of people. We stayed in a rest area. We made our ablutions, performed our Prayer in the *masjid*, and had a little rest. When all of us returned to the van, Gülen was missing. After a couple of minutes, he came with some biscuits and nuts in his hands. He told us that we used the rest area's water, the *masjid* and had little rest on the carpets of masjid without paying anything. I did shopping to contribute some income to the owner of the rest area." We realised that how cautious Gülen is regarding others' rights. He also taught us a great lesson by such an action in terms other peoples' rights.

Mehmet Eldem recalls: In 1974, I went to hajj with Gülen and few friends. All of us were staying at the same unit in Mecca. The unit was untidy and unclean especially the kitchen and bathroom. We were exhausted. Immediately, we went to bed and slept. When we woke up, we saw that bathroom and kitchen were cleaned. Later, we realised that Gülen did it. One of us put his soap in the bathroom. When Gülen wanted to use the soap, he asked permission for using it. Gülen does not

---

411   Ünal, *Bir Portre Denemesi*, 144.

use anything, even the smallest thing, without consent. Gülen teaches through actions more than his words.

Malik Ejder recalls. Gülen is very sensitive about even slightly interfering with another's belongings and property. Once, when passing one person's land to another, he took off his shoes at the border and dusted off the soil from the first person's land, so that he would not carry it over to the second person's land.

İbrahim Hasgür, a professor and former Vice Chancellor of one of the universities in Turkmenistan, has known Gülen since 1970. He recollects:

"The first time, I met Gülen, in a student house. We then shared the same unit for three years. I was so impressed with his humility and knowledge which was not just in theological disciplines but also secular sciences. Also, I was inspired by his firmness in the faith. In the early 1970s irreligiosity was a fashion among the university students. Being well versed in the secular sciences, Gülen was able to respond university students' questions about Darwinism and other issues related to religion, science, or modernity scientifically and with satisfaction. He was addressing not just hearts but also minds. The university students were so pleased by Gülen answers. By the time, they became addicted to his talks and sermons. Gülen conquered hearts and minds through his actions or his representation of Islam. He preached what he firmly believed and practiced what he preached."

İrfan Yılmaz stated that Gülen is so generous but, on the other hand, he is very contented. He is a perfectionist. We learned from him how to deal with family problems. Yılmaz recalls. '*Sızıntı*' magazine began publishing and few of us were asked to write articles for it. When we wrote articles, we did not want anyone else to edit or do changes. Gülen was writing the editorial. He brought his article and told us to feel free for doing any changes. Then all the authors did not mind having their articles revised or edited. I saw the influence of Gülen's leadership through his *tamthil*. Osman Şimşek, a pupil of Gülen, says that Gülen is so pleased when any of his students ask some revision in his writing.[412]

Alaattin Kaya recalls: Once, Gülen was called to a court for testifying on an issue. The judge asked his home address. Gülen did not have a home or a permanent address to give, but he did not want to lie

---

412   Osman Şimşek, *Yanık Yürekler* (Izmir: Işık Yayınları, 2010), 86.

either. He looked at me with eyes of filled with tears. I realised that he wanted to give my home address. I nodded my head. He turned to the judge and asked if he could give his friend's home address because he has no home and no permanent place to live. The judge was shocked and asked why the leader of the biggest faith-based movement does not even have a house. Then, Gülen gave my home address with the consent of the judge.

While Gülen recommended his followers to have a dialogue with non-Muslims, he did not neglect to build a good relationship with Muslim leaders and groups. According to one of his close associates, in 2013, he sent Eid cards to twenty-one prominent religious leaders in Turkey, but only one of them replied to him. Despite the fact that they did not reply to him, Gülen has been sending Eid cards for many years. He also actively encourages his followers to visit not just faith-based groups but also secular or non-practicing Muslim groups as well.

In 1980, Gülen's students were arrested and tortured in the police station and military camp. Their feet were tied together, and they were beaten on their soles. They tied their feet in bastinado, a punishment inflicted by beating the soles of the feet and then beaten with birch. This continued until the bones were sticking out of their skin. Then Gülen's students were forced to walk on salt and rocks with their feet in that condition. When they were released, they were driven home. They could not walk to the house. When Gülen saw them in such condition, he fainted.

During the parliamentary election in 2014, the leader of ruling AKP and former primary minister and current president Tayyip Erdoğan initiated a five months' campaign against Gülen—more than against the opposition parties in eighty cities throughout Turkey. Erdoğan accused Gülen of being the head of a terrorist organisation, an imposter, a fake prophet, false messiah, a leech, an agent of foreign governments, a fake scholar, an evil-doer, and a fake sheikh. Pro-Erdoğan and state media called Gülen a CIA agent, a Mossad spy, a British agent, a secret cardinal (the one who has a mission to Christianise Turkey through dialogue with non-Muslims), a crypto Armenian, a vile so-and-so, and so on. Gülen was silent for about four months during all of these accusations and slandering. Gülen issued a statement, saying that "These words do not suit someone who is a prime minister." For the other accusations, he made a brief statement through his lawyer in philosophical principles and according to law.

When Gülen is critical of someone, he will not mention the name in his statements or talks. Also, his criticism is constructive rather than destructive. When Gülen is critical of someone's opinion or deeds, he also shows alternative ideas.

Since January 2014 this anti-Gülen and anti-Hizmet campaign continued without ceasing. According to some sources, they fabricated about three thousand news items, accusations, slanders, and insults. Despite all of that, Gülen has not changed his position against them. So many times, he even stated that he forgave them and asked his followers or sympathisers to forgive and to disregard them as well. Before 2013, I googled Fethullah Gülen, with Turkish letter, there were less than one million comments but, when I googled again in a search engine in November 2016, there were 7,767,000 million. When I researched the English version of Gülen, it was 2,240,000. Similarly, when I typed in Tayyip Erdoğan's name in a search engine, it was over sixteen million. Although Gülen is a cleric and not a politician, his name appears almost half the number of times in comparison with Tayyip Erdoğan who has been in politics more than three decades. That shows the degree of the negative campaign against Gülen by the Turkish media since December 2013.

Since mid-July 2016, the unsuccessful military coup (of which Gülen has been accused of being the mastermind), he has been interviewed by more than three dozen leading media groups. All of his interviews are constructive without making any polemics and promoting hatred despite the arrest of over sixty thousand, the interrogation of over sixty-two thousand Hizmet people, and the closure of more than three thousand Hizmet educational institutions (including schools, dormitories, mosques, universities, childcare centres, and hospitals). His responses have been according to the philosophical principles. Gülen's responses to all accusations, slandering, oppression and tyranny shows his degree of *tamthil*.

Through a successful *tamthil*, first Gülen believed and he caused people to believe for serving humanity without any expectation. Therefore, he has been able to mobilise hundreds of thousand people for educational purposes. If the people did not see his *tamthil* or role modelling at the *ihsan* degree, trustworthiness, altruism and compassion, none would help so many great educational projects.

5.4 Institutionalization of *tamthil*

For greater success, the institutionalisation of *tamthil* is necessary. For Gülen, every good and beautiful idea should be institutionalised.[413] As Muslim individuals are responsible for being role models for their fellow human beings; similarly, institutions of all fields must be operated in the most useful and productive ways and should serve as role models for other institutions. In this section, Gülen's views about the institutionalisation of *tamthil* will be briefly touched upon. The detail of institutionalisation of *tamthil* could be a chapter or even a PhD research topic in the light of Gülen's work and philosophy.

According to Gülen, for a required *tamthil*, firstly, institutions must have a humanist vision and serve all human beings. Secondly, they should be a place where people are spiritually and morally elevated.[414] Thirdly, they should be based on public support rather than that of the state. Finally, those who work for institutions must not use institutions for their worldly ambitions.

While they are competing with similar institutions, on the other hand, they should be at the service of humanity for a common and greater good. This can be done with a team which is among the best in their field and represent their mission accordingly. For Gülen, the degree of institutional *tamthil* is based on the extent of its benefits for humanity. Otherwise, if they are seen just for making money or profit, the compassionate dimension of institutionalisation of *tamthil* will be missing. Institutions must have a compassionate mission in their service rather than materialistic policy. In regard to this mission, all staff members should be reminded so often by the head of their institution. Otherwise, if the aims of the institution are forgotten, then gradually it will become unproductive and finally will collapse.

Institutions should serve all humanity for guiding to a right path. The aim should be to show humanity the beauty and perfection through the *tamthil* of the institution. There is a seed of goodness in the nature of every human. Through institutions, this seed can be nurtured and eventually open a pathway to *al-insan al-kamil*, the perfect human. Through the service of an institution, people can be motivated

---

413　Gülen, *Çağ ve Nesil* 4, 121.

414　Gülen, *Asrın Getirdiği Tereddütler* 4, 88.

for the common good, a better society, and a civilised nation.

According to Gülen, the institution as a non-profit organisation mostly must not rely on the power of the state and operate by dictating as it is done in undeveloped countries. Most Hizmet organisations are funded by donations and the in-kind help of people. Osman Şimşek mentions a story. For many years, Gülen told people not to rely on the financial support from any governments. In the early 1970s, Gülen asked the board member of a *waqf* not to rely on anyone for help except the people, especially the local ones. At that time, the Hizmet community was building a dormitory for poor and disadvantaged students. When some board members asked Gülen to seek help from some governments outside Turkey, he said: "Let's not to be in debt to any government but rely on the support of the community. This community has enough resources to build this dormitory. We must not be dependent on anyone." On hearing this, Yusuf Pekmezci, one of the board members stood up with tearful eyes and supported Gülen's view. He said that "Please do not worry sir, I will sell my house, my business and donate to dormitory. I will beg money from people. So, we will not be dependent on anyone (or any government)."[415] For the dignity of institutions, the support of the community is crucial. By the support of the community, the institutions have a greater chance to be successful.

For Gülen, a non-profit institution belongs to the whole community. This means it belongs to God. The staff must feel a big responsibility on their shoulders and accountability towards people and God.[416] With the full capacity, institution must be allocated for the people. Those who work must not have any financial expectation, except their salary.

In the Hizmet Movement educational institutions Gülen recommends that, those who run them, provide scholarships for twenty percent of students who enrolled. Before it was closed down, over two hundred tutoring centres were offering free preparation courses for university exams, specifically in poor suburbs and the south-east of Turkey where conflict is still going on. Over two hundred thousand students were getting free tutoring. Most of the teachers were also volunteers from the Hizmet Movement.

---

415   Gülen, *Çağ ve Nesil* 8, 16.
416   Fethullah Gülen, *Kırık Testi* 3 (Izmir: Nil Yayınları, 2011), 183.

In summary, all institutions (specifically non-profit ones) must provide services to the community regardless of their faith, ethnicity, or social status. By operating such way, Hizmet's institutions look similar to the *waqf*s of Golden Age of Islam. The *tamthil* of institutions is more important than individual *tamthil* in Gülen's philosophy. To him, if institutions are not represented as required, their collapse is inevitable. If the successful members of a government or experienced executives of a state or institution demand the lion's share of benefits in consideration of their abilities and accomplishments, the government is paralysed, the state collapses, and the institution descends into chaos.[417]

5.5 Analysis

The truths of religion can be conveyed in the best way through the *tamthil*, particularly the principles such as faith in God, the Hereafter, angels, hell and heaven, and so on. Without perfect *tamthil*, these articles of faith cannot be understood or believed. Therefore, there was a need for prophets for role modelling. God sent prophets to show the religion through *tamthil*. Nursi argues that the truth can be understood if it is clothed with the cloth of *tamthil*.[418] Otherwise, it will be like a utopia which will be seen as impossible to put into practice. If the *tamthil* is not perfect, the religion cannot be understood properly. If religion is only conveyed through proselytising, then it will become like an ideology and will not persist (like fascism and communism).

Tamthil can be classified in two ways. The first is a metaphor-like narration of saintly stories. The second is true *tamthil* that is shown or displayed in living examples. The second leaves permanent marks on the human soul and spiritual life because it addresses the sight, reason, heart, and soul. Since the human being is a small universe and God's caliph on earth, it is necessary to be a role model. Therefore, the human being has an obligation to serve in the best way, which can be the combination of heavenly and worldly *tamthil*.

In Gülen's works, *tamthil* can be categorised in three aspects: namely, *iman* (faith), Islam, and *ihsan*. *Tamthil* of faith is having a sound

---

417   Fethullah Gülen, Pearls of Wisdom, available at www.fgulen.com/en/fethullah-gulens-works/thought/pearls-of-wisdom/24551-love-of-status.

418   Nursi, *The Words*, 619.

aqida and being firm in it. The *tamthil* of Islam is a complete practice of fulfilling obligations and refraining from unlawful things. At the degree of *ihsan*, *tamthil* means always being conscious that God is watching. If the *tamthil* is done at the level of the heart and soul or *ihsan*, then it will be able to set moral emotions and will lead to a sincere practice of religion. The perfect *tamthil* is a combination of all in an individual's life.

In Gülen's works, the levels of *tamthil* are *kulli tamthil*, the perfect or universal representation, which is at the degree of Prophethood. *Zilli* (shadow) *tamthil*, which resembles *kulli tamthil*, is a saintly representation. *Taqlidi* (imitative) *tamthil*, which resembles the second (*zilli tamthil*), can be for ordinary believers. Finally, *nifaqi tamthil* is just by appearance. It contradicts the inner dimension; that is, it is hypocrisy.

For Gülen, *tamthil* is a prerequisite for those in positions of leadership because they represent the collective personality of congregations, groups, movements, and nations. If *tamthil* is not done properly, then it will have an enormous negative impact and will weaken spirituality. However, if *tamthil* is done appropriately, it will bring unity, lead to acceptance of the truth by the reason, heart and soul, and elevate to a higher rank spiritually. Without good *tamthil*, the essence of truth will not be understood in a world where science and materialism dominate.

In my humble understanding, without the ascetic life and *tamthil* of Gülen and his close associates, the Hizmet Movement would not grow. Since Gülen represents the collective personality of the movement, he has to be much more vigilant about role modelling than anyone else, like all great spiritual leaders in the history of Islam. According to Nursi, a human can reach the degree of perfection through *tamthil*, and faith-based movements are elevated to the degree of the *Qutb* (Spiritual Pole) of the time.[419] However, to keep such level of spirituality, it is essential not use *tamthil* for any world ambitions.

Such a spiritual degree of *tamthil* can be considered a Divine gift. Whoever attains it, as Gülen states, he or she will be at the spiritual degree of resignation (*rida*). This spiritual level is achieved by those purified, saintly scholars who are pleased with what pleases God.[420] According to

---

419   Nursi, *Tarihçe-i Hayat*, (Istanbul: n.d.), 309.

420   Gülen, *Key Concepts in the Practice of Sufism* 1, Rida, available from, www.fgulen.com/en/fethullah-gulens-works/sufism/key-concepts-in-the-practice-of-sufism-

Dhu'l-Nun al-Misri (796–859), resignation means preferring God's wishes over one's own in advance, accepting His decree without complaint, based on the realisation that whatever God wills and does is good, and overflowing with love of Him even while in the grip of misfortune.

This degree of *tamthil* can be acquired only with an individual's conscious decision to exercise free will in constant striving and struggle. To have such an ideal lifestyle is extremely difficult but not impossible. However, not many people can achieve it as it is necessary to sacrifice many things for which every human desires and works, or even sometimes fights. It is essential to have a very firm faith at the level of *ihsan* with deep *ma'rifatullah* (gnostic knowledge of God), *muhabbatullah* (love of God), and *makhafatullah* (fear of God). For Gülen, the highest level of *ihsan* is the spiritual degree when a person can feel the ninety-nine Names of God are always present. It also necessitates deep devotion in worship and a total commitment to mission without retreat, as Sayyid Nasimi (1369–1417) said:

> I am a suffering lover, O dear One, I will not abandon You;
> Even if You cut through my chest with a dagger, I will not abandon You.
> Even if they cut me into two from head to foot like Zachariah,
> Put your saw on my head, O Carpenter, I will not abandon You.
> Even if they burn me into ashes and blow away my ashes,
> They will hear my ashes sigh: "O Veiler (of sins), I will not abandon You."

According to a saying of Prophet Muhammad (pbuh), "Indeed, Allah created Adam in the form of the Most Merciful,"[421] This degree can be achieved with perfect *tamthil*. If the Companions of the Prophet were successful in a short period, it was because of this degree of *tamthil*, representing Islam in the most beautiful way. For Gülen, believers must strive to increase their level of faith and should struggle to have the highest degree of *tamthil* until their last breath.

Conclusion

Fethullah Gülen's philosophy of *tamthil* or role modelling and its appli-

---

1/24747-rida-resignation. Retrieved 21.11.2016.

421   Narrated by Bukhari and Muslim.

cation in his daily life is remarkably idealistic. The influence of Gülen's philosophy may be attributed to his active practice of the eleven characteristics of *tamthil* outlined in this chapter. He leads an ascetic life, sleeping only a few hours every night, and devoting the rest of the night to prayer, worship, study, contemplation, and writing, despite his diabetes, heart problems, and high blood pressure. For Gülen, those who are in any type of leadership position have to be more vigilant. If they neglect any part of their duties (including a spiritual one, even for one hour), then the congregation or followers will be careless the whole day. Gülen says that "those who lead the way must set a good example for their followers. Just as they are imitated in their virtues and good morals, so do their wrong and improper actions and attitudes leave indelible marks upon those who follow them."[422] Based on his close associates' testimonials, Gülen has been an ideal role model since a young age. Despite all the accusations against him over decades, his influence has grown. It can be said that Gülen sees the primary problem of the Muslim world as the lack of proper representation of Islam in all fields. Therefore, those who claim to be struggling with the crises of the Muslim *umma* have to begin with themselves by applying the principles of *tamthil*.

Gülen refers to Nursi's saying as a reflection of his life, "In my eighty-year life, I have not tasted anything of worldly pleasures."[423] Whenever Muslim leaders follow these principles, they have influenced others, conquered people's minds and hearts, and attained success in their endeavours. Despite all obstacles, stereotyping, accusations, oppression, and injustice against Gülen and the Hizmet Movement since the late 1960s by most Turkish governments, none of them has been able to prevent their activities entirely or create an alternative to Gülen's ideas. Thus, they try to stop them by injustice, using force, and oppressing Hizmet participants and supporters. However, all the oppression and injustice have become fertiliser for Gülen's ideas and the movement. The secret of his success is in the *tamthil* which also does not contradict the laws of creation in worldly matters.

It can be argued that Gülen is reintroducing the way of the *Salaf*

---

422   Fethullah Gülen, *Pearls of Wisdom*.

423   Nursi, *Tarihçe-i Hayat*, 629.

al-Saliheen in the service of humanity through his works and exemplary life. He is also injecting ascetic love into *tamthil* to serve Islam. As al-Ghazali injected spirituality into the dry body of Islamic theology and renewed religious sciences, Gülen has infused spirituality, altruism, asceticism, hope, and modernity into the dry body of faith-based activism through *tamthil* in the last half century. So, it can be said that he is one of the leading revivalists of our time.

CHAPTER 6

FETHULLAH GÜLEN'S EFFECTIVE ALTRUISM

Fethullah Gülen's Effective Altruism

Ithar (altruism or preferring others to one's self) is one of the major principles of all religions and an ethical principle of moral philosophy. It has a significant place in the Qur'an and *Sunnah* of Prophet Muhammad (pbuh). *Ithar* is a major characteristic of all prophets who are at the pinnacle of altruism. It is also considered an indispensable moral value to establish a civilisation. Fethullah Gülen views *ithar*, along with sincerity, as a pillar of serving both religion and humanity. His philosophy of *ithar* is based on the Qur'an and *Sunnah* and the *Salaf al-Saliheen*'s interpretations. To him, without the practice of *ithar*, particularly by scholars and rulers, the Muslim world cannot overcome contemporary crises. This chapter argues that Gülen's philosophy of *ithar* and its practice is effective and highly idealistic. It is very difficult to practice in a materialistic society in which human beings are motivated by self-interest. It is possible, however, that a creative and devoted minority can apply it in their lives.

This chapter has three aims. First, it will analyse the verses about *ithar* in the light of major Qur'anic exegeses and the *Sunnah*. Second, it will examine Gülen's philosophy of *ithar* and how it is applied in his daily life. Finally, Gülen's view of *ithar* will be compared with the *Salaf al-Saliheen*. This chapter argues that Gülen has maintained a high standard of *ithar* in everything he has pursued.

The term *ithar* means altruism, self-sacrifice, self-denying, preferring others over oneself. The Cambridge Dictionary defines altruism as "willingness to do things that bring advantages to others, even if it results in disadvantage for yourself."[424] The term is used as the contrary of "self-interested" or "selfish" or "egoistic."[425] *Ithar* is one of the important characteristics of all Prophets, their disciples, or companions, great scholars and spiritual leaders in human history. All civilisations are established and expanded by altruistic people. It is an important ethical principle of moralists' philosophy. In psychology, it is demonstrated as prosocial behaviour for helping, comforting, sharing with others, and performing community service.

---

424 Cambridge Dictionary, dictionary.cambridge.org/dictionary/english/altruism. Retrieved 28.04.2017.

425 Richard Kraut, Stanford Encyclopedia of Philosophy, plato.stanford.edu/entries/altruism. Retrieved 28.04.2017.

According to al-Ghazali, *ithar* or sacrifice for others is the high-est stage of generosity.[426] Gülen defines altruism (*ithar*) as preferring others to oneself when doing a good deed and refers to the act of giving preference to others over oneself.[427] For him, those who prac-tice *ithar* are considered as abiding by the highest degree of nobil-ity. Moralists define it as seeking benefit for the community before thinking about one's own needs. Sufis express this concept using the term *tafani*. Said Nursi defines *tafani* as "annihilation in the [Mus-lim] brother."[428] This means that a person forgets the feelings of his own carnal soul and lives as part of a collective personality, a *jama'a*, and ultimately, the *umma*. In that way, each person is like a bodily organ working together with other organs without harming one an-other. Just as the hand does not harm the eye, but protects and cleans it, the believers protect and support each other.[429] Other Sufis define *ithar* as preferring the lives and happiness of others over one's own. A person who conducts *da'wa* strives for the well-being and comfort of the community.[430] The antonyms of altruism are the stinginess and selfishness that arise from avarice and attachment to this world.[431] Such a person is "self-interested, lazy, and always seeks material ben-efit, is a bad manager of time, and acts according to other people's wishes during the whole of his or her life," as Gülen states.[432]

In Islam, *ithar* is considered a necessary principle for serving religion and humanity. It has a very strong relation with *iman* (faith), the *Sunnah* of the Prophet, devotion, sincerity, spiritual satisfaction, and happiness, ac-

---

426　Al-Ghazzali, *Ihya Ulum-id-Din, Revival of Religious Learnings*, trans. Fazl-ul Karim, Vol. 3, p. 194–196, available at ghazali.org/ihya/english/ihya-vol3.htm.

427　Salih Yücel, "Istighna and Ithar: Two Forgotten Principles of Da'wah from the Per-spective of the Hizmet Movement", in Salih Yücel and Ismail Albayrak, *The Art of Coexistence: Pioneering Role of Fethullah Gülen and Hizmet Movement* (New Jersey: Tughra Books, 2014), 137.

428　Nursi, *The Flashes*, 216–217.

429　Nursi, *The Flashes*, 216–217. A hadith states, "The example of the believers in their af-fection and compassion and benevolence is like the body; if one part of it becomes ill the whole body comes to its aid with fever and sleeplessness." (Bukhari and Muslim)

430　Fethullah Gülen, *Sızıntı*, 16–192 (1995): 1–2.

431　Fethullah Gülen, *Yeni Ümit*, January (1995): 1–2.

432　Gülen, *Enginliği ile Bizim Dünyamız*, 58.

cepting the truth, and healing the spiritual diseases. *Ithar* is reflected in the Qur'an as the self-sacrifice of the prophets in various forms, particularly, Prophet Muhammad (pbuh) (Qur'an,18:6; 26:3), Abraham, Ismael, and Jonah. An analysis of all the Qur'anic verses related to *ithar* is beyond the scope of this chapter. It will focus specifically on the Qur'anic verses 59:9 and 76:8–9, which are commonly known as "the *ithar* verses."

In Gülen's works[433] and speeches, *ithar* is mentioned under the topic of self-sacrifice, altruism, and selflessness which are synonyms with slight differences. Also, Gülen first strongly relates *ithar* with *iman* (faith), sincerity, self-negation, accepting the truth, devotion and overcoming spiritual diseases.

Secondly, Gülen finds a strong correlation between *ithar* and social harmony, peaceful society and the life span of a group, a movement, a nation, and establishment of a civilisation. It can be argued that, for Gülen, *ithar* is an indispensable moral value in the service of religion, humanity, and social transformation by all means.

Before examining Gülen's philosophy of *ithar*, it is necessary to look at *ithar* in the Qur'an and *Sunnah* briefly, specifically, the interpretation of the above-mentioned verses in the classical period and according to some prominent contemporary scholars.

6.1 *Ithar* in the Qur'an and *Sunnah*

> "Those who, before their coming, had their abode (in Madinah), preparing it as a home for Islam and faith, love those who emigrate to them for God's sake, and in their hearts do not begrudge what they have been given; and (indeed) they prefer them over themselves, even though poverty be their own lot. (They, too, have a share in such gains of war.) Whoever is guarded against the avarice of his own soul, those are the ones who are truly prosperous." (Qur'an 59:9)[434]

To understand a Qur'anic verse in depth, it is necessary to look at its historical context and the occasion of revelation (*asbab nuzul*). The first part of the above verse (59:9) was revealed about the spoils of the war with the Banu Nadir, a Jewish tribe. The Prophet consulted with the *Ansar* (Helpers) about the distribution of the spoils. If they wished,

---

433 All Turkish and Arabic sources in this chapter are translated by the author.

434 *The Qur'an with Annotated Interpretation in Modern English* translated by Ali Ünal is used in this chapter.

he could distribute the them to the *Muhajirun* (Migrants – the Meccan Muslims), so they would not be dependent on the *Ansar*, or if they wished, he could divide the spoils equally between all Muslims, including the *Ansar* and *Muhajirun*. The *Ansar* asked the Prophet to give them to the *Muhajirun* and also said that they would still like to continue to share their own houses and wealth with the *Muhajirun*.[435]

   Al-Tabari commented on this verse, referring to the Helpers, who shared everything they owned with the Migrants, that they preferred their Meccan brothers' well-being over their own.[436] Ibn Kathir states that it means the Helpers gave the Migrants preference over themselves even though they were in desperate need.[437] According to Al-Qurtubi, the second part of the verse referred to the incident of Abu Talha, one of the Companions, and his guest. A poor man came to the mosque in Medina and told the Prophet that he had not eaten for three days. Prophet Muhammad (pbuh) asked his wives one by one if there was anything to offer this man at home. They stated they had nothing. Then the Prophet asked his Companions to feed the poor man. Abu Talha took up the offer and invited the man to his house. Abu Talha's wife whispered that there was only enough food for one person. Abu Talha told his wife to turn out the light and bring the food. In the darkness, Abu Talha and his wife made it seem as if they were eating while the guest ate until the food was finished. After the *Fajr* (Morning) Prayer the next day, the Prophet asked, "What did you do last night that Allah praised you?" Then he recited the verse above which was revealed that night (59:9).[438] Commenting on this verse, Sayyid Qutb says that to give preference to others when one is in need oneself is a high summit to reach, one which the Helpers scaled in a way unknown anywhere in

---

435   Waqidi, Maghazi, v. 1, p. 379, Balazuri, Futuhu'l-Buldan, v. 1, p. 22) In addition, they said that even the Prophet could distribute their wealth to Muhajirs as well. (Waqidi, Maghazi, v. 1, p. 379, Balazuri, Futuhu'l-Buldan) Due to their preference, the following verse was revealed. (Waqidi, v. 1, p. 382, Balazuri, Futuhu'l-Buldan, v. 1, p. 21 in Mustafa Asım Köksal, *İslam Tarihi*, (Istanbul: Köksal Yayınları, 1987).

436   Al-Tabari, *Jamiu'l-Bayan*, www.altafsir.com. Retrieved on December 22, 2010.

437   Ibn Kathir, *Tafsir al-Quran al-Karim* www.qtafsir.com. Retrieved 1.10.2016.

438   Al-Qurtubi, *Tafsir al-Qurtubi*, www.altafsir.com. Retrieved on December 22, 2010.

human history.[439] The two verses below are also considered by Islamic scholars to be about *ithar*:

> "They give food, however great be their need for it, with pleasure to the destitute, and to the orphan, and to the captive, (saying): "We feed you only for God's sake; we desire from you neither recompense nor thanks (we desire only the acceptance of God)." (Qur'an, 76:8–9)

There are two narrations for the reason of revelation of these verses. The first narration says that they were revealed after the Battle of Badr. Although the Muslim soldiers were hungry, they fed the prisoners of war with what they had.[440] They asked them to ride their camels or horses, while they walked. Such kind treatment to prisoners of war was not known and had never been seen before. It was unimaginable in Arab tribal culture at that time. The second narration says that these verses were revealed about Ali ibn Abi Talib and his wife Fatima, the daughter of the Prophet. Both were fasting and a short time before *iftar*, or the breaking of the fast, a poor man knocked at the door and asked for some food. They gave what they had, so both broke their fast with water only. On the second day, an orphan, and on the third day, a prison of war asked for food before the *iftar*. They gave what they had for *iftar* each time on the three consecutive days. The angel Gabriel brought these verses, which praise their altruism, and let the Prophet know what both did.[441] According to ar-Razi, even though they were revealed for Ali and Fatima, these verses include all generous and righteous people.[442]

According to Gülen, the prophets are at the pinnacle in practicing *ithar* in their whole lives. For him, Prophet Muhammad (pbuh) practiced *ithar* during every moment of his life. Gülen says that the Prophet's Ascension into heaven and return to the earth demonstrates *ithar* at the highest degree. His return from the realms beyond the heavens to be among people who oppress and kill Muslims is such a great degree of altruism that nobody else has ever been able to

---

439 Sayyid Qutb, *In the Shade of the Qur'an*, vol.16 p 435, available on futureislam.files. wordpress.com/2012/07/volume-_15-16-17_surahs_40-77.pdf

440 Al-Tabari, ibid. altafsir.com. Retrieved 23.12.2016.

441 Ar-Razi, Mafatihu al-Gayb, altafsir.com. Retrieved 14.08.2016.

442 Ar-Razi, ibid. altafsir.com. Retrieved 14.08.2014.

achieve it.[443] When Gülen refers to the *ithar* of Prophet Muhammad (pbuh), he mentions Abdul Quddus Gangohi's (1456–1537) statement: "Muhammad of Arabia ascended the highest heaven and returned. I swear by God that if I had reached that point, I should never have returned."[444] The Prophet's *ithar* is not just in this world but also in the Hereafter. He would think his community[445] when everyone thought of himself or herself. Nursi considers his Ascension from the creation to the Creator as the inner face of sainthood, and his returning from the Creator to the creation as his Messengership,[446] which is the highest degree of altruism. Gülen says this is the difference between a saint and a Prophet. A Prophet would always think of his community even if he is in heaven.[447] Also, on the resurrection day, while everyone thinks of him- or herself, Prophet Muhammad (pbuh) will think of his community, saying, "My community, my community."[448] The altruism and self-sacrifice of the Prophet reflected on his Companions in different degrees. It is important to give a few examples.

When the Prophet suggested giving charity, he gave away everything, including his upper body garment, which he gave to some-

---

443 *Sufism* 2 www.fgulen.com/en/fethullah-gulens-works/sufism/key-concepts-in-the-practice-of-sufism-2/25734-ithar-altruism. Retrieved 20.12.2016.

444 Abd al-Quddus Gangaohi, *Lata'if-i Quddusai,* ed. Shaikh Rukn al-Di`n, LaÇâfah 79; quoted in Iqbal, *The Reconstruction of Religious Thought in Islam,* p 54. See Chapter 7, " Two Forgotten Principles of Da'wah: Istighna and Ithar and the Hizmet Movement", in Yücel, Salih, and İsmail Albayrak. *The Art of Coexistence: Pioneering Role of Fethullah Gülen and the Hizmet Movement.* (New Jersey: Tughra Books, 2014).

445 Allah's Messenger (pbuh) said, "For every Prophet there is one invocation which is definitely fulfilled by Allah, and I wish, if Allah will, to keep my that (special) invocation as to be the intercession for my followers on the Day of Resurrection." Sahih al-Bukhari 7474 *sunnah*.com/bukhari/97/100   22.08.2016.

446 Said Nursi, *The Words,* trans. Şükran Vahide, (Istanbul: Sözler Publications, 2001)547.

447 Yücel and Albayrak, *The Art of Coexistence,* 138.

448 Bukharî, Tawhid, 36; Muslim, Îmân: 326, 327

one who asked for it. He had nothing to give but that garment.[449] He then had nothing to wear and therefore he could not go out of his home. Allah warned him not to do that.[450]

During the Battle of Yarmuk, Harith ibn Hisham, Ikrimah ibn Abu Jahl, and Ayyash ibn Abu Rabi'ah were severely wounded and were lying on the ground. Harith asked for water. One of the soldiers brought water. Harith noticed that Ikrimah was looking at him because he was in need of water. Harith said, "Give the water to Ikrimah." The soldier took the water to Ikrimah, who noticed Ayyash was asking for water, and said, "Give the water to Ayyash." The soldier went to Ayyash, but he had already died. The soldier returned to Ikrimah, who had also died. He finally went to Harith, who had died too.[451]

Abu Ubayda was the head of the Muslim army stationed in Damascus when Caliph Umar visited him. At Abu Ubayda's house, the caliph did not find anything else at the house beside a sword, shield, and a mount. When the caliph asked Abu Ubayda, "Wouldn't it be better if you had some belongings (for your needs)?", Abu Ubaydah replied, "O Commander of the Believers, these things will be sufficient for us until our final rest."[452]

Just like the Prophet, his many Companions and the great leaders in Islamic history would receive many gifts and spoils of war, as well as income, but they would prefer others over themselves and give those things to others straight away, keeping either a small amount for their needs or nothing at all. There are numerous examples from the Prophet's and the Companions' lives, but due to limitations of space, they will not be explored further here.

Due to the altruistic character of the Companions and their sincerity and because they always acted for the sake of God, they built trust in

---

449   Al-Qurtubi, ibid. altafsir.com. Retrieved 5.9.2016

450   Ismail Haqqi, *Ruhu'l Bayan*, altafsir.com. Retrieved 5.9.2016

451   *Kenzü'l-Ummal*, V/310; Hakim, *Müstedrek*, III/242, İstiab, III/150, cited in Muhammad Yusuf Kandehlevi, *Hayatu's-Sahabe*, (Istanbul: Akçağ Yayınları, 1982)1–313.

452   Ebu Nuaym el-Isfehani, *Hilyetu'l Evliya*, trans. into Turkish by Said Aykut, (Istanbul: Sule Yayınları, 1995), 231.

the conquered lands. As a result of this, they brought peace, justice, and security. For these reasons, many people converted to Islam in a short period.[453]

Gülen argues that the seed of altruism and self-sacrifice is in every human being's nature and everyone has the potential to develop it.[454] Some studies support his view of altruism and self-sacrifice in human nature.[455] Research shows that altruism reduces depression, anxiety and somatisation.[456] The Companions developed this seed under the supervision of the Prophet and made it part of their nature and reflected it completely in their daily lives. Their altruism, self-sacrifice, sincerity, trustworthiness, and always acting for God's sake brought peace and safety to the conquered lands, which led very many to convert to Islam rapidly.[457] In other words, this explains how a small group of Muslims (compared with the armies of the empires of that time) were able to spread Islam in three continents in a short period and rule them for centuries.[458] For Gülen, self-sacrifice was not the only part of the nature of the Companions but there was also their ecstatic love. Those who have such character will continue to serve Islam even in the hardest times and they will achieve their goals. He argues that the degree of self-sacrifice of a believer depends on the degree of his or her faith.[459] Whoever reaches

---

453 Gülen, *Enginliği ile Bizim Dünyamız*, 58.

454 Gülen, *Ölçü ve Yoldaki Işıklar*, 237.

455 See K.R. Monroe, *The Heart of Altruism* (NJ: Princeton Press,1996), 13; A. Knafo and R. Plomin, "Prosocial Behavior from Early to Middle Childhood: Genetic and Environmental Influences on Stability and Change", *Developmental Psychology*, 42, (2006), 771–786); Dabie Haskhi Levental, "Altruism and Volunteerism: The perceptions of altruism in four disciplines and their impact on the study of volunteerism", *Journal for the Theory of Social Behavior*, Vol. 39, Issue 3, September 2009, pp. 271–299; J. Philippe Rushton, "Genetic similarity, human altruism, and group selection", *Behavioral and Brain Sciences*, 12, (1989), pp. 503-559.

456 K. I. Hunter and M.W. Hunter, "Psychosocial differences between elderly volunteers and non-volunteers", *The International Journal of Aging and Human Development*, 12 (3) (1980), 205–213.

457 Gülen, *Asrın Getirdiği Tereddütler* 2, 118.

458 Ibid., 117–118.

459 Gülen, *Fasıldan Fasıla* 1, 177; *Yeni Ümit*, October–December, Vol. 4, Issue (1995), 30.

the level of *haq al-yaqin* (certainty), will also have an ability to reach the highest degree of *ithar*.[460] Following in the footsteps of the Prophet and his Companions, most of the great scholars in the first three generations of early Islam, practiced *ithar* in various degrees. Gülen says:

> They are the heroes of altruism who have completed their ascension toward God by going down among the people to guide and spiritually educate them. They think of nothing other than guiding people to God; they encourage hearts always to do good, and they erect spiritual barriers before evils. They try to confront possible misfortunes through prayers and supplications, and they are ready to sacrifice themselves for the good of people or to prevent disasters. Their hearts always beat with feelings of self-sacrifice, compassion, and tender care for others. Since they have dedicated their lives to the happiness of others, they live a life overburdened with the troubles of others and sigh for them. Even if there are times when they feel happy at the news of others' happiness, they are always sorrowful because of what they have witnessed or heard concerning the sufferings of people. In respect of their mission, they are heirs to the Prophets. The Prophets are the pinnacle of *ithar*.[461]

According to Gülen, there are degrees of *ithar* depending on the level faith and quality of the representation of Islam:

> - To look after others while neglecting oneself, such as feeding others while remaining hungry. Observing the rights of all humans and being careful not to tread on any person's rights. This raises a person to a state of perfection. I would call this *"ithar bil aql"* (altruism with the reasoning).
> - Despite everything, to use all bounties, including time, money, health, and personal abilities, only to earn Allah's pleasure, and then to keep these acts to oneself, or even forget the acts so as to remain humble. This degree is above the first. I would call it *"ithar bil aql wa qalb"* (*ithar* with the reasoning and heart).
> - The third degree is the highest level of devotion to the community. Gülen points to the sacrifice of Prophet Muhammad (pbuh) during the Ascen-

---

460 Gülen, *Ölçü veya Yoldaki Işıklar*, 237.

461 Gülen, *Key Concepts in the Practice of Sufism* 2, www.fgulen.com/en/fethullah-gulens-works/sufism/key-concepts-in-the-practice-of-sufism-2/25734-ithar-altruism. Retrieved 23.11.2016. Ibid.

sion. The Prophet had entered *Janna* and came close to the Divine presence, but returned to the world to save his *umma* from hell and to take his *umma* to Paradise. This state is a type of annihilation of one's self.[462] The last degree of *ithar* can be called *ithar "bil aql wal qalb wa'r-ruh"* (*ithar* with the reasoning, heart and soul). It can be called pure *ithar* as well.

According to Sufis, *ithar* is the total annihilation of self in the interests of others. This is reflected in different degrees. The highest degree of ithar is sacrificing one's soul for the sake of God. Showing warmth, speaking soft and kind words, being of use to others, and being the means of various instances of good—these are examples of altruism that almost anyone can strive for in any situation.[463] Mawlana Jami (1414–1492) summarises this degree of *ithar*:

> It is easy to show generosity with gold and silver
> Worthy of respect is he who shows generosity with his soul[464]

6.2 *Ithar* and spirituality

According to Gülen, there is a very strong relationship between *ithar* and faith, sincerity, and love. Individuals who have enlightened their hearts with faith and filled them with knowledge of God[465] will feel compassion and deep ascetic love for all humans and the whole universe.[466] For Gülen, such faith led the Companions of the Prophet to be

---

462   Gülen, *Sızıntı*, 3, 1980.

463   Gülen, *Key Concepts in the Practice of Sufism* 2.

464   Cited in ibid.

465   "According to travellers on the path of God, it is the station where knowing is united with the one who knows, where knowing becomes second nature, and where each state reveals what or who is known. Some have defined ma'rifa as the appearance and development of knowledge of God in one's conscience, or knowing God by one's conscience. In other words, one has attained self-realization and has realized his or her humanity with all of its intrinsic values and dimensions", Fethullah Gülen, *Key Concepts in the Practice of Sufism* 1, available at www.fgulen.com/en/fethullah-Gülens-works/sufism/key-concepts-in-the-practice-of-sufism-1/24757-marifa-spiritual-knowledge-of-god. Retrieved 18.10.2015.

466   Gülen, *Yeni Ümit*, October–December 1995, Vol. 4, Issue, 30.

altruistic. A strong faith means further altruism.[467] So a person can be altruistic to the degree of his or her faith. A firm faith will lead to devotion and self-purification. Gülen states that *ithar* is a necessity for serving faith.[468] *Ithar* is very important for persuasiveness. It is the shortest way of self-purification and the best way to serve the faith and humanity. Like Said Nursi, Gülen believes that serving the faith and the Qur'an is the shortest and safest way to reach the Reality (*Haqiqa*). Consequently, this will strengthen the faith. For Gülen, an altruistic person must always seek to strengthen his or her faith. If one is at the degree of *ilm al-yaqin* (certainty of reasoning), one should strive for the degree of *ayn al-yaqin* (state of belief based on personal witness), and then the aim should be to reach the degree of *haqq al-yaqin* (absolute certainty).[469]

Analysing the stories of the prophets in the Qur'an, Gülen argues that people who were not even a little altruistic and did not want to give up their unlawful material benefits, social status, and carnal desires, rejected the Divine message. He says that altruism leads to acceptance of the truth.[470] Likewise, meanness will lead to rejection of the truth.

Altruism enhances forbearance, compassion, sincerity, and love. Those are the fruits of the faith. For Gülen, achieving such qualities is dependent on the level of sincerity, pure intention and detachment from racism and racial fanaticism.[471] Nursi refers to this level of *ithar* as the peak and views it as a precondition for sincerity. For him, having any worldly ambition in the service of faith and the Qur'an damages sincerity.[472] He does not limit the giving of material items, but continues,

> Choose your brothers' souls to your soul in honor, rank, acclaim, in the things you enjoy like material benefits. Even in the most innocent, harmless benefits like informing a needy believer about one of the subtle, fine truths of belief. If possible, encourage one of your companions, who do not want to inform him, so that your soul does not become conceited. If you have a desire like "Let

---

467   Gülen, *Fasıldan Fasıla* 4, 159.

468   Gülen, *Fasıldan Fasıla* 1, 182.

469   Gülen, *Yeni Ümit*, October–December 1995, Vol. 4, Issue, 30.

470   Gülen, *Enginliği ile Bizim Dünyamız*, 387.

471   Gülen, *Ölçü ve Yoldaki Işıklar*, 237.

472   Nursi, *The Flashes*, 216.

me tell him this pleasant matter, so I'll gain the reward," it surely is not a sin and there is no harm in it, but the meaning of sincerity between you could be damaged.[473]

Nursi continues that for serving the religion, worldly benefit may not even be sought through the tongue of disposition by desiring it with the heart or expecting it.

Following Nursi, Gülen says that, while serving religion, to expect any material and even spiritual benefit in this world will harm sincerity.[474] If *ithar* is not sincere, it may lead to ostentation and hypocrisy. Hypocrites, even though they sometimes may practice *ithar* for worldly ambitions, never like it. For Gülen, however, a believer should enjoy *ithar* at the degree of ascetic love. This requires a long time and a constant spiritual struggle, and it develops in the midst of altruistic friends or groups.[475] Otherwise, it will gradually weaken and then disappear. A religion without *ithar* and love will become a set of rules and regulations only.

For Gülen, even "Paradise can be left for the sake of a peaceful world."[476] This statement spiritually is highly altruistic. To gain this spiritual rank needs constant struggle against the carnal soul and devotion to worship, not just doing all one's obligations but also supererogatory Prayers.

According to Gülen, there is a relation between the *Tahajjud* Prayer and *ithar*. In the Qur'an, they are mentioned in the same verse:

> Their sides forsake their beds at night, calling out to their Lord in fear (of His punishment) and hope (for His forgiveness, grace, and good pleasure), and out of what We have provided for them (of wealth, knowledge, power, etc.), they spend (to provide sustenance for the needy and in God's cause, purely for the good pleasure of God and without placing others under obligation)." (Qur'an, 32:16)[477]

---

473   Nursi, *The Flashes*, 216.

474   Gülen, *Kırık Testi* 9 (Istanbul: Nil Yayınları, 2011), 221.

475   Gülen, *Fasıldan Fasıla* 1, 143.

476   Gülen, *Fasıldan Fasıla* 5, 102.

477   Gülen, *Enginliği ile Bizim Dünyamız*, 36–37.

It can be said that those who perform the *Tahajjud* will be able to practise self-sacrifice and prefer others over themselves.

6.3 *Ithar* in the formation of Islamic civilisation

Altruistic people laid the foundation of all civilisations.[478] Similarly, the *ithar* of early Muslims has a prominent place in the establishment of Islamic civilisation. The ideal and pure *ithar* of the Prophet Muhammad (pbuh), the enormous altruism of his Companions and the early Muslims (*Salaf al-Saliheen*) was one of the major factors in its formation. Although the Prophet was the head of state, he lived as one of the poorest in Medina.[479] His Companions followed in the footsteps of the Prophet in different degrees. Although they knew the spiritual virtues of living in Mecca and Medina, almost ninety percent of them migrated to various cities on three different continents. For Gülen, without these heroes of *ithar*, Islamic civilisation would not have been established. According to Arnold Toynbee, civilisations fell or died because they failed to respond to the ethical challenge of altruism versus egoism.[480] When altruism declines, a faith group, movement, nation or civilisation declines as well.

Travelling has an important place within Islamic faith and tradition in connecting with the Divine.[481] Gülen states that all Islamic disciplines are the product of the extraordinary effort and *ithar* of the early Muslim scholars. They travelled to different cities to collect and compile the material in very difficult conditions and sometimes put their lives at risk. In order to ascertain the authenticity of a hadith or a saying of a Companion and to understand the meaning of a Qur'anic verse, these lovers and heroes seeking knowledge and the truth would travel for weeks or

---

478 Prominent British historian Arnold J. Toynbee analyses the establishment and collapse of 28 civilisations. He mentions the importance of altruism and self-sacrifice in the formation of them. See Arnold J. Toynbee, "A Study of History", in William Eckhardt, "Civilizations, Empires, and Wars", *Journal of Peace Research*, Vol. 27, No. 1 (1990): 9–24; Toynbee, Arnold J. and Daisaku Ikeda, T*he Toynbee–Ikeda Dialogue: Man Himself Must Choose* (New York: Kodansha,1976), 315.

479 Gülen, *The Messenger of God*, 268.

480 William Eckhardt, "Civilizations, Empires, and Wars", Journal of Peace Research, Vol. 27, No. 1 (Feb, 1990), pp. 9–24.

481 Tittensor, "Islam's Modern Day Ibn Battutas".

months.[482] Similarly, some altruistic leaders also contributed significantly to the development of Islamic civilisation. These creative, altruistic scholars and leaders influenced society, and they became an engine of progress, prosperity, social harmony, and a peaceful society. For example, as mentioned in Chapter 5, Gülen refers to Hasan (r.a) as exemplifying *ithar* in his political decision making.[483] He chose "we" over "I" or communal benefit over his leadership. This is clearly seen in his choice of declining the highest political and spiritual position in Islam as caliph in order to prevent bloodshed.[484] Although he had the majority of the community on his side, Hasan (r.a) did not want to endanger people's lives and risk the community's stability by accepting their widespread support.[485] Also, due to following very strictly the principle of *ithar*, Caliph Umar ibn Abdu'l-Aziz (682–720) brought peace and prosperity to the Muslim community. Even the extremist Kharijites stopped fighting.

In an Islamic community in which *ithar* is applied as an ethical principle, wealth would never become a fortune circulating only among rich people.[486] This is a Qur'anic principle.[487] According to ar-Razi, not applying this principle will be considered an act of *Jahiliyya* (a pre-Islamic custom). The rich and those who were powerful would manipu-

---

482 Gülen, *Kırık Testi*, 9, 224.

483 For detail, see Yücel, "The Spiritual Role Model in Gülen's Educational Philosophy".

484 Yaqubi 2:226, Zahabi 2: 260 in Demircan, "Hz Hasan ve Halifeliği", *Harran İlahiyat Fakültesi Dergisi*, Vol. 2, (1995): 94–106.

485 Hasan (r.a) said, "I hate to be caliph if it means people will be killed. I gave up the caliphate so that the blood of the community of Muhammad (i.e. Muslims) does not spill." Even though Hasan took part in the Battle of Siffin, he did not engage in direct combat. (Abu Nuaym al Isfahani, Hilyetul Evliya va tabakatu'l Asfiya 2. 37 and Ibn Manzur Vol. II, 35 cited in Demircan, "Hz Hasan ve Halifeliği", *Harran İlahiyat Fakültesi Dergisi*, Vol. 2, (1995), 94–106.

486 Gülen, *Enginliği ile Bizim Dünyamız*, 291.

487 "And what Allah restored to His Messenger from the people of the towns—it is for Allah and for the Messenger and for [his] near relatives and orphans and the [stranded] traveler—so that it will not be a perpetual distribution among the rich from among you. And whatever the Messenger has given you—take; and what he has forbidden you—refrain from. And fear Allah; indeed, Allah is severe in penalty." (Qur'an, 59:7)

late wealth for their own benefit.[488] For Gülen *ithar* is essential for peace and social cohesion because each individual will be generous and prefer others over him/herself. The Prophet said, "A man is not a believer who fills his stomach while his neighbour is hungry."[489]Commenting on this hadith, Gülen states that a *mu'min* (believer) will embrace such character and will not eat until his Muslim brother is satisfied.[490] *Ithar* leads to strong social bonds and is an exalted human feeling, and what generates it is love. In contrast, meanness causes hatred and weakens social bonds.

6.4 Testimonials from friends

Gülen was raised in a very altruistic family. He says, "I grew up in a family in which all members were heroes of generosity, and I don't know any stingy person in my family and relatives."[491] Based on the information I obtained from twenty of Gülen's close associates, he always has been the pinnacle of altruism in the movement since the late 1960s when they came to know him. All agreed that they never saw anyone as altruistic as Gülen in their lifetime. Gülen would cook for the students, clean the dormitory, and work as a labourer voluntarily when institutions were being built. He would help his students who were in need. He would feed others while he went hungry. Gülen does not own any worldly possessions. His close friend, Suat Yıldırım, the former Dean of the School of Divinity at Sakarya University, lived together with Gülen at a young age. He says that when Gülen was an imam in Edirne, he would give half of his salary to poor students. Sometimes, he would give all his money and leave nothing for himself.

Gülen recalls the challenges he faced in the early 1970s: "Once, the police raided a house where a study circle was held. The aim of the raid was to arrest me. However, the police could not find me there and arrested all the people in the house including İbrahim Efendi who was a truck driver. İbrahim had never been arrested before. I felt very sorry for him. He was arrested because of his affiliation with me. My primary

---

488   Ar-Razi, *Mafatihu'l Gayb*, altafsir.com.

489   Al-Adab Al-Mufrad, 112, *sunnah*.com/adab/6/12 retrieved 26.08.2016

490   Gülen, *Enginliği ile Bizim Dünyamız*, 2, 29.

491   Ünal, *Bir Portre Denemesi*, 86–88.

concern was that İbrahim was poor and would not be able to look after his family as long as he was under arrest. I knew that to feel sorry for him was not sufficient. I borrowed a car and drove to the police station and parked it at the front. I wanted to be seen by the police. I took a great risk. The police let İbrahim know that I was waiting in front of the police station. My action boosted his morale and later he was released without any charge. İbrahim later told his friends that after he heard Fethullah was in front of police station and waiting for him, he thought, 'by God; at that time, I felt that I don't mind if I spent sixty years under arrest.'[492]

Most importantly, Gülen applies *ithar* through example. According to İsmail Büyükçelebi, from the over sixty (now over seventy) best-selling books Gülen has written, Gülen has donated almost ninety percent of his earnings to scholarship funds for the institutions established by his followers or for humanitarian aid. Gülen himself focuses on generosity and very often encourages his followers to be more generous like the Companions of the Prophet.[493]

Erdoğan Tüzün who has known Gülen since 1967 recalls that he had no money to rent a house and therefore stayed with Gülen for six months in 1968. At that time, Gülen was living in a small hut next to the Kestanepazarı Mosque. He gave his friend the bed in the hut to sleep in, but Gülen himself slept on a rug at the door of the hut.[494]

According to his biographer, Ali Ünal, Gülen would always cook and serve food to his guests. This continued until he developed diabetes, heart disease, and hypertension.[495] Between 1999 and 2007, I spent approximately six months with Gülen. I observed many examples of his *ithar*.

Once, Gülen came down from the second floor to the dining room, and he looked happy. Mostly, his face looked sorrowful. His doctor asked the reason for his happiness. He indicated he had had a nightmare three days earlier and had been worried about his dream, but this morning his dream had come true. Then his doctor asked what his dream was. He said that in his dream, the toilet in his room overflowed. Upon hearing

492   Şimşek, *İbretlik Hatıralar*, 169.

493   Yücel, "Fethullah Gülen: Spiritual Leader in a Global Islamic Context", 1–19.

494   Ünal, *Bir Portre Denemesi*, 503.

495   Ibid., 507.

this, one of the people in the room wanted to go up and fix the bathroom. Gülen said that there was no need. He had fixed the toilet and washed the carpet in the bathroom by himself. Another person would have called the plumber instead of doing it by himself. Despite his chronic illnesses and being in his seventies, he did not seek the help of others for his own work.

Gülen says that "it is one of the important and greatest of aims of my life to achieve unity between the East and West (Islamic and Western worlds) on a common ground. Even if I were about to enter Paradise, if I were to receive news indicating that both worlds were coming together and united on common ground based on mutual understanding and respect, this would be the most enjoyable and beautiful news of my life. It is possible that I would change my mind and not enter Paradise (to return to this world). As once I saw in a dream, if I was placed in heaven with all necessary food, I would think that I must return to the world to achieve the greatest aim of my life if there were anything that I could contribute to bringing these two worlds together with my work because it is needed with my tears. So, since there is a lot that I can present to humanity for this purpose, I would leave Paradise at this stage."[496]

Gülen views *ithar* not only as personal altruism but also prefers other groups over the Hizmet Movement. Nezir İpek has known Gülen since the early 1970s. He recalls, "The board members of one of the *waqf* (charity foundation) wanted to donate an empty building. There was another religious group who are called the students of Süleyman Tunahan. They also wanted the same building to open a Qur'an course. But the foundation board made the decision to give the building to the Hizmet Movement. When Gülen heard the building had been given to Hizmet Movement instead of the other religious group, he felt sorry and talked to the person in charge to return the building. He also told him to speak to the board and give the building to the students of Süleyman Tunahan. Gülen preferred another religious group over the Hizmet Movement."

This type of altruism is called *ithar* by souls, which is the highest degree, as Mawlana Jami states. Gülen views such preference as a principle of sincerity. When he hears of other religious groups doing any activities and opening any institutions, it makes him happy. Nezir İpek says

---

496 Gülen, *Fasıldan Fasıla* 5, 102.

that when he prays, he prays for Gülen's parents before he supplicates for his own. He says it is "because I learned how to respect my parents, love, show my compassion to others from him. Therefore, I feel indebted to Gülen."

The degree of many Hizmet-affiliated people, particularly the close associates of Gülen and those who are in leading positions, resembles the Companions of the Prophet Muhammad (pbuh). Despite a very good educational background, they sacrifice most of their income and time for educating people. Some of them work four to six hours voluntarily daily to establish these institutions. They did not sacrifice their time and income only but also where needed they worked as labourers. Most of those who have been in leading positions in the last thirty or forty years do not own a house and have no possessions. They have a simple life. I have witnessed hundreds of altruistic examples in the last twenty-five years. It will give an idea to mention just a few them.

We had a fund-raising program for establishing a school in Sydney in 1994. There were about fifty people, mostly Hizmet affiliated people, which included nine small businessmen and the rest were employees of high-tech companies, a few teachers, labourers and students. One of the post-graduate students donated around 400 dollars in cash and pledged a thousand dollars with tearful eyes. The student was the father of two children and had no income except for his scholarship. I asked him how much money he had left for his family. He said, "I left only one dollar in my bank account because I did not want my account to be closed." Another person wanted to donate the only house which he owned. The attendees pledged around six hundred thousand dollars. I had never heard of such altruism in the history of Muslims in Australia. The school opened, and the principle, who had a doctorate, worked for eight months without a salary. Currently, there are sixteen Hizmet-affiliated schools educating around six thousand students in various cities of Australia. There are many similar stories for each school. Their altruism could be a doctoral research topic. Such altruism is not unique to Australia. It is seen in all the Hizmet Movement's institutions all over the world. Gülen's altruism has inspired all Hizmet affiliates. Sometimes they have put their lives at risk when they have opened institutions in countries or cities where there is no security.

Mehmet Şevki Erol, an imam and a preacher, recalls with tearful eyes: "Gülen taught *ithar* through his actions and exemplary life. We sent thirteen teachers and mentors to a country [he was reluctant to name the country). All were single. After nine months a few of us went to visit them. These teachers and mentors had opened a school. After a while, their money had run out. They were not receiving any money from Turkey either. They had a meeting and made the decision not to ask any money from the local people. It would be a dishonour for them. They came to help and not to ask for help from others. They collected all their clothes and sold them one by one. They purchased only bread and ate it with water. For nine months, they survived by eating bread. They also fasted every Monday and Thursday. All of these teachers graduated from good universities, and they could have had very easy lives. But they were suffering for others. Gülen trained these students."

Gülen's exemplary altruistic life is another key concept that has made the Hizmet Movement successful. Historically, all successful political, religious and social movements apply the *ithar* principle, specifically during their formation. It can be said that through his effective altruistic life style, he reintroduced *Salaf al-Saliheen*'s altruism. They do not sacrifice only their rest, money and time but also their souls. In Gülen, the philosophy of altruism which combines heart, mind, and soul can be called effective *ithar*. As mentioned above, all civilisations are established on altruism. But this is effective altruism. However, as Ibn Khaldun (1332–1406) argues in the life of later generations *ithar* gradually diminishes and then civilisations collapse.

Conclusion

Ithar is an important principle of all major religions in various ways and a set of values of moral philosophy. It is the foundation of all civilisations, including Islamic civilisation, throughout history. Gülen's philosophy of *ithar* and its practice is based on the Qur'an and *Sunnah*. It is highly idealistic, and it can be practiced by a creative and devoted minority only; however, the seed of *ithar* is part of human nature, and it can grow in an altruistic environment. For Gülen, *ithar* is not just a principle to be applied in daily life but also a moral value which must be loved by all. Also, it is an essential ethical rule for social cohesion and a peaceful society. When *ithar* is applied in a community, particularly by scholars and rulers, it leads to an amicable society. Gülen views *ithar* as the source of progress and the base of the development of sciences. All Islamic disciplines are products of the *ithar* of scholars. *Ithar* is a fundamental principle which prolongs the life span of a movement, a society, and a civilisation. When a civilisation becomes egoistic in nature instead of altruistic, first it declines, and then it collapses.

Gülen's philosophy of *ithar* can be classified as the pure and effective altruism which was practiced in the highest degree by the Prophet, then his Companions, and then the *Salaf al-Saliheen* at different levels. While most human beings are motivated by self-interest, the first three generations of Islam were mostly motivated by *ithar*. The degree of altruism in Gülen's thought shows that sometimes there is risk to life, which Monroe calls pure altruism (which is helping another, even at risk to one's self).[497] In Gülen's works, along with sincerity, *ithar* can be considered a pillar of serving religion and humanity. To him, *ithar* is a prerequisite for overcoming the crisis of the Muslim world as well. *Ithar* is a high Islamic goal which believers should strive for until their last breath.

---

497   Monroe, *The Heart of Altruism.*

CHAPTER 7

ISTIGHNA AS A NEGLECTED PILLAR OF ISLAMIC SERVICE

Istighna as a Neglected Pillar of Islamic Service

One of the major of problems of serving religion in the Muslim world is the lack of *istighna* or contentedness of scholars and clergies towards governments and people. This is a forgotten or neglected and probably the most important principle of religious service after sincerity. The Qur'an and *sunnah* place particular emphasis on *istighna* because it is considered one of the major characteristics of all prophets, their companions, saints, great leaders, and scholars. This principle is seen as an indispensable prerequisite by all the great Islamic scholars in the history of Islam for serving humanity in order to be effective and successful. This chapter argues that Fethullah Gülen has reintroduced the *istighna* principle of *Salaf al-Saliheen*, not just in theory but also for practice in one's daily life and in the Hizmet Movement. He believes that one of the major reasons for the decline of the *umma* was not applying the *istighna* principle.

This chapter will first examine the Qur'anic verse which is related to *istighna*, "I ask you for no wage; my wage is only due from God" (Qur'an, 10:72), in the light major exegeses of the of classical and modern periods. Second, it will examine Gülen's philosophy of *istighna* and its practice, which is similar to the way of Umar, the second caliph. Third, I will analyse how this principle is implemented broadly in the modern day by Gülen and Hizmet representatives locally and globally. Finally, this chapter argues that Gülen's *istighna* philosophy and its practice is highly idealistic and difficult to apply, but it is not impossible. His personal practice of *istighna* is based on the peak of *taqwa* (piety) rather than *azimah* (strictness)[498] or *rukhshah* (dispensation).[499]

Istighna is serving the cause of Islam by all means without any expectations of reward, whether material, social, or otherwise. This means sacrificing resources, including time, money, abilities, and networks for

---

498   *Azimah* is the rule or the law that the Lawgiver issued for every liable person in every condition in first place. See Recep Doğan, *Usul Al-Fiqh: Methodology of Islamic Jurisprudence* (New Jersey: Tughra Books, 2013), 168.

499   A law or rule is considered *rukhshah* if it is exempted from the general law and brings ease in difficult circumstances.

the purpose of serving. In return, a Muslim should desire Allah's pleasure alone.[500] *Istighna* is defined by moralists as seeking benefit for the community before thinking about one's needs. The early Muslim scholars sought no benefit with their knowledge except the pleasure of Allah.[501] For Gülen, *istighna* means "not to be indebted to anyone except Allah. It is contentedness of the heart or ego."[502] Wanting a financial return and hoping for a political, religious, spiritual, or social position is contrary to *istighna*. Desiring respect for one's deeds, or receiving a special title such as *efendi, ustad, alim,* master, or *pir* will weaken sincerity in religious service. Even expecting not to fall into difficulties, experience loss and suffering, or receive criticism is against the principles of *istighna*. Gülen goes as far as stating that not applying *istighna* principles has caused the fall of the *umma* and the overall decline of Islamic civilisation.[503]

In the Muslim world, imams or religious workers may expect financial, material benefit, and social status from the people in return for their religious services. These may be referred to as *ikramiyya* and *sharafiyya* in Arabic, *khayraat* and *nadhraana* in Persian, *hadya* in Urdu, *hadiah* and *upah* in Malay, *hak* or *hediye* in Turkish and *hedija* in Bosnian.

After examining the Qur'anic verse referring to *istighna* (10:72) of the *Sunnah* and classical and modern period Qur'anic exegeses, I will briefly touch on the life of some great Islamic leaders regarding *istighna* principles and their application, such as Umar ibn Abdu'l-Aziz (682–720), Tariq ibn Ziyad (689–720), Salah ad-Din Ayyubi (1138–1193) and Osman Ghazi (1258–1324). Finally, the views of the imams of the four *madhhab*s (schools of thought) as well as prolific scholars, such as Hasan al-Basri (642–728), Imam al-Ghazali (1058–1111), Abdulqadr al-Jilani (1077–1166), Muhammad Jalal ad-Din Rumi (1207–1273), Imam Rabbani (1564–1624) and Said Nursi (1877–1960) will be examined. This chapter will end with an in-depth look at Gülen's philosophy of *istighna*

---

500   Yücel, "Two Forgotten Principles of Da'wah," in Salih Yucel, Ismail Albayrak, "The Arts of Coexistence: Pioneering Role of Fethullah Gülen and The Hizmet Movement", Tughra Books, New Jersey, 2014 p131-147.

501   Al-Ghazali, *The Book of Knowledge*, trans. Nabih Amin Faris (Kuala Lumpur: Dar al Wahi Publication, 2013), 80.

502   Gülen, *Çağ ve Nesil* 4, 42.

503   Gülen, *Kırık Testi* 1, 101.

and how he applies it in his daily life as well as how it has been taken up in the Hizmet Movement.

7.1 Qur'anic verses on *istighna*

There are twelve verses stating that the prophets refrained from asking for worldly rewards when they conveyed or taught the message of God. Verses 10:72, 11:29 and 26:109 refer to Prophet Noah; 11:51 and 26:127 refer to Prophet Hud; 26:145 refers to Prophet Salih; 26:164 refers to Prophet Lot; 26:180 refers to Prophet Shuaib; 36:20 refers to two un-named Prophets or possibly disciples of Prophet Jesus; 6: 90, 34:47 and 12:104 refer to Prophet Muhammad (pbuh) with *The Words*, "I do not ask any reward for it." All of these verses have very similar form and meaning. The *istighna* verse in the earliest reference mentions Prophet Noah. There are three verses refering to Noah, who conveyed the message of God for close to a millennium according to the Qur'an. This first reference and length of time points to Noah as a role model for this principle and amplifies the standard of *istighna* due to his service being the longest among the Prophets.

Prominent Qur'anic exegetes unanimously draw from these verses to show that reward or return must not be sought or expected when making *da'wah* or *tabligh*. According to al-Tabari [504] [505] and Ibn Kathir (1301–1373),[506] *tabligh* is a [religious] duty, so a benefit must not be sought. Zamakhshari (1704–1143) elaborates on this, saying that the prophets sought neither personal gain, nor any elevated social status or position, and never desired anything else that would place them above others.[507] From this, he concludes that Muslims must follow their examples. Fakhr al-Din al-Razi (1149–1209) goes further, asserting that a person should not even desire a reward by the heart.[508] Al-Qushayri (986–1074) adds that when serving religion, refraining from asking for anything is the *sunnah* of the prophets and a major principle of all Com-

---

504   All Arabic and Turkish sources are translated by the author.

505   Al-Tabari, *Jamiu'l Bayan*, altafsir.com. Retrieved 6.8.2016.

506   Ibn Kathir, *Tafsiru'l Qur'an al-Karim*, altafsir.com. Retrieved 6.8.2016.

507   Zamakhshari, *Al-Kashaf*, altafsir.com. Retrieved 6.8.2016.

508   Fakhruddin al-Razi, *Mafatihu'l Ghayb*, altafsir.com. Retrieved 6.8.2016.

panions and saints.[509] Al-Alusi (1802–1854) states that Noah was ordered not to take anything from disbelievers, and he said that he would never disobey this command of God.[510] In his commentary on the verses mentioned above, Nursi states that if *da'wah*, which he calls *hidhmati imani-yya wa Qur'aniyya* (service to the faith and the Qur'an), is undertaken with the aim of obtaining material advantages (by breaking the *istighna* principle), it will slowly destroy sincerity and will have detrimental results.[511] Nursi believed that sincerity is a condition for success in service to the faith and the Qur'an and *istighna* is necessary for sincerity. Sayyid Qutb (1906–1966) states that Noah did not fear that his compensation would be reduced as a result of people's turning away. He completely surrendered to God and did not expect anything from his tribe.[512]

Ibn Ashur (1879–1973) asserts that the Noah tribe was materialistic. This verse shows that Noah totally relies on God's help.[513] Muhammad Mutawally al-Sa'rawi (1911–1998) says that "I ask you for no wage; my wage is only due from God" is the statement of all prophets. Noah asked for his reward from the One who has the infinite treasure.[514]

Commenting on the above verses related to *istighna*, Gülen says that this principle is like a covenant between God and every prophet. It is an oath not to have any expectations, not even a successful result at the end, for conveying the message of God. It is an obligation for those who serve religion not to seek anything from anyone due to their service to Islam.[515] If the prophets and saints influenced people and conquered hearts with their words and exemplary life, it is due to their strict application of *istighna* principles. This may even be applied to contemporary scholars and leaders who do not implement these principles and hence,

---

509   Al-Qushayri, Lataif al-Isharat, altafsir.com. Retrieved 6.8.2016.

510   Al-Alusi, Ruhu'l Maani, altafsir.com. Retrieved 4.8.2016.

511   Nursi, *The Flashes*, 218.

512   Sayyid Qutb, *In the Shade of the Qur'an*, Vol. 9, p 106, available at www.kalamullah. com/Books/InTheShadeOfTheQuranSayyidQutb/volume_9_surahs_10-11.pdf.

513   Ibn Ashur, *At-Tahrir Wat-Tanwir*, altafsir.com.

514   As-Sa'rawi, Khawatir Muhammad al-Mutawally as-Sa'rawi, altafsir.com. Retrieved 4.8.2016.

515   Gülen, *Asrın Getirdiği Tereddütler* 4, 66.

as a result, are not effective in bringing about change.[516]

7.2 *Istighna* as a characteristic of Prophethood

As a pillar of serving Islam, *istighna* is a component of prophetic character, as well as a significant practice of the companions of all prophets, saints (*awliya*), and great leaders in Islamic history. Prophet Muhammad (pbuh), his Companions, and great scholars applied the *istighna* principle very strictly. The Prophet lived by the principle of *istighna*. Despite remaining hungry for days, he would not ask others for food and other needs, relying on God alone and fearing the expectation of return from those whom he served.[517] He would sleep on a thin straw mat. When Umar ibn al-Khattab saw that it left marks on the Prophet's back, he cried, "When the kings of the Persians and Romans live in palaces, can't you at least have a bed?" and the Prophet replied, "O Umar! Wouldn't you desire that this world be theirs and the next world be ours?"[518]

His life of poverty was not due to a lack of support. Whenever he received charity or a gift, however, he would always give it away to the poor and needy. This powerfully conveyed to others that he would not partake in any potential return or reward because of his service to the faith.

One night during the final days of his life, he could not sleep. He asked his wife Aisha if there were money in the house. She replied that someone who owed them money had brought seven dinars not long be-

---

516   Ibid., 67.

517   All hadiths from six authentic books in this article are taken from the following website: www.usc.edu/schools/college/crcc/engagement/resources/texts/muslim/ hadith/. Hadith narrated by 'Aisha, that she said to Urwa, "O, the son of my sister! We used to see three crescents in two months, and no fire used to be made in the houses of Allah's Messenger [i.e. nothing used to be cooked]." 'Urwa said, "What used to sustain you?" 'Aisha said, "The two black things [i.e. dates and water], except that Allah's Apostle had neighbours from the Ansar who had some she-camels, and they used to give the Prophet some milk from their house, and he used to make us drink it." (Bukhari)

Ibn Hanbal, cited in Fethullah Gülen, *The Messenger of God*, 37.

518   Ibid.

fore. The Prophet requested that it be given out right away, which Aisha did.[519] He then said, "The upper (giving) hand is better than the lower (receiving) hand."[520] This is the degree to which he practiced *istighna*. It may be viewed as the peak of his *taqwa* and his desire to please God.

It is worth mentioning Gülen's unique comment on the situation wherein the Prophet's shield was being held by a Jewish neighbour as collateral for a debt he owed him. Gülen says, "The pinnacle of *istighna* is that the Prophet Muhammad (pbuh) at the time was in need of money to feed his family. If he borrowed money from Muslims, they would never consider holding his shield for a debt (and give to the Prophet freely). He did not want to be in debt to any Muslims and hence applied *istighna* strictly."[521]

7.3 The *istighna* of great leaders and scholars

The first Caliph Abu Bakr donated all his wealth and property to the cause of Islam. In his will, he asked his inheritors to pay back the salary he received while in office.[522] Although they were the heads of state, Umar, Uthman, and Ali, did not leave any inheritance. Khalid ibn Walid was chief of staff but did not leave any inheritance when he died. Other well-known examples of leaders and scholars include Umar ibn Abdu'l-Aziz, Tariq ibn Ziyad, Salah ad-Din Ayyubi, Imam al-Ghazali, Abdulqadr al-Jilani, and Mawlana Jalal ad-Din Rumi,[523] as well as Ottoman rulers from

---

519   Ibn Sa'd, v. 2, p. 237–238, Ahmed, Müsned, v. 6, p. 104, cited in Asım Köksal, *İslam Tarihi*, (Istanbul: Köksal Yayınları 1981), www.darulkitap.com/oku/tarih/islamtarihi/islamtarihiasim/indexana.htm. Retrieved on December 24, 2010.

520   Sunan an-Nasai, Hadith No: 2553, www.*sunnah*.com/urn/1077110. Retrieved 23.04.2017.

521   Fethullah Gülen, Toplumsal Cinnet, fgulen.com/tr/turkce/264-hitabet/bamteli-dosyalari/49975-toplumsal-cinnet. Retrieved 12.6.16.

522   Tabaqat Ibn Sa'd, VI, 130 vd.; Ibnu'l-Athir, II, 115, cited in Asım Köksal, İslam Tarihi, (Istanbul: Köksal Yayınları 1981), www.darulkitap.com/oku/tarih/islamtarihi/islamtarihiasim/indexana.htm. Retrieved on December 24, 2010.

523   For detailed information see Ebu'l-Hasan En-Nedevi, *İslam Önderleri Tarihi 1*, (Istanbul: Kayıhan Yayınları, 1995), 453, www.darulkitap.com/oku/tarih/islamonderleri/indexaan.htm. Retrieved on January 8, 2011.

the founder Osman Ghazi to Süleyman the Magnificent (1594–1566).[524] All these leaders led a very simple life, gave away or shared what they received as gifts or spoils of war, and did not leave any inheritance.[525]

On the first day of Umar ibn Abdu'l-Aziz's caliphate, some gifts, including musk for the previous caliph Sulaiman ibn Malik (674–717), were received. When Umar smelled the fragrance of musk, he closed his nose with his arm and asked for the gifts to be taken away immediately. He did not even wish to benefit from the smell of the gift.[526] When he died, he had only 14 dirhams, sufficient only for his funeral service.[527] Similarly, among Salah ad-Din's possessions at the time of his death was a piece of gold and forty pieces of silver.[528] He had given away his great wealth to his poor subjects, leaving almost nothing to pay for his funeral.

Hasan al-Basri warns, "Do not be included within those persons who are learned in wisdom and knowledge but are equal to the ignorant in actions."[529] He meant the scholars who do not apply the *istighna* principle for serving religion. He continues, "The death of the heart is a search for the world with the actions of the Hereafter."[530] A leading figure of the *tabiun* (those who saw the Companions), Yahya ibn Muaz, states that if the world is sought by one with learning and wisdom, his light goes gradually. Saeed ibn Musayyab (642–715) a leading scholar of the *tabieen*, views the frequent visit of the learned man to the houses of rulers as a robber.[531]

Imam Azam Abu Hanifa (699–767), would never accept anything for his teaching and religious services. Abdullah ibn Mubarak (736–797) said that if the treasures of the world were given to Imam Abu Hanifa

---

524   Gülen, *Prizma* 1, 81.

525   Yücel and Albayrak, *The Art of Coexistence*, 132.

526   Al-Isfahani, *Hilyatu'l Awliya*, Ibn Jawzi, Sifatu's Safwa, trans. Said Aykut et al., Vol. 2 (Istanbul: Sule Yayınları, 2003), 277.

527   Ibid., 283.

528   Bahā' al-Dīn Ibn Shaddād, *The Rare and Excellent History of Saladin* (London: Ashgate, 2002), 19.

529   Al-Ghazali, *Ihya*, trans. Fazl-ul Karim, Vol.1, p. 64, available at ghazali.org/ihya/english/ihya-vol1-C1.htm. Retrieved 6.10.2016.

530   Al-Ghazali, *The Book of Knowledge*, 190.

531   Al-Ghazali, *Ihya*, 64.

he would flee from them. Muhammad ibn Shuja said that Caliph Abu al-Mansur (714–775) ordered 10,000 dirhams to be given to Imam Abu Hanifa but he declined the offer. He refused any financial benefit, as well as the social and religious status of *Qadi al-Quddat*, the chief judge of the caliphate. Rabi'a ibn Asim said, "Caliph Yazid (d. 683) once sent me to Abu Hanifa wanting to appoint him as cashier of the state treasury. On his refusal to accept the post, he was flogged twenty times. He fled a prize post and, as a result, he received punishment."[532]One day, when the caliph's representative came to deliver some material wealth, he covered his body with a cloth after Prayer and did not talk to anybody. The representative went to him with dirhams, but Imam Abu Hanifa did not talk with him. One of the people present said, "This is his habit never to accept any material benefit from anyone. He never accepts gifts from anyone."[533] Caliph al-Mansur sent him a small pouch of gold. Imam Abu Hanifa again did not accept, adding that "even if you cut off my head, I would never take that."[534]

Imam Malik (711–795) rejected Caliph Harun al-Rashid's (763–809) money given to him so they he might purchase a house. The caliph also offered him some financial benefit and social status in Baghdad, but Imam Malik declined and said, "Over the whole world, I prefer nothing more than the city of the Messenger of God."[535] When, as a result of his diffusion of knowledge and the dispersal of his companions, great wealth began to come to him from different corners of the earth, he used to distribute it in charity.[536] He died without leaving any inheritance.[537]

Imam Shafi'i (767–820) once went to Yemen with some men and returned to Mecca with 10,000 dirhams. A tent was fixed for him in the outskirts of Mecca, from where he did not move until he distributed all the dirhams among the people who came.[538]

Imam Ahmad ibn Hanbal (780–855) never accepted any gifts from

---

532   Ibid., p. 38.

533   Al-Isfahani, *Hilyatu'l Awliya*, Vol. 4, 287.

534   Ibid., 29.

535   Al-Ghazali, *Ihya*, 43.

536   Ibid., 44.

537   Al-Isfahani, *Hilyatu'l Awliya*, Vol. 2, 352.

538   Al-Ghazali, *Ihya*, p. 40.

rulers.[539] He would not accept money given to him by a teacher, friend, prince or caliph.[540] If he ran out of food during his travels, he would work as a porter to survive, and he would never accept anything from anyone.[541] When he received 10,000 dirhams, he could not sleep until he donated this money to poor people.[542] When a caliph gave him a garment, he sold it immediately and donated the money to a poor person.[543] He stated that his happiest days in his life were the days on which he had nothing to eat or wear at home.[544] When he died, he left six or seven objects which could be wrapped in a cloth and had no value.[545]

Imam al-Ghazali, when he was in Jerusalem, took an oath not to take money from any rulers and never broke this oath until death.[546] He said, "How can a man be counted as a learned man who persists in the pathways of this world although his journey is towards the next world? The sign of the learned man of the next world is that his words and actions are the same. In short, the learned men of the Hereafter seek and acquire knowledge, but the learned men of the world are engaged in the acquisition of wealth and name and fame and give up those learnings for which God sent the prophets."[547] When he returned to his teaching position after his seclusion, he declined the salary offered.

Mawlana Jalal ad-Din Rumi believed scholars must not study to please princes or attain worldly benefit, fame or position, but instead, pursue learning for the sake of the truth. When their actions and words spring from the truth that they have learned, this will in turn lead them to become blessed with the guidance of the Prophets.[548]

Imam Rabbani views "the cleric who did not apply the *istighna*

---

539 Ebu'l-Hasan En-Nedevi, *İslam Önderleri Tarihi 1*, (Istanbul: Kayıhan Yayınları), 132-141.

540 Adil Salahi, Ahmad ibn Hanbal, muslimheritage.com/article/imam-ahmad-ibn-hanbal. Retrieved 24.12.2016.

541 Al-Isfahani, *Hilyatu'l Awliya*, Ibn Jawzi, Sifatu's Safwa vol. 3, 185

542 Ibid., 207.

543 Ibid., 208.

544 Ibid., 200.

545 Ibid., 189.

546 Al-Isfahani, *Hilyatu'l Awliya*, Vol.7, 40.

547 Al-Ghazzali, *Ihya*, Vol. I, p. 72, ghazali.org/ihya/english/ihya-vol1-C1.htm.

548 Rumi, Discourse of Rumi, 4

principle as lovers of this ephemeral world. They are the lowest of low and thieves of the faith and religion."[549] Particularly, if clerics have any financial aim or worldly expectations from their students, they can never have any influence on them.[550]

 Fatih Sultan Mehmet offered his Shaikh Akshemseddin the position of vizier (minister) after the conquest of Istanbul, but he declined and spent the rest of his life in Göynük, a small village close to the city of Bursa.[551] The spiritual founder of the Nur Jamaat, Said Nursi, lived an ascetic life and died in 1960 with 35 kuruş (less than half a Turkish Lira), only enough to pay for his burial shroud. Mustafa Kemal Atatürk offered Said Nursi the position of Member of Parliament or a preacher position in southeast Turkey with a salary of three hundred gold coins and a car, but he declined.[552] He strictly followed *istighna* principles and did not even accept gifts. If he accepted a gift, he would pay for it.[553] He would sell his own things in order to purchase a copy of his own books from his friends or rent clothing from them.[554]

7.4 Testimonials from friends

I asked more than twenty of his close associates about Gülen's *istighna* and analysed about fifty interviews produced by Irmak TV and Mefkure TV. This series consists of testimonials by Gülen's friends who have known him since the late 1960s or the early 1970s. I have also added my personal observations from the total of six months I spent near him in Pennsylvania where he resides.

 Since his childhood Gülen has followed the *istighna* principle very strictly, but it is since 1960 that Gülen's character has been observed and recorded by his associates, students, friends and foes. In the early 1970s, and after a military coup in 1980, he was accused by the secularist media of possessing millions of dollars in property and farms. From June

---

549 Imam Rabbani, *Maktubati Rabbani*, 59.

550 Ibid., 212.

551 Ismail Köksal, "Hoca Efendinin Hukuk Anlayisi", in *Bir Alim Portresi Etrafında*, ed. Hamza Aktan (Istanbul: Ufuk Yayınları, 2014), 138.

552 Said Nursi, *Tarihçe-i Hayat*, (Ankara: 1978), 141.

553 Yücel and Albayrak, *The Art of Coexistence*, 131–145.

554 Sahiner, Son sahitler, available at www.nur.gen.tr. Retrieved 31.10.2106.

1999, the secularists' media outlets in Turkey campaigned against him and the Hizmet Movement for a few months. Again, Gülen was accused of controlling billions of dollars. After two ministers' sons were arrested because of corruption in late December 2013, pro-government, secularist and state media outlets which are controlled by the Turkish government began an anti-Gülen and Hizmet Movement campaign. Gülen was accused of owning twelve tons of gold and controlling over $70 billion in assets. Gülen denied these accusations through his lawyer but has not been able to sue them because there is no rule of law and the judicial system is now working like a government department. The government appoints all judges and there is no separation of powers in the current regime in Turkey.

Gülen's close friend Suat Yıldırım, the former Dean of School of Divinity at Sakarya University, lived together with Gülen when they were young. He witnessed that when Gülen was an imam in Edirne, he would not go to the Mufti's office to get his salary. The clerk would bring his salary. Gülen did not view himself worthy or deserving of the salary, and hence did not go to collect it. While he was doing his mandatory military service, he did not eat from the food which was provided for all the soldiers. Not wanting to partake from public wealth, he would purchase enough food to get by.

When Gülen worked as a teacher at the Kestanepazarı Qur'anic boarding school in Izmir, he would never ask for any payment for his overtime. According to all the twenty close associates that I interviewed, Gülen never used Hizmet institutions or money for himself. Gülen paid for the water he used to perform ablutions at the mosque. While staying at Hizmet or public institutions, he has always paid rent, often more than required and even if he only stayed overnight. He has been paying rent for his room at the retreat centre in Pennsylvania where he has been secluded since 1999. These actions are based on *istighna*, which involves not partaking of public property or assets that belong to others. This means avoiding indebtedness and seeing himself as a servant. By applying the *istighna* principle strictly, Gülen wanted to educate his students and future leaders.

Gülen himself has never had personal wealth. He was so poor that for some years he lived in the corner of a local mosque in Izmir with barely enough space to lie down. In addition to never having any personal wealth, he prayed for his relatives to remain poor so as not to raise any suspicions of gaining from his influence. He is the author of more than seventy books. Almost all are bestsellers, and many of them translated into more than forty languages. His book about the Prophet Muhammad (pbuh) sold about two million copies. To understand how strictly Gülen apples the *istighna* principle, it is important to mention some testimonials of his close friends and brothers.

Cemalettin Bölükoğlu from Turgutlu recalls how Gülen spent his days when he visited his town. Gülen would never eat the meal which had been prepared for students in the dormitory. Bölükoğlu continues, "It was Gülen's principle not to eat from the food which the *waqf* [religious endowment or foundation] provides." Instead of that he would cook for himself and eat. Yusuf Pekmezci, who was a board member at Kestanepazarı, says that "when Gülen was teaching at Kestanepazarı Qur'an course, he never ate from the students' meal." It was a tradition that the teacher partakes of the meal which was cooked for the students. For almost six years, I never saw him having the student meal."

İsmail Gönülalan, who attended Gülen's study circle, asserts that Gülen would not eat the food which was given to him by the congregation. The students never saw such *istighna* from any other teachers.

Sabri Çolak from Erzurum describes one instance: "Gülen's brother was sick in the hospital. I joined Gülen to visit him. During the visit, Gülen wanted to write a *dua* [supplication] which his brother could read for healing. Someone gave him a piece of paper but Gülen did not want to use this paper. Initially, I could not understand why Gülen did not want to use it. Later, I realised that Gülen does not want to use *waqf* paper. Then he wrote the dua on the empty page of a book which his brother was reading at the hospital."

Gülen is very cautious not to use any public things for himself or his family. Mehmet Eldem who has known and been close to Gülen since the early 1970s recalls: "Some of his friends stored Gülen's things in a small room in a dormitory which belongs to a Hizmet foundation. Gülen did not feel comfortable, and he has been paying rent for this little room for many years."

Gülen's brother Kutbettin stated that Gülen visited their mother as often as he could. Sometimes, he would use the foundation's car and he would pay the people in charge for using it. Once, Kutbettin visited Gülen in the United States. Gülen was aware that his brother did not have sufficient money for travelling. He asked him where he got the cost of his flight. Kutbettin said that a businessman from the Hizmet Movement had purchased his ticket without asking for anything from him. Gülen paid the cost of the flight from the income of his books and asked his brother to return the money to the businessman. Then he told him, "You must not be indebted to anyone." Kutbettin said, "Whenever I visited him and stayed in the foundation building, my brother calculated the days which I stayed and the food that I consumed and he would pay for it."

Kutbettin says, "I assume Gülen learned such a principle from my father. He would stay hungry or thirsty but would never have anything from anyone without the owner's consent." Gülen's brother Sıbgatullah, recalls that "none of the family members ever benefited from the Hizmet Movement because we promised Gülen," as mentioned in Chapter 4. He went on, "I enrolled my children at the Hizmet tutoring centre and then Aziziye College in Erzurum. Because I am Gülen's brother, the administration did not want to take the tuition. But I paid it and I am still keeping the receipts, because like all of his brothers and sisters, we promised not to get benefit from Hizmet or any Hizmet institutions nor would our children get any benefit from the movement." He adds, "We are nine siblings; none of us are rich and we do not even own a house, except for two of us. I have a disabled son and therefore I had to purchase this simple house for him."

Özgür Öztaş who has known Gülen for more than forty years, stated, "I have never seen Gülen using any *waqf* or public property. Once he visited a dormitory and a cup of tea was served to him. He drank the tea because he did not want to be disrespectful towards us. However, he paid ten times more than a cup of tea costs."

Mustafa Türk, who has been close to Gülen since 1966, recalls that Turgut Özal, who later became Prime Minister and President of Turkey, was a candidate of an Islamic party in Izmir for the parliamentary election in 1977. He listened to Gülen's sermon and then both went to Türk's home for lunch. Özal mentioned to Türk that since he had begun his election campaign, everyone had asked for something from him, except Gülen.

For Gülen, those who serve religion at any time anywhere are obliged to follow *Ulul'azm Anbiya'* (the Arch-Prophets—those who came with scriptures). He says, "After piety the most important quality of a believer is *istighna*."[555] He states that the degree of those who serve religion and their effectiveness is dependent on their altruism, serving without any expectation, and avoiding indebtedness to others. *The Words* of those who would desire any benefit will be ineffective on hearts and minds.[556] Gülen describes those who serve Islam without any expectations as heroes: "These heroes of religious service are those who abstain from extravagance and luxurious lifestyle and always live with contentment by following the *istighna* principle. They see attaining honour in this world not as coming through worldly possessions but through devotion to their faith. Even if these heroes live in a tent instead of a house, ate a piece of dry bread every day and wore old clothes, they are the ones who conquer heart and minds by the grace of God."[557]

In particular, those who serve the faith and the Qur'an are obliged to accustom themselves to frugality. Otherwise, it will lead to loss of reputation and trustworthiness in the eyes of people. For Gülen, loss of credibility means loss of everything.[558]

Based on an examination of Gülen's works, TV interviews, and personal observation, for Gülen those who serve religion must have five essential characteristics in order to follow the *istighna* principle properly.

First, they must lead a simple life and absolutely avoid being in debt to anyone except God.[559] Desiring respect for the acts done or receiving a unique title such as *efendi*, *üstad*, *alim*, master or *pir* would weaken their *istighna*.

Second, they must not have any worldly ambitions. Leaders, including spiritual leaders, should live like the poorest members of their community.[560]

Third, they must be altruistic. One of their characteristics is choos-

555 Fethullah Gülen, "Sığ Görünen Deryalar", www.herkul.org/kirik-testi/sig-go-runen-deryalar/. Retrieved 5.08.2016.

556 Gülen, *Asrın Getirdiği Tereddütler* 4, 66–67.

557 Fethullah Gülen, "Hesabını verebilecek misin?" www.herkul.org/kirik-testi/hesabi-ni-verebilecek-misin/. Retrieved 2.08.2016.

558 Fethullah Gülen, "Adanmış Ruhlar ve İktisat-İstiğna Mesleği", www.herkul.org/kirik-testi/hesabini-verebilecek-misin/. Retrieved 12.06.2016.

559 Al-Isfahani, *Hilyatu'l Awliya*, Vol. 4, 68.

560 Gülen, *The Messenger of God*, 251-252.

ing "we" over "I" and placing the needs of others over themselves or choosing the greater communal benefit over all kinds of personal benefits.[561] To Gülen, the ideal clerics or religious servants are those who burn like candles, melting away despite themselves and illuminating others. He states that those who serve religion are charged with following the prophets in disseminating the truth and hence must never use this service for their own interests. A resolute religious servant should always work for others' happiness but have no time to think of himself or herself.[562]

Fourth, they must, in *The Words* of Nursi, see this world "as a guesthouse and view it as the abode of service, not the place of pleasure, reward and requital."[563]

Finally, they must not leave any inheritance when they die or aim to enrich their children but should provide them with a very good education.

7.5 Analysis

After researching the *istighna* principle in Gülen's works and analysing his life, it can be said that his philosophy and application of *istighna* is very similar to *Salaf al-Saliheen*. He has been trying to apply the way of the second caliph, the *Umari* way. According to Muslim historians, once Umar saw a thin and scruffy toddler girl. He asked his son who she was and why she was not being looked after well. His son Abdullah told him that she was his daughter and he asked his father to provide some help to take care of her. Umar responded to him, "By God, you will not receive the state's help more than any other citizen. I cannot give tax payers' money to my children more than they deserve."[564] Those who act like Umar are called the followers of the *Umari* way. Despite Gülen's credibility and being the spiritual leader of the biggest transnational faith-based movement in the world, he has not provided any benefit for himself nor for his relatives at all.

He is also reintroducing the caliph, Umar ibn Abd al-Aziz's state

---

561   Yücel, "Spiritual Role Models in Fethullah Gülen's Educational Philosophy".

562   Fethullah Gülen, *Çağ ve Nesil*, V.7, (Izmir: Nil Yayınları, 2011), 254

563   Said Nursi, The Flashes, trans. Şükran Vahide, (Istanbul: Sözler Publication, 2001), 23

564   Şimşek, *İbretlik Hatıralar*, 176–178

policy by not allowing Hizmet leaders or representatives, whom Gülen calls "*khadim*" (servants), to engage in trade or business as an ethical principle because it brings profit. This principle is only for the leaders and does not include the business community, affiliates, or sympathisers in Hizmet. Not having any worldly ambition, Gülen is trying to apply the way of the *Salaf al-Saliheen*. Not having valuable worldly possessions himself, Gülen strives to be a role model particularly for those who serve faith and humanity, just as Imam Malik, Abu Hanifa, Imam Ahmad ibn Hanbal and Imam Shafi'i. Gülen's philosophy of *istighna* rejects not only material benefits or worldly ambition but also titles, fame, praise, applause, respect, or being held in high regard or spiritual positions. Because the *istighna* of the soul, is a higher spiritual station than the *istighna* of the body and it is considered as the peak of *taqwa* (piety).

Viewing the *istighna* principle as a requirement in service and emphasising it heavily, Gülen wants this principle to become part of human nature.[565] Once it has become natural, it will lead to the best *tamthil*, or representation. *Istighna* and *tamthil* are two sides of one coin and one cannot exist without the other. *Tamthil* cannot be complete without *istighna*. Also, it is necessary to reach the Reality and spiritual satisfaction. The way to reach the Reality is to rely on sincerity,[566] and one of the most important principles of sincerity is *istighna*. Without *istighna*, a believer will not be able to have *iman* (faith) at the degree of *yaqin* or certainty.

There is a relationship between *istighna* and *iman* (faith). A believer will have *istighna* at the degree of his or her faith. Strong faith means less indebtedness to others. Likewise, there is a relationship between *istighna* and success in the serving of faith and humanity. The level of success is inversely proportional to the degree of *istighna*. It can be argued that all major Muslim leaders and scholars, particularly *Salaf al-Saliheen*, chose the peak of *istighna* rather than *azimah*, strictness or *rukhshah*, dispensation, in its application. Gülen, like *Salaf al-Saliheen*, chooses mostly

---

565   Al-Isfahani, *Hilyatu'l Awliya*, Ibn Jawzi, Sifatu's Safwa V.4, 70.

566   Thomas Michel, *Insights from the Risalei Nur: Said Nursi Advices for modern Believers*, (New Jersey: Tughra Books, 2012), 198

the peak of *istighna* or *azimah* rather than *rukhshah* for the service of faith, the Qur'an, and humanity. However, while he acts according to the peak of *istighna* for himself, Gülen recommends *azimah* or *rukshah* for others.[567] Some scholars have applied *rukhshah* instead of *azimah* in serving religion in Islamic history. Those scholars are called *khalaf* who have accepted the permissibility (*jaiz*) of some particular financial benefit for serving Islam. Al-Qurtubi discusses the permissibility of acceptance of *ujrah*, fee or financial income, in detail from the point of view of various scholars when he comments on the verse "And (you scribes, fearful of losing your status and the worldly benefit accruing from it) do not sell My Revelations for a trifling price (such as worldly gains, status and renown)" (Qur'an: 2:41).[568] However, during the crisis of Muslim world applying *azimah* rather than *rukhshah* particularly by the scholars and leaders is crucial for overcoming difficulties. It can be said that an individual cannot gain *istighna* without sacrificing his wealth and time for the common good.

Conclusion

In today's world, the philosophy of serving one's own interests is widespread and includes the Muslim world and its leaders. Gülen, like other scholars, is fully aware of this spiritual disease and its damage to religion and faith. Muhammad Awwamah calls scholars who do not apply the principles of *istighna* deviants who patch up this world with their religion.[569] They contradict themselves with what they teach and what they preach. Each of them damages the faith more than a thousand ignorant people would. The people who misguide others accuse religious scholars of making their teaching and religion a means of livelihood for themselves.

As Nursi states, it is necessary to show this to be false by action.[570] There is no greater asset than *istighna* for the children of Adam. "A per-

---

567 Osman Şimşek, *Yanık Yürekler*, (Izmir: Işık Yayınları, 2010), 90.

568 Al-Qurtubi, *Al-Jamiu li Ahkami'l Qur'an*, altafsir.com. Retrieved 6.11.2016

569 Shaikh Muhammad Awwamah, *The Influence of the Noble Hadith*, trans. by Mariam Madge Conlan (London: Turath Publishing, 2014), 143.

570 Said Nursi, *The Letters*, trans. Şükran Vahide, (Istanbul: Sözler Publication, 1996) 32.

son without indebtedness to others, even if he has no worldly possession, is the richest in the world," Gülen says.[571] Accepting any gifts from people, particularly from the rulers without paying for it, will damage the credibility of Islamic scholars, clerics, and reigious workers in society and this will weaken their spirituality and religious practice in society. Therefore, it is the almost unanimous opinion of all great scholars to follow the i*stighna* principle. *Istighna* is a gate to the palace of contentment. For contentment, it is necessary to follow strictly the *istighna* principle. Therefore, contentment and *istighna* are two sides of one coin and cannot be separated.[572]

For Gülen, not just scholars but all Muslims must aim to apply *istighna* as the essence of their spiritual life.[573] Like every individual, however, they need an income to survive. Gülen calls what is given to teachers in Hizmet schools and other employees of the Hizmet Movement a scholarship instead of a salary. They are expected not just to work eight hours daily during the week but also to do more hours of overtime voluntarily, during weekends and holidays. Based on my research, the teachers at one of the Hizmet-affiliated schools in Australia do voluntary work for between eight and 20 hours weekly.[574] This volunteerism shows that they do not teach for the financial benefit only in the eyes of the parents and people. Historically, whenever the leader of the Muslims and those who serve religion practice *istighna*, they have effectively influenced others, conquered people's minds and hearts, and attained success in their endeavours. Therefore, Gülen's first and last advice to people is to serve their religion, homeland, nation, state, and humanity at any level, and not to expect anything in return. Being independent of people is one of the indispensables principles of Gülen's life.

---

571 Fethullah Gülen, "Rüzgarlar ve Mümince Duruş," www.fgulen.com/tr/abd-soh-betleri/bamteli/49809-muhalif-ruzgarlar-ve-mumince-durus 18.06.16 retrieved 8.8.2016

572 Said Nursi, *Tarihçe-i Hayat*, (Istanbul: Sözler Nesriyat, 1987) 14.

573 Fethullah Gülen, *Kırık Testi*, 7, (Izmir: Nil Yayınları, 2011). 208.

574 For detail of the research, see Yücel, "Spiritual Role Models in Fethullah Gülen's Educational Philosophy", available at file:///C:/Users/SN/Downloads/Spiritual_Role_Models_in_Fethullah_Gülen.pdf.

CHAPTER 8

GÜLEN'S SELF-EXILE IN PENNSYLVANIA

Gülen's Self-Exile in Pennsylvania

Following the 1996 elections in Turkey, the Islamic-oriented Welfare Party (Refah) under the leadership of Necmettin Erbakan formed a coalition government with the liberal True Path Party (Doğru Yol). The army and the secularists' camp, including the media and judiciary, were uncomfortable with the result of the election. At the same time, the global growth of the Hizmet Movement was seen as a threat by militant secularists. Thus, they became aggressive not just towards the Welfare Party but also towards all religious leaders and faith-based groups including Fethullah Gülen and the Hizmet Movement. Initially, their campaign was against Erbakan and his party. Erbakan could not resist the secularists' camp and eventually stepped down. The Welfare Party was closed down by the courts. Then the campaign turned against religious groups, particularly the Hizmet Movement.

The National Security Council, which consists of the heads of the armed forces, the president, prime minister and foreign minister, put pressure upon the new government to apply a Jacobin-style secularism. If not, İsmail Hakkı Karadayı, the chief of staff of the Turkish Army, threatened the government with a possible civil war like in Algeria, where more than 200,000 people were killed in the early 1990s due to military intervention against the Islamic Salvation Front (FIS) after the 1989 election. The Turkish government could not resist the military pressure and banned the *hijab* in all educational institutions, universities and even in the religious high schools and Qur'an courses run by the state. Almost half of the religious high schools were closed down. Those who were praying or fasting in the army, police, some government departments, and educational institutions were profiled by the military or national intelligence service. Many of those who practiced the religion were sacked from the army, police and educational institutions. All civil rights were threatened. Most of the non-governmental religious organisations and other NGOs which were not allied with the military and secularists were in peril. Religious organisations were not even allowed to provide humanitarian aid after the earthquake in which over twenty thousand people died in 1999. Some politicised religious groups were fuelling the tension which the military could use to justify the oppressive form of secularism they preferred. Gülen tried to reduce tension between secularists and religious organisations.

It was a difficult time for Gülen and the Hizmet Movement. Gülen's health was deteriorating. He needed heart surgery, but he was hesitating. On the recommendation of one his friends who was a doctor in the United States, he went to have a medical examination at the Mayo Clinic so he could decide whether to have heart surgery or not.

After Gülen had left for the United States with this intention in March 1999, the secularists' camp, with the full endorsement of the media and military, initiated an anti-Gülen campaign in June 1999. It was claimed that Gülen was going to overthrow the secular state and establish an Islamic state like Iran or Saudi Arabia. It was initially designed to last about two months. However, the cold war against Gülen and the Hizmet Movement continued for over a decade. These claims were not new. Gülen had been accused many times before and even prosecuted for such accusations but he was always acquitted. Gülen was prosecuted for infiltrating the secular state.[575] The public prosecutor Nuh Mete Yüksel asked for the death penalty for Gülen. Unofficially, most of the businessmen who donated to Hizmet's educational institutions were intimidated. The people were afraid to buy or read Hizmet Movement's daily newspaper, *Zaman*. The circulation dropped from four hundred thousand to one hundred seventy thousand in four months. The movement could not do any fund-raising in public.

To divert public attention from their corrupt activities, the government and media conglomerates would obsess over Gülen and the Hizmet Movement. To discredit Gülen, the military used all sorts of tools. Hundreds of thousands of CDs, which consisted of anti-Gülen propaganda, were distributed to all social, religious and political groups. They promoted the idea among religious groups that Gülen was a Mossad agent, secret cardinal, or the American representative of watered-down Islam. The evidence for their claims was that some American teachers

---

575 Gülen was prosecuted many times for similar claims before 1999. However, all cases were dismissed. For detail, see Examples of Court Decisions, www.fgulen.com/en/press/court-decisions/25017-examples-of-the-court-decisions. Retrieved 27.11.2016.

were teaching English in Hizmet-affiliated schools in Central Asia and that Gülen was living in the United States. Gülen's meeting with Pope John Paul II in 1998 and his dialogue initiatives with non-Muslims in Turkey and abroad were presented as more evidence for their claims. Furthermore, they propagated among secularists, particularly the Alawites, a Shi'a sect, the idea that Gülen had aims to bring *sharia* law to Turkey. The anti-Gülen campaign was promoted among the nationalists by accusing him of betraying Turkey's national interests.

Hundreds of news reports were fabricated in June and July 1999. On several occasions secularists wrote that Gülen had died and his family was preparing for his funeral. Gülen's approach was to minimise tension between his followers and secularists. About three months after the campaign, in October 1999, he wrote an article indicating that he forgave all his personal rights to those who attacked him during what is now known as "the June Storm." He wrote, "Let's not be enemies of each other."[576] The secularists' cold war against Gülen and the Hizmet Movement continued to some extent. They tried to put pressure on the United States government after 9/11, indicating that Gülen was more dangerous than Osama bin Ladin. Gülen, through some media interviews, sought to calm down the political and religious tension of years in Turkey. Finally, all the charges against Gülen were dismissed in 2005, and further appeals were rejected by the General Council of the Supreme Court of Appeals on January 24, 2008.[577]

Whenever secularists wanted to change the political agenda, they would attack Gülen, up until the referendum in 2010, which changed some articles of the constitution. In this way, the people's attention would be diverted towards him instead of the terrorism and major economic, social, and other problems facing the country. Gülen responded through his lawyer or sometimes via the media in a diplomatic way or with philosophical principles. Because of the political and religious tension, Gülen did not return to Turkey but stayed in the United States voluntarily. He did not want to be used to raise political tension and create disunity in Turkey. Since then, he has considered himself to be "self-exiled."

---

576 Fethullah Gülen, *Sızıntı*, October, 1999.

577 Loye Ashton and Tamer Balcı, "A Contextual Analysis of the Supporters and Critics of the Gülen/Hizmet Movement," (Washington DC: Georgetown University conference proceedings, 2008), 113.

8.1 Gülen's daily routine

Gülen spends most of his time in his private room at the retreat centre in Pennsylvania. Although he is considered the spiritual leader of the largest global faith-based movement, he does not spend more than four to five hours with his followers or audience per day. On some days, he spends less than two hours with them. After one of my academic friends had visited him, I asked his view about the visit. He said that his expectation was to see many rooms full of staff with computers and various departments. Since the retreat centre is the headquarters of the Hizmet Movement, there ought to be many staff but all he saw was people reading books, having friendly conversations and being vigilant about congregational Prayers and the *Tahajjud*. People were not using their computers, phones, and tablet devices.

Gülen speaks little and studies and worships abundantly. He spends most of his time in reading, writing, worshipping and contemplating in his twenty-metre-square private room. He eats little and sleeps two to three hours daily. According to his close associates and the students in his study circle, Gülen does not sleep more than three hours per day. Some nights he does not sleep at all. According to Necdet Başaran, who has been close to Gülen since the early 1970s, Gülen once told him, "Everyone wishes for something worldly from God. Some may ask to be wealthy while others may ask a good position. If I were to ask something from God for this world, I would ask for two to three hours of straight sleep."[578] Gülen cannot sleep for three hours without a break.

According to my observations, Gülen would divide his day into the following segments: Sometimes an hour or two prior to dawn, he would get up, pray the *Tahajjud*, read a minimum of one *juz* (twenty pages of the Qur'an) per day, supplicate in the way of the Prophet Muhammad (pbuh) and make *awrad* or *dhikr* (remembrance of God) which includes reciting the Names of God. He reads *al-Qulubu ad-Daria* (The Broken Hearts) supplications, which consist of the supplications of the Prophet, some Companions and most of the great spiritual leaders in Islamic history. After every *Tahajjud* Prayer, he would make supplication for those who requested that he pray for them. Then he would perform the *Fajr* (the Morning Prayer in the congregation). After Prayer, he would again

---

578   Personal communication, May 2004

make *awrad* and *dhikr* for fifteen to twenty minutes followed by recitation of the end of *Surah Al-Hashr*. He would converse with the visitors for a few minutes before his teaching session began. He would then ask his students to read from Said Nursi's *Risale-i-Nur* (the Epistles of Light) collection and expound on the particular reading of the passage.

The study period would last approximately one hour. After performing the *ishraq* or supererogatory prayer, Gülen would continue reading different books, writing essays for portions of his books or poetry, and contemplating the activities of the movement. I was told that Gülen sometimes takes a short nap before the study circle begins. About two hours before the Midday Prayer, he would teach *tafsir* (commentary on the Qur'an), hadith, jurisprudence, *aqidah*, and the theology and history of Islam to a select group of students who have graduated from divinity schools in Arabic. The study circle is similar to the traditionalists' way, in which students would sit on the ground, but using modern technology such as computers and projectors. Gülen's schedule is based around the daily *Salat* (obligatory Prayers), which are always performed in the congregation on time followed by a ten or fifteen minutes of *dhikr*, invocation of God's Names.

After teaching, he would have a short conversation with the students or audience before the Noon Prayer (*dhuhr*). Then he would return to his room to read books or prepare his future publications. At times, he would invite individuals to discuss their requests further with him. He would then pray the Afternoon Prayer (*Asr*) in congregation and make *awrad* and *dhikr* with his congregation for about forty-five minutes. There would be another short question and answer session lasting about half an hour. He would then walk on the treadmill in his room for forty minutes. While on the treadmill he would make *dhikr*.

After the congregational dusk Prayer (*Maghrib*), he might or might not eat with others. After the congregational Night Prayer (*Isha*) he would return to his room and continue his usual activities of reading, writing, supplicating and *dhikr* until 11 p.m. and later. Sometimes he would speak privately with visitors after the *Isha* Prayer.[579]

Gülen leads a life of seclusion. He has three illnesses: hypertension, diabetes, and heart disease. Due to these medical conditions, he has di-

579   Yücel, "Fethullah Gülen: Spiritual Leader in a Global Islamic Context", 1–19.

etary restrictions and is under a doctor's supervision all day. In the last seventeen years, he has left his residence in a small town in Pennsylvania only for medical treatment. In an interview with a reporter from Turkey, Gülen said that in the last five years, (now seventeen years), he had only stepped out onto his balcony a few times. If the weather was beautiful, he would sometimes go out to the trellis and have a cup of coffee or tea there.[580]

Relations between Gülen and the AKP (JDP)

In this section, I will briefly elaborate how the relations began between Gülen and the AKP (Justice and Development Party or JDP) and how they were sundered and turned into oppression and tyranny by the ruling party. Then, I will analyse the reasons for the split.

Before establishing the JDP, both Recep Tayyip Erdoğan and Abdullah Gül visited Gülen in Pennsylvania on August 14, 2001. Later, from 2003 onward, many members of parliament from the party visited Gülen out of respect for him. The economic crisis in 2001 led people to look for an alternative party in the November 2002 election. This allowed the JDP to achieve a significant victory. However, they had no bureaucrats prepared to assign to positions and the JDP mainly relied on educated people from Hizmet.

The JDP leader Recep Tayyip Erdoğan claimed many times that they were not an Islamic party and that their program was pluralistic, inclusive and that they were aiming to join the European Union and in favour of extending human rights. These claims meant that they received some support from the European Union and the United States. The Hizmet Movement had suffered under militant secularism for decades, and so it supported the JDP with its media. Initially, the JDP took steps to bring about democratic reforms, including freedom of expression, human rights, and economic development. The JDP made some progress in democratisation and economic development with the help of the European Union. Foreign Minister Abdullah Gül's "Zero problems with neighbours" policy built good relation and minimised the differences with surrounding countries. Turkey's model gradually inspired other Muslim countries. This policy was coherent with the Hizmet Move-

---

580   Mehmet Gündem, "My interview with Gülen," *Milliyet*, January 27, 2005.

ment's ideals. The Hizmet Movement continued to grow globally and open more educational institutions throughout the world. Again, the secularists' camp was uncomfortable with the victory of the JDP and the growth of the Hizmet Movement. They attempted a military coup three times but due to the government's democratisation policy, economic progress, and Hizmet's media and bureaucratic support of the JDP, they were not able to carry off a coup.

The court dismissed the long-standing case accusing Gülen of plotting to introduce sharia in 2005. Some secularists and a strong secularist element in the army were not happy with the dismissal of the case. In 2006, the National Security Council, which consists of five top generals, the president, the prime and foreign ministers passed a resolution naming Gülen and the Hizmet Movement as enemies of the state, along with the PKK, a terrorist organisation responsible for the deaths of thousands of soldiers and civilians.[581] Prime Minister Erdoğan and Foreign Minister Abdullah Gül signed the resolution. Gülen did not say anything against either and thought positively about them. He thought that neither was able to stand up to the other members of the Security Council.

Despite being the greatest faith-based movement in Turkey, Gülen did not encourage Hizmet participants to be involved in politics directly. His cousin applied to the JDP to be a candidate for member of parliament without the approval of Gülen. However, JDP did not accept him. In 2011, the JDP asked the Hizmet Movement to assign some people to be candidates for election. Although they asked for more, only three individuals who are affiliated with the Hizmet Movement became candidates and all three won a place in parliament. İlhan İşbilen, who was elected from Izmir as a member of parliament, later mentioned that the JDP was expecting at least thirty Hizmet people to become candidates.[582] When they asked, Gülen said that three would be enough. In my view, by accepting that three Hizmet participants would stand as members of parliament, the aim was to improve direct communication with the government and not for any other purpose.

---

581 www.crisisgroup.org/europe-central-asia/western-europemediterranean/turkey/
turkey-s-pkk-conflict-death-toll. Retrieved November 21, 2017.

582 İlhan İşbilen stated that during his visit to Sydney in 2015.

On the other hand, the JDP was not happy with the growth of the Hizmet Movement and its influence. JDP leaders often reflected on this in their private circles. However, the Hizmet Movement continued to support the government, expecting the JDP to prepare a civil constitution which it had promised many times since the 2002 election and then to hold a referendum for the approval of the people. All previous constitutions in Turkey's history had been drawn up by the army. In 2011, an electronic eavesdropping device was found in the prime minister's office. Erdoğan indirectly blamed the Hizmet Movement but also rejected an investigation by the courts. Despite that, the Hizmet Movement continued to support the government until October 2013. In March 2014, Gülen mentioned that their "excessive trust in the JDP leaders was a mistake."

In October 2013, Erdoğan proposed a resolution to close about three thousand tutoring centres. In Turkey, it is very competitive to pass the university exams and enrol in a university. Only one third of the students can study at university. Therefore, there was and still is a high demand for tutoring centres. Initially, Erdoğan said that the aim of closing them down was to reform the education system. However, later he said that the goal was to close down over 750 of the Hizmet Movement's tutoring centres where about 750,000 students were receiving education. About two hundred of these centres were providing free tutoring in economically undeveloped cities or towns where the PKK terrorist group was active. With the closure of the tutoring centres, over 100,000 teachers lost their jobs.

In December 2013, the police arrested the sons of two ministers on corruption charges and a Turkish-Iranian businessman who had smuggled approximately twenty billion dollars in gold from Turkey to Iran in breach of the Western countries' economic embargo. Erdoğan blamed Gülen and the Hizmet Movement and declared war on the movement. In one of his public speeches during the election campaign, Erdoğan said, "We will not give even a cup of water to people of Hizmet." In Turkish culture, this expression is used to refer to the Karbala tragedy, where Hussain, the grandson of the Prophet, was martyred. Yazid's army did not allow Hussain and his family to have even a cup of water from the river. Erdoğan then continued to attack Gülen and the Hizmet Movement throughout the whole five-month election campaign in about seventy regions. He called Gülen an imposter, fake prophet, leech, false messiah, hypocrite, betrayer of the country, and so on. He called Hizmet participants people *hashashin*—assassins, terrorists, worse than the PKK and a "parallel state."[583] Gülen was called a fictitious scholar, evil-doer and pseudo-sheikh. Erdoğan continued, "Whoever does not cut off relations with Hizmet will pay the price." The JDP mayors and regional governors of cities did not give permission to the people of Hizmet to conduct any activities including conferences and seminars about the Prophet Muhammad (pbuh). Pro-Erdoğan and state media repeated the same accusations as some secularists and Islamophobes have been doing since the early 1970s but with a sharper rhetoric after December 17, 2013. Gülen did not respond to the accusations for about three months. In his interview with *Zaman* newspaper, he said, "Such words do not suit a prime minister."[584] The public prosecutor opened a case against Gülen in 2014 and asked for a five-hundred-year sentence for establishing a terrorist organisation.

All state media which is run by the government and secular, Islamophobic, Maoist, communist and pro-government media initiated a massive campaign against Gülen and the Hizmet Movement. The government reassigned over thirty thousand police officers, changed most of the bureaucrats and intimidated more than fifty thousand middle-class individuals in businesses who had donated their alms (*zakat*) and charity (*sadaqa*) to the Hizmet Movement. Later, the JDP government confiscated Banka Asya, the biggest Islamic Bank in Turkey, which was set up by Hizmet Movement affiliates and supporters. This was quickly followed by closing all Hizmet-associated media, confiscating Hizmet publishing companies and banning over seventy of Gülen's books and hundreds of publications about the Hizmet Movement, including translations of the Qur'an in many languages and Gülen's book about the Prophet Muhammad (pbuh). People threw the books into rubbish bins because having them at home meant the risk of arrest and prosecution. Those who were known to read Gülen's books were interrogated. About six weeks prior

---

583   For Gülen's responses to slander, see *Today's Zaman*, March 22, 2014, www.fgulen. com/en/press/news/43567-todays-zaman-gulen-offers-more-explanations-of-his-views-against-slanders.

584   Ibid.

to the failed military coup on July 16, 2016, a resolution which called the Hizmet Movement a terrorist organisation was passed by the National Security Council. As the military coup attempt was progressing, Erdoğan accused Gülen and the Hizmet Movement of being behind it. Gülen strictly denied any involvement with it. He said that he is ready to be prosecuted in an international court and if he is found ten percent guilty, he is ready to be executed. After the coup failed, the public prosecutor asked for a 3500-year prison sentence for Gülen. The requested sentence length is the highest in Islamic history and the seventh highest in human history.[585] The sentences of those who caused the killing of millions during the Second World War were not as long as the sentence for Gülen.

Within a week of the coup attempt, over 3,000 Hizmet educational, health and humanitarian aid institutions including 16 hospitals, primary, secondary and high schools, 13 universities, over a thousand dormitories, where mostly poor students stayed, and many childcare centres were closed down and the buildings were confiscated. Some of them were later appropriated by President Erdoğan's son. Over 140,000 people were interrogated and about 62,000 of them were arrested, including judges, lawyers, teachers, military officers, businessmen, imams, journalists, over seventeen thousand women and six hundred thirty of them with babies, and some elders, one of whom was over ninety years of age. The government revoked the university degree of over 20,000 Hizmet-affiliated teachers. Due to military coup over 150,000 Hizmet-affiliated people were laid off or lost their jobs and were not allowed to work even in any private companies. Some Pro-Erdoğan media groups published a telephone hotline number to report to law enforcement any Hizmet-affiliated people their readers might know. Some of those who were arrested were tortured and deprived of food and water. Some were not allowed to pray during interrogation or in jail. All their basic human rights were denied. Turkey has been classified as a "not-free country" by world-leading human rights organisations. The government confiscated or assigned administrators (*kayyım*) over small and large businesses to

---

585   For comparison, see Chris Langton, "Top 15 Longest Prison Sentences Ever Issued", www.therichest.com/rich-list/most-shocking/top-15-longest-prison-sentences-ever-issued/. Retrieved 3.1.2017.

the value of billions of dollars which belong to Hizmet participants, supporters, and donors. Ertuğrul Özkök, the editor-in-chief of the biggest staunchly secularist newspaper *Hürriyet*, wrote that in 1996 the secularist military coup's main target was Gülen and the Hizmet Movement. However, the 1996 coup was not as successful as Erdoğan at crushing the movement's capacity.[586] He praised Erdoğan highly for his success. Also, Doğu Perinçek, the leader of a Maoist Party, has said many times that Erdoğan has been applying their plan for the destruction of the Hizmet Movement and offered his full support to Erdoğan.

Despite this, Gülen has repeatedly told his followers to be patient and forgive everyone who has wronged them in his talks, which are available online.[587] Once, he said, "I hope I can do something good to those who did wrong to me before I die."[588] He gave over thirty interviews to different media groups throughout the world after the failed military coup. Gülen's responses to President Erdoğan's accusations were tactful. I have also listened to all his weekly speeches in Turkish since the failed military coup.[589] He has not mentioned President Erdoğan in his talks at all, but indirectly was critical of some of the attributes possessed not just by Erdoğan but by others as well. However, if Gülen speaks about the characteristics of hypocrisy, the pro-Erdoğan media will interpret this as, "Gülen called Erdoğan a hypocrite" and take his words out of context.

This is followed by the question which everyone asks, that is, why did this split happen? In my humble view, there are six primary reasons for the early split, and later it led to aggression and tyranny against the Hizmet Movement through the Turkish Intelligence Service (MIT), police, military, judiciary, ninety percent of the media, the Presidency of Religious Affairs, all of the diplomatic corps, and most of the NGOs in Turkey.

---

586 Ertuğrul Özkök, "28 Şubat kararları uygulanabilseydi bugün darbe girişimi olmazdı," 19 October 2016, t24.com.tr/haber/ertugrul-ozkok-28-subat-kararlari-uygulanabilseydi-bugun-darbe-girisimi-olmazdi,365898. Retrieved 8.12.2016.

587 All of his interviews are available on Gülen's official website. For detail of interviews, see www.fgulen.com/en/press/columns. Retrieved 26.11.2016.

588 Personal communication, 26.12.2016

589 All of his talks in Turkish are available on ozgurherkul.org/ under Bamteli. Retrieved 26.11.2016.

The first reason for the split and point of separation always existed, though in varying degrees. A fundamental principle of Gülen and the Hizmet philosophy is that religion must not be used for any political gains and worldly ambition. This principle was inspired by Nursi, who viewed using religion for any other purpose as tantamount to killing it.[590] After the 2010 referendum which reduced the military's power over politicians, the JDP began using religious rhetoric heavily to gain the favour of the public, which enabled them to carry out their corrupt activities and nepotism. Through legal and illegal means, they funnelled tax payers' money to their allies in the business community. Gülen and Hizmet participants were uncomfortable with such policies. Among many reasons, they saw how a religious-seeming administration was harming the perception of Islam among the secular community in Turkey and abroad. Gülen acted diplomatically and stated his criticism in his online talks, although he avoided mentioning any names. Erdoğan and his camp were not happy with this criticism given the size, power and influence of the movement. Thus, Erdoğan moved to weaken the movement by using state power to the full.

The second reason is jealousy. The Hizmet Movement has been educating millions for the last forty years. It has a great deal of credit in the eyes of people as well as in the world. Gülen and the Hizmet Movement have mobilised millions of people for educational purposes and they have been highly successful. Many children of JDP ministers, members of parliament, and other national and local leaders, including Erdoğan's own daughter, were educated or stayed in Hizmet institutions. Jealousy is a spiritual disease of the heart that can cause more destruction than heresy. Cane killed his brother Abel because of jealousy. Prophet Joseph's brothers threw him into the well and then sold him as a slave because of jealousy. Hussein, the grandson of the Prophet Muhammad (pbuh), was martyred for similar reasons. Despite Gülen's warnings on numerous occasions about the jealousy of others, the necessary steps were not taken by the local and regional leaders of the Hizmet Movement.

In 2008, about 830,000 Turkish Lira (400,000 USD) was donated to the JDP which had over 16 million voters throughout Turkey. How-

---

590   Nursi, *Sünuhat*, 336, www.erisale.com/index.jsp?locale=tr#content.tr.15.336. Retrieved 22.04.2017.

ever, about three hundred Hizmet volunteers—middle-class individuals in businesses, teachers, students and other volunteers—donated twice as much money as that given by all JDP voters just for education purposes in the city of Adıyaman, a small town located in the south-east of Turkey. Such altruism throughout Turkey caused jealousy and conspiracy theories about the financial resources of the Hizmet Movement.

Initially, the JDP tried to create an alternative to the Hizmet Movement as secularists have been doing for more than forty years. They opened dormitories and encouraged other religious groups to open private schools and humanitarian aid organisations. Also, the government transformed many secular public high schools into *İmam Hatip Lisesi* (religious high schools) but still people kept sending their children to the Hizmet schools. The government asked the Minister of Religious Affairs to open students' houses and established study circles similar to those of Hizmet. However, none of them was as successful as the Hizmet institutions. They gradually put pressure on Hizmet participants and their institutions. All of them were audited and some of them were fined. The government officially started a campaign based on fearmongering and intimidation to prevent people from sending their children to Hizmet institutions. It was thought that by doing so they would be able to dismantle the movement. Even three months after the beginning of the anti-Hizmet campaign in December 2013, State Minister Beşir Atalay, a close ally of Erdoğan said, "Hizmet is dead; now there is a funeral service going on."

An idea can be discredited or weakened by a better idea. However, the JDP could not produce an idea or a movement like Hizmet. Then, as previous rulers applied harsh oppression to stop the activities of faith-based movements in Islamic history, the government began to apply similar methods and implemented a Machiavellian political game which the movement could not play or resist because it stuck to its Islamic ethics and principles. Therefore, Hizmet people have suffered.

The third reason is that Hizmet-affiliated bureaucrats did not accept bribes and acted as an obstacle for corruption. These bureaucrats were altruistic and donated money for the common good throughout their lives. Those who always give their time and money to the community or nation would not accept bribes. As it stood, the decrease of corruption from 2002 to 2008 had led to Turkey's economy developing rapidly. Gross Domestic Product, exports and imports had tripled. Refusing bribes was not liked by some of those who had worldly ambitions around Erdoğan and in the JDP. In time, they turned against the Hizmet Movement and Hizmet-affiliated bureaucrats. To get rid of these bureaucrats, they needed a scapegoat.

The fourth reason was that from time to time Gülen would remind JDP leaders including Erdoğan in a friendly or diplomatic way about some of the issues which were important for the whole society or Turkey and the region. For example, Gülen asked Erdoğan to stay neutral and use diplomacy instead of supporting the revolt of Syrian rebels militarily with the assistance of some external powers. One of the reasons for this was a request from Ramadan al-Buti (1929-2013), the well-known Syrian scholar, to Gülen. According to Ali Bulaç, the former Erdoğan adviser and *Zaman* newspaper columnist, before he was killed Ramadan al-Buti sent letters to Erdoğan and asked him not to support the Syrian conflict by allowing weapons and fighters to pass through Turkey's border. Al-Buti also asked Gülen to persuade Erdoğan. However, Erdoğan neglected both scholars' requests. The Syrian conflict has resulted in over 300,000 deaths, most of which were civilians. An additional four million have been displaced, with half the houses in Syria destroyed. A Western expert said that the destruction is equivalent to having used four atomic bombs in Syria. The country has become a home for terrorist activities. Over two thousand Turkish citizens have died in the conflict and terrorist attacks. Most likely Syria will be split into three small states. Turkey is hosting over two million refugees with the economic cost of war for Turkey exceeding fifty billion dollars so far. How these events are going to affect Turkey is not foreseeable, but most likely it will have only negative repercussions. In December 2016, Erdoğan accepted talks with Bashar Assad and met with him later. Events have shown again and again that al-Buti and Gülen were right but Erdoğan's policy has resulted in a disaster for the region.

The fifth reason is that almost all highly influential scholars have been seen as a threat by most rulers in Islamic history and in undemocratic or semi-democratic countries in the contemporary Muslim world. There are two major reasons for this. First, influential scholars do not approve their corruption, injustice and tyranny. The second is that they are not silent but critical of their wrongdoings and unlawful actions.

Gülen is also very influential and has consequently been seen as a threat by secularists since 1970. In recent times, political Islamists have joined ranks with them as well. Those who refrain even from killing an ant, have no worldly ambition, and dedicate their lives to the common good or educating people are seen as threats by those who have worldly ambition, and by jealous sheikhs, corrupt leaders, dictators, and tyrants. This was not the destiny of Gülen only but also the fate of many great scholars such as Imam Azam Abu Hanifa, Ahmad ibn Hanbal, Imam Shafi'i, Imam Rabbani and most recently Hasan al-Banna and Said Nursi.

The final reason is that Gülen is not understood by his contemporaries as many great scholars of the past were not understood. Gülen is reviving the methodology of serving Islam in the light of the *Salaf al-Saliheen*'s works and practices. When Gülen opened dormitories in the early 1970s, political Islamists and some religious groups were severely critical because it was mandatory to hang Atatürk's portrait on the wall in educational institutions. Islamists were against hanging Atatürk's picture and therefore against opening educational institutions. When the Hizmet Movement opened private schools, tutoring centres and universities without Islamic education in the curriculum (as it was not allowed in Turkey), again some religious groups and Islamic parties were highly critical of Gülen and the movement. For them, Muslim scholars should open Qur'an courses and mosques but not secular schools. Later, those who were critical of Gülen opened dormitories, private schools, and universities similar to Hizmet's educational institutions. They saw the benefit of these secular schools. Hizmet teachers conveyed the message of Islam through their actions rather than proselytising the religion, which was not allowed in Turkey. Similarly, other groups have imitated Hizmet's model.

When Gülen initiated dialogue with non-Muslims and secularists in Turkey Islamic parties and some religious groups accused him again of selling the religion. The Director of the Presidency of Religious Affairs began dialogue with non-Muslim groups in Turkey ten years later. When the Hizmet Movement opened schools in many countries, once again they received very severe criticism for spending Muslims' money and using human resources for educating non-Muslims. Now the Turkish government and all religious groups are trying to open institutions throughout the world. However, none has been as successful as the Hizmet Movement. The success of the Hizmet Movement, which is based on altruism, hard work and financial sacrifice, has excited great jealousy after not being understood initially.

The JDP philosophy, like that of other political parties, revolves around benefit for itself and its members, and its policy has become more populist since 2010. It can be said that, initially, from 2002 until 2010, the party allowed the due separation of powers not purely, but mainly, for the public good. Therefore, the economy was boosted; Turkey became a model for others, and even inspired the Arab Spring. But once the JDP had gained total control of the military, intelligence service, police and media, then the party gradually inclined towards benefit for individuals. It was not only Gülen who issued a friendly warning to the JDP about corruption. Numan Kurtulmuş, a close ally of former Prime Minister Necmettin Erbakan for many years and the leader of the (Islamic-oriented) HAS Party, warned Erdoğan and the leaders of JDP about corruption in 2009. He said, "When the JDP leaders began to run the country in 2002, they were poor like Prophet Aaron, but seven years later they have become like Qarun." Qarun was the richest person in Pharaoh's court in the time of Prophet Moses. The significant risk is that the JDP has been doing this in the name of Islam or with an Islamic political identity.

For Gülen, there were three options in relation to JDP policy. First, use diplomacy and give a friendly warning, as he did about the Mavi Marmara flotilla, corruption, involvement in Syria and Iraq. But this did not work. He had also warned the government about various terrorist groups such as the PKK, al-Nusra, ISIS, and al-Qaida operations in Turkey. The JDP did not take these into consideration. The second option for Gülen was to play the "three monkeys policy," that is, not to hear or see and to remain silent about the JDP policies which were harmful to Islam, society, Turkey, the region and, in the long term, the world, in order to spare himself and the Hizmet Movement. In that case, everyone, including most Hizmet participants, supporters and volunteers would ask, "What have we striven and suffered for, and why did we work hard, and what will be our responsibility in the life Hereafter?" This would be a denial of the spiritual, ethical, and universal principles of Islam for which Gülen and the movement have been striving over the last sixty years. If Gülen accepted and agreed with JDP policy, then all of these wrong ideas and anti-Islamic ethical principles would spread and flourish in generations to come. The final option was to speak the truth and suffer the power of the state and the JDP's Machiavellian machinations. Gülen, like many great scholars in Islamic history, chose the most difficult path, that is, the last option—to suffer instead of denying Islam's ethical principles in practice.

Conclusion

In summary, in the last hundred years in the Muslim world, there is no one who has been as discriminated against, despised, accused, slandered, insulted, oppressed, imprisoned, and exiled as Gülen by a wide range of political, social, religious, nationalist, and communist groups. What he has faced is very similar to or even harder than what other great scholars and saints in Islamic history have faced.

Since the day he was born, Gülen has been discriminated against and has not been allowed to rest. Future historians will have difficulties understanding how Gülen could have borne such a life filled with pain, suffering and the shedding of tears. Despite these obstacles, he has acted positively, like his spiritual master Said Nursi, and has not revolted but expressed himself by shedding tears for the last sixty years. In my humble understanding, one of the reasons for his success is hidden in his suffering and tears. He has faced his destiny, which is similar to that of Said Nursi, who said, "I have known no worldly pleasures during my lifetime of eighty years and more. I have lived out my entire life either on the battlefield, in captivity, in dungeons or prisons, or in the courts of my native land. I have encountered all kinds of suffering and pain. I have been treated as a criminal at courts martial and exiled from one province to another like a vagabond. I have not been allowed visits in confinements, and I have been poisoned time and time again [19 times] and insulted in many ways, to the extent that sometimes I have preferred death over life. If our religion had not forbidden us to commit suicide, perhaps Said Nursi today would be buried under the earth. You see, my life has passed through many sufferings, trials, calamities, and disasters. I have devoted myself and my life to the cause of the faith, belief, security and salvation of the nation… I claim nothing and I do not call down curses upon them because in this way the *Risale-i Nur* [his work] has become a means to save the faith of some hundred thousand or a million people. I would save only myself by dying, but by enduring such sufferings and trials I was able to help save the faith of a great many people. All thanks be to God, the Exalted, I would sacrifice my salvation for the safety of the faith of the society."[591]

Gülen has also encountered all sorts of suffering and pain. He has been under police, intelligence or military surveillance since the age of eighteen. He was treated like a communist terrorist for six years after the military coup in 1980. He was a fugitive for six years in his native land for no reason. All his books were banned by political Islamists although they had nothing to do with politics. As mentioned above there is no one in the last hundred years of Muslim world history who has been slandered as much as Gülen by all camps, including ultra-secularists, Maoists, communists, atheists, political Islamists, radical religious groups, Islamophobes, Islamic extremists and ultra-nationalists. He has been subject to all kind of slander. As mentioned in Chapter 1, the staggering number of fabricated news reports about him since the early 1970s is more than KGB produced about capitalism or the CIA invented about communism in the almost seventy years of the Cold War.

There have been many attempts by ultra-secularists, political Islamists and other terrorist organisations to kill him. Still, it is not known how many. He has been labelled as the greatest criminal in Islamic history in the courts in Turkey. The public prosecutor asked for a 3,500-year prison sentence for Gülen, which is twenty times more than for all twenty-eight Nazis tried at Nuremberg.

When I began to write this book, I realised that it was beyond my capacity to comprehensively reflect on Gülen. In this situation, I recall a story I was told. An ant was carrying water in its mouth to extinguish the fire that had been lit to burn Prophet Abraham. Someone told the ant that the water it was carrying in its mouth would not put out the fire. The ant answered, "I know, but it is my task to do what I can." Similarly, I know that my book is not up to truly presenting Gülen's scholarship and leadership, but, like the ant, I have tried to carry out my moral task.

Gülen and the Hizmet Movement have suffered under the rulers of Turkey, mainly because of its weakness against Machiavellian political games, and the existing fear, misunderstanding, jealousy, and hatred of Islam. This is not just the destiny of Gülen and the Hizmet Movement.

---

591   Nursi, Tarihçe-i Hayat, 629.

All great scholars and revivalist movements have shared the same fate. Gülen has shared the destiny of the great scholars (*Salaf al-Saliheen*) such as Imam Malik, Imam Azam, Imam Shafi'i, Ahmad ibn Hanbal, al-Sarakhsi, Imam Bukhari, Imam al-Ghazali, Abdulqadr al-Jilani, Baha ud-din Naqshband, Imam Rabbani, Said Nursi, Hasan al-Banna, and so on.

Despite all the suffering so far, Gülen has said many times, "I have forgiven all those who have harmed me. I pray God enables me to return their evil with good before I die."

History shows that if a spiritual or religious movement, a school of thought or an order is not moulded with tears of pain and suffering, it will have a short life span. Therefore, Gülen's suffering and shedding of tears for sixty years will prolong the life span of the Hizmet Movement like that of the four schools of law in Islamic jurisprudence, the Ash'ari and Maturidi in theology and the Qadiri and Naqshbandi orders in Sufism. With the JDP's most recent oppression and tyranny of Gülen and Hizmet participants, the movement's life span will be prolonged for centuries. Due to his works, dedication to education, piety, altruism and suffering for humanity, his influence will continue to grow. It can be said that all of Gülen's products are due to *ilm mawhiba* (gifted knowledge), *aqli mawhiba* (gifted intellectualism), *qawli mawhiba* (gifted speech) and *akhlaqu mawhiba* (gifted character), which are blessings from God who has bestowed these characteristics upon many great scholars. However, Gülen has never claimed such qualities.

Gülen does not want to be known and wants to be forgotten. As mentioned at the end of the first chapter, Dexter Filkins, a journalist in the United States, asked Gülen how he thought he would be remembered. Filkins says, "He gave me an answer the like of which I have never heard from another leader in politics or religion." Gülen said, "It may sound strange to you but I wish to be forgotten when I die. I wish my grave not to be known. I wish to die in solitude with nobody actually becoming aware of my death and hence nobody conducting my Funeral Prayer. I wish that nobody remembers me."[592] These words of Gülen's remind me of a conversation between Baha ud-Din Walad—the father

---

592 Dexter Filkins, Turkey's Thirty-Year Coup, New Yorker Magazine, October 17, 2016,

available at www.newyorker.com/magazine/2016/10/17/turkeys-thirty-year-coup.

of a great saint Mawlana Jalal al-Din Rumi—and Aladdin Kayqubad (1190–1237), the Sultan of the Seljuks. The sultan asked him what would happen to both when they die. Baha ud-Din Walad told him, "O king, both of us are sultans.[593] However, your sovereignty endures as long as your eyes are open. Mine will begin when my eyes close forever."[594] May God give long life to Gülen. When he closes his eyes, his spiritual sultanate will truly flourish.

---

593   Baha ud-Din Walad is known as the Sultan of Ulama (the Sultan of the Scholars).

594   For detail, see Franklin D. Lewis, *Rumi: Past and Present, East and West: The Life, Teaching and Poetry of Jalal al-Din Rumi* (London: Oneworld Books 2008), 41–49.

Appendix

Selected Passages from Fethullah Gülen's Works

Bibliography

Index

Selected passages from Fethullah Gülen's works

Islam is a universal religion, and the significance it gives to rights is inclusive of all creation.

***

Rather than party politics or cliquishness, people needs disciples of knowledge, morality, and virtue who are well equipped with faith and hope, full of enthusiasm, and who have divested themselves of any wish, desire, and distress, be it material or immaterial, pertaining to this world or the other.

***

An ideal in the hands of an ideal man reaches the most elevated values and turns into the charm of victory and accomplishment.

***

Those who live without thinking are the objects of the philosophy of others.

***

The generations of hope, which are, with respect to the present, the representatives of science, knowledge, faith, morality, and art, are also the architects of the spirits of the people who will succeed us.

***

Hope consists of a man finding his spirit and seeing the potentiality that lies within it.

***

The daytime for one who has enduring hope is as colourful as the garden of Paradise, for his heart is set upon a brightness as unfailing as the sun.

***

Everything has come into existence through compassion and by compassion it continues to exist in harmony.

***

Human has a responsibility to show compassion to all living beings as a requirement of being human. The more they display compassion, the more exalted they become.

***

A soul without love is impossible to be elevated to the horizon of human perfection. Even if he lived hundreds of years, he could not make any advances on the path to perfection.

***

How happy and prosperous are those who follow the guidance of love. How unfortunate are those who are unaware of the love deeply innate in their souls and lead a "deaf and dumb" life!

***

Events in this life are no more than dreams, so quickly do they pass: it is a life without permanent foundation and flows away like a river.

***

If only we had been able to remember and learn the terrible lessons of the past, then we should have been better prepared.

***

The real guide and teacher is he who first experiences the truth in his own heart, then pours out the fire of his inspiration to ignite the hearts of his listeners.

***

Each scene from the past is valuable and sacred only so long as it stimulates and enthuses us, and provides us with knowledge and experience for doing something today.

***

There is no reason for man to be afraid of science. The danger does not lie with science itself and the founding of a world in accordance with it, but rather with ignorance, and the irresponsibility of scientists.

***

Mankind have never suffered harm from a weapon in the hands of angels. Whatever they have suffered has all come from deprived, ambitious souls who believe only that might is right.

***

Every new idea or message has always been resisted where it has appeared, and those who have offered it have usually been welcomed in new places where their pasts were unknown.

***

The best sort of knowledge to be acquired in the school must be such that it enables pupils to connect happenings in the outer world to their inner experience.

***

The new man is a conqueror and discoverer: conqueror of himself, conqueror of thoughts and conqueror of hearts, and discoverer of the unknown in the universe.

***

Belief, with the will-power to struggle, is the first and foremost condition for success in life.

***

Tariq (ibn Ziyad) was victorious, not when he defeated the Spaniards' army of ninety thousand men with a handful of self-sacrificing brave men, but when he stood before the wealth and treasures of the king and said: "Be careful, Tariq. You were a slave yesterday. Today you are a victorious commander. And tomorrow you will be under the earth."

***

People are not guided to God as they were during that blessed era of the Prophet (pbuh), because the words emitting from the mouth do not take a visa from the heart.

***

Repentance is an oath of virtue, and holding steadfastly to it requires strong willpower.

***

Self-criticism resembles a lamp in the heart of a believer, a warner and a well-wishing adviser in his or her conscience.

***

Self-criticism attracts Divine mercy and favor, which enables one to go deeper in belief and servanthood, to succeed in practicing Islam, and to attain nearness to God and eternal happiness.

***

Reflection is a vital step in becoming aware of what is going on around us and of drawing conclusions from it. It is a golden key to open the door of experience, a seedbed where the trees of truth are planted, and the opening of pupil of the heart's eye.

***

Be like earth so that roses may grow in you.

***

The individual's body is the physical dimension of his or her existence, while one's heart constitutes its spiritual dimension. For this reason, the heart is the direct, eloquent, most articulate, splendid, and truthful tongue of the knowledge of God. Therefore, it is regarded as more valuable and honored than the Ka'ba, and accepted as the only exponent of the sublime truth expressed by the whole of creation to make God known.

***

Belief is the life of heart; worship is the blood flowing in its veins; and reflection, self-supervision, and self-criticism are the foundations of its permanence.

***

Sorrow or sadness arises from an individual's perception of what it means to be human, and grows in proportion to the degree of insight and discernment possessed by one who is conscious of his or her humanity.

***

The Almighty considers hearts, not outward appearances or forms. Among hearts, He considers the sad and broken ones and honors their owners with His presence, as stated in a narration: "I am near those with broken hearts."

***

Fear and hope are two of the greatest gifts of God that He may implant in a believer's heart. If there is a gift greater than these, it is that one should preserve the balance between fear and hope and then use them as two wings of light to reach God.

***

The concept, even the actual word, of taqwa (piety) is unique to the Qur'an and the religious system of Islam. Its comprehensive meaning encompasses the spiritual and material; its roots are established in this world, while its branches, leaves, flowers, and fruits are located in the Hereafter.

***

Piety is an invaluable treasure, the matchless jewel in a priceless treasure of precious stones, a mysterious key to all doors of good, and a mount on the way to Paradise.

***

Taqwa (piety) is the heavenly water of life, and a muttaqi (pious one) is the fortunate one who has found it.

***

Servanthood is a cause of honor and dignity for men and women. Nothing is more esteemed and valuable than being honored with servanthood and devotion to God. Although other, more valuable ranks may be conferred for a limited time, servanthood is constant and continuous, and therefore the most valuable rank.

***

Sincerity is one of the most significant qualities of those most faithful or loyal to God; loyalty is regarded as a source, and sincerity as a sweet water originating from it.

***

If we consider a deed to be a body, sincerity is its soul. If a deed represents one wing of pair of wings, sincerity is the other. A body without soul is of no worth, and nothing can fly with only one wing.

***

If people claim progress on the path to the Truth but are not straightforward in their state and conduct, all efforts will be in vain, and they will have to account in the Hereafter for the time spent without straightforwardness.

***

Commitment and confidence are the highest degrees of reliance on God. Those who have attained these degrees have entirely submitted their reason, logic, and belief, as well as their outer and inner feelings, to God's commandments. As a result, they have become "polished mirrors" in which His Names, Attributes, and acts are reflected.

***

The signs of good nature have been summarized as follows: a person possessing this quality does not hurt anybody by either word or deed, overlooks those who hurt him or her and forgets the evils done, and returns evil with good.

***

Do not boast of yourself in a way to see yourself as greater than others. As creatures are equal in being distant from being worshipped, so also are they equal in that they are all created.

***

Truthfulness is the firmest road leading to God, and the truthful are fortunate travelers upon it.

***

True thankfulness in one's heart is manifested through the conviction and acknowledgment that all bounties are from God, and then ordering one's

life accordingly.
***

Patience is an essential characteristic of those believers who are the most advanced in belief, spirituality, nearness to God, and who guide others to the truth.
***

Love is based on two important pillars: that which is manifested by the lover's acts (a lover tries to comply with the Beloved's desires), and the lover's inner world (a lover should inwardly be closed to anything not related to Him). True men and women of God mean this when they talk about love.
***

Futuwwa (youth and chivalry) is a treasure obtainable by climbing high beyond all the "highest mountains of the world."
***

True freedom is attainable only by freeing one's heart from worldly worries and anxieties about the things of this world, and so being able to turn to God with one's whole being.
***

Since the day it was revealed, the Qur'an has encountered many objections and criticisms. However, the Qur'an has always emerged unscathed and so continues to reflect its victory.
***

Religion and science are, in fact, two faces of a single truth. Religion guides us to and along the true path leading to happiness. Science, when understood and used properly, is like a torch that provides us with a light to follow the same path.
***

The really long-lived are not those who live long but those who can make their lives as fruitful as possible.
***

The true life is the one lived at the spiritual level. Those whose hearts are alive, conquering the past and the future, cannot be contained by time.
***

One of the most important ways to conquer the hearts of people is that one always seeks an opportunity to do others good and once such an opportunity appears, makes use of it without delay.

***

Ignorance is like a veil drawn over the face of things. The unfortunate ones who cannot remove this veil, will never be able to penetrate into the truths of creation.

***

Love is one of the subtlest blessings that the All-Merciful One has bestowed upon humanity. It exists in everyone as a seed.

***

Love is the most direct and safest way to human perfection. It is difficult to attain the rank of human perfection through ways that do not contain love and yearning.

***

It is impossible to express love with words, for love is an emotional state that can be understood only by the lover. Much of what is said concerning love is only the expression of its outward manifestations.

***

Humble and modest people are highly regarded by the created and the Creator. Haughty and self-conceited people, who belittle others and are arrogant, are always disliked by the created and punished by the Creator.

***

Those who do not seek or claim great prestige in their community sooner or later attain high ranks and are honored. Those who have a superiority complex are repudiated by their community and eventually become strangers in it.

***

People reveal themselves through their words, and manifest their spiritual rank through their manners.

***

Criticizing and objecting to everything means an attempt to destruction. If you do not like something, try to make something better than it. Being destructive causes ruins, while being constructive brings about prosperity.

***

Smart and prudent people envisage all possible drawbacks and problems, and then figure out how to solve them or deal with them appropriately if they should arise.

***

Efforts to secure a goal, as well as precautions taken to realize it, are invitations for the Almighty's help.

***

Educators who have not been apprenticed to a master and have not received a sound education are like blind people trying to light the way of others with lanterns.

***

The first school for children, whose souls are as bright as mirrors and as quick to record as cameras, are their homes. Their first educators are their mothers.

***

The communities which will dominate the future are those that pay close attention to the family institution and their young people's education, not those who are more advanced in technology.

***

Those who oppress the weak are defeated even if they seem to be the victors; those who are right are victorious even if they seem to be the losers.

***

Parents have the right to claim their children as long as they educate and equip them with virtue. They cannot make such a claim, however, if they neglect them.

***

One should not marry for reasons of wealth or physical beauty; rather, marry for spiritual beauty, honor, morality, virtue, and character.

***

A home is a small nation, and a nation is a large home. One who successfully manages a home and who has raised its members to a level of humanity can manage a large organization with little effort.

***

Those who value their parents and regard them as a means to obtain God's mercy are the most prosperous in both worlds.

***

Avoiding the positive sciences fearing that they will lead to irreligion is naivety, and seeing them as contradictory with religion and faith and as vehicles for the rejection of religion is prejudice and ignorance.

***

Since "real" life is possible only through knowledge, those who neglect learning and teaching are considered "dead" even though they are physically alive, for the most important purpose for our creation is to learn and to communicate what we have learned to others.

***

The purpose of learning is to make knowledge a guide for your life, to illuminate the road to human perfection.

***

National development only occurs when a nation's people have the same goal.

***

Civilization does not mean being rich and putting on fine airs, nor does it mean satisfying carnal desires and leading a luxurious, dissipated life. What it really means is being civil and courteous, kind-hearted, profound in thought, and respectful to others.

***

Communities based on the joining of science and morality have always established true civilizations.

***

The civilization of the future will have to be founded upon a combination of Western science and Eastern faith and morality.

***

Do not stop doing good, even to those who have harmed you. Rather, treat them with humanity and nobility, for harming someone is brutish behavior. Returning evil with evil implies a deficiency in character; returning good for evil is nobility.

***

The happiest and most fortunate people are those who are always intoxicated with ardent desire for the worlds beyond. Those who confine themselves within the narrow and suffocating limits of their bodily existence are really in prison, even though they may be living in palaces.

***

Like a flower worn on the breast, a beautiful woman may receive admiration and respect for some short period. But, if she has not been able to get the seeds of her heart and spirit to blossom, she will eventually fade and, like falling leaves, be trampled underfoot.

***

Freedom allows people to do whatever they want, provided that they do not harm any being and that they remain wholly devoted to the truth.

***

Art is the spirit of progress and one of the most important means of developing emotions.

***

It is art which inspires human beings to travel in the depths of oceans and heavens. By means of art, humanity sets sail for the outer limits of the earth and sky and reaches feelings beyond time and space.

***

Art makes iron more valuable than gold, and copper more valuable than bronze. Thanks to art, the most worthless metals become more valuable than gold, silver, and diamonds.

***

All the fine arts are eternal gifts of blessed souls to humanity.

***

Noble thoughts and lofty subjects must be explained with a style to penetrate minds, excite hearts and receive acceptance from spirits.

***

A poem that grows in the thought of infinity and flies in the skies of pure thought with the heart's wings and the spirit's strength does not pay too much attention to positive thought.

***

The media should avoid serving individual fancies and interests, for their main purpose is to enlighten and serve the nation as a whole.

***

Be so tolerant that your heart becomes wide like the ocean. Become inspired with faith and love for others. Offer a hand to those in trouble, and be concerned about everyone.

***

Ask someone who knows; two lots of knowledge are better than one.

***

Love and good relations between friends continue as long as they understand each other, practice self-denial, and make sacrifices within permissible limits.

***

Hearts are created as safes for keeping secrets. Intelligence is their lock; willpower is their key. No one can break into the safe and steal its valuables if the lock and key are not faulty.

***

Magnificent nations produce magnificent governments.

***

Those who understand politics as political parties, propaganda, elections, and the struggle for power are mistaken. Politics is the art of management, based on a broad perspective of today, tomorrow, and the day after, by seeking people's satisfaction and God's approval and good pleasure.

***

Do not remember the promises that others have failed to keep; instead, remember your own promises that you did not fulfill.

***

We applaud every good deed and attempt made in the name of the people, and stand behind the fortunate people who serve it.

***

Sincerity or purity of intention determines the quality of the deed and of the one who performs it, and whether or not God will accept it.

***

The people of service see, before anybody else, their own selves responsible and answerable for any work left undone, and are considerate and fair-minded to everyone who hastens to help and support the truth.

***

Those who lead the way must set a good example for their followers. Just as they are imitated in their virtues and good morals, so do their bad and improper actions and attitudes leave indelible marks upon those who follow them.

***

Only those who overflow with love will build the happy and enlightened world of the future. Their lips smiling with love, their hearts brimming with love, their eyes radiating love and the most tender human feelings—such are the heroes of love who always receive messages of love from the rising and setting of the sun and from the flickering light of the stars.

***

Humanity is a tree, and nations are its branches. Events that appear as heavy winds hurl them against each other and cause them to clash. Of course, the resulting harm is felt by the tree. This is the meaning of: "Whatever we do, we do it to ourselves."

***

The pen is a golden channel for the light of thought. This light descends from the mind to the arm, and therefrom to the finger, and finally comes out from the pen.

***

Poverty is not only the lack of money, for it can assume the form of a lack of knowledge, thought, and talent. In this respect, wealthy people who lack knowledge, thought, and talent can be considered poor.

***

Glasses are a vehicle for the eyes to see, and the eyes are a vehicle for the mind, the mind is a vehicle for insight, and insight is a vehicle for the conscience. The conscience is an outlet through which the spirit can observe, and a vehicle through which it can see.

Bibliography

Al-Alusi, *Ruhu'l Ma'ani*, www.altafsir.com

Al-Kasani, *Bada'i al-Sana'i*, v.7 , Beirut: Daru'l Kitab al-Arabi, 1974

Aktan, Hamza, *Bir Alim Portresi Etrafında*, Istanbul, Ufuk Yayınları, 2014.

Awwamah, Shaikh Muhammad, *The Influence of the Noble Hadith*, trans. by Mariam Madge Conlan London, Turath Publishing, 2014.

Ashton, Loye & Tamer Balci, 2008, "A Contextual Analysis of the Supporters and Critics of the Gülen/Hizmet Movement," (Washington DC: Georgetown University conference proceedings, 2008)

Al-Baqliyyyu, *A'raisu'l Bayan*, *www.altafsir.com.*

Beekun Rafiq I & Badawi, Jamal. *Leadership: An Islamic Perspective*, Beltsville, Maryland: Amana Publication, 1999.

Bulac, Ali. Önsöz, Foreword for Fethullah Gülen, *Ölümsüzlük İksiri*, Izmir: Kaynak Yayınları, 2011.

Al-Isfahani, Abu Naim. *Hilyetul Awliya (Allah Dostlari)* translated by Sait Aykut, Istanbul: Sule Yayınları, 2003.

Al-Ghazzali, Imam. *Revival of Religious Learnings, Imam Ghazzali's Ihya Ulum-id-Din*, trans.
      Fazl- ul- Karim, www.alghazali.org.

_____. *Revival of the Religious Sciences, On Conduct in Travel*, trans. Leonard Librande. Cambridge: Islamic Texts Society, 2015.

_____. *The Book of Knowledge* trans. Nabih Amin Faris, Kuala Lampur: Dar al Wahi Publication, 2013.

Al-Jilani, Abdu'l Qadir. *Tafsir al-Jilani*, www.altafsir.com

Ar-Razi, Fakhrud Din. *Mafatih'ul Ghayb*, www.altafsir.com

Al-Qurtubi, *Al-Jamiu'l Ahkam*, *www.altafsir.com*

Al-Qushaiyri, *Lataif al-Isharat*, *www.altafsir.com*

Al-Tabari, *al-Jamiu'l Bayan*, *www.altafsir.com*

Al-Zimakshari, *al-Kashaf*, *www.altafsir.com*

Alsharawi, *Muhammad Metwali* , *Khawatir Muhammed Metwali Al-sharawi*, *www.altafsir.com*

Barazangi, Mimat Hafez, M. Zaman Raquibuz and Omar Afzal, *Islamic Identity and the Struggle for Justice*, Gainsville, University of Florida Press, 1996.

Bursawi, Ismail Haqqi, *Ruhu'l Bayan*, *www.altafsir.com*

Carroll, Jill, *A Dialogue of Civilizations: Gülen's Islamic Ideals and Humanistic Discourse*, NJ: Tughra Books, 2007.

Gurkan Celik & Yusuf Alan, "Fethullah Gülen as a servant leader." This paper was presented at "Second International Conference on Islam in the Contemporary World: The Fethullah Gülen Movement in Thought and Practice" March 4-5, 2006, Southern Methodist University, Dallas, Texas, USA,

Celik, G, Kirk, K, Alan, Y, "Gülen's Paradigm on Peaceful Coexistence: Theoretical Insights and Some Practical Perspectives." Paper presented at "International Conference on Peaceful Coexistence: Fethullah Gülen's Initiatives for Peace in the Contemporary World," Erasmus University of Rotterdam 2007.

Çetin, Muhammed, *The Gülen Movement: Civic Service without Borders*, New York: Blue Dome, 2010.

_____. "Is the Gülen Movement a Civil Society Initiative?" *Today's Zaman*, Sunday, 19 April 2009.

Celik, Gurkan & Alan, Yusuf. "Fethullah Gülen as a servant leader." Paper presented at second international conference on "Islam in the Contemporary World: The Fethullah Gülen Movement in Thought and Practice," March 4-5, 2006, Southern Methodist University, Dallas, Texas, USA.

Demircan, Adnan, "Hz Hasan ve Halifeligi," *Harran Ilahiyat Fakultesi Dergisi*, V 2, 1995.

Dogan, Recep, *Usul Al-Fiqh: Methodology of Islamic Jurisprudence* New Jersey: Tughra Books, 2013.

En- Nedevi, Ebu'l-Hasan, *İslam Önderleri Tarihi* 1, Istanbul: Kayıhan Yayınları, 1995.

Fontenot, Karen A. & Fontenot, Michael J., "Fethullah Gülen as a Transformational Leader: Exemplar for the 'Golden Generation.'" Paper presented at "Islam in the Age of Global Challenges: Alternative Perspectives of the Gülen Movement," November 14-15, 2008, Georgetown University, Washington, D.C.

Gülen, Fethullah. *Al- Qulubu Dari'ah*, Izmir: Define Yayınları, 2013.

_____. *Asrın Getirdiği Tereddütler 1*, Istanbul: Nil Yayınları, 20011

_____. *Asrın Getirdiği Tereddütler 2*, Istanbul: Nil Yayınları, 20011

_____. *Asrın Getirdiği Tereddütler, 3*, Izmir: Nil Yayınları, 2011.

_____. *Asrın Getirdiği Tereddütler 4*, Istanbul: Nil Yayınları, 2011.

_____. *Beyan*, Izmir: Nil Yayınları, 2011.

_____. *Çağ ve Nesil 1*, Izmir: Nil Yayınları, 2011.

_____. *Çağ ve Nesil 2, Izmir: Nil Yayınları, 2011.*

_____. *Çağ ve Nesil 3, Izmir: Nil Yayınları, 2011.*

_____. *Çağ ve Nesil 4, Izmir: Nil Yayınları, 2011.*

_____. *Çağ ve Nesil 5, Izmir: Nil Yayınları, 2011.*

_____. *Çağ ve Nesil 6, Izmir: Nil Yayınları, 2011*

_____. *Çağ ve Nasil 7, Izmir: Nil Yayınları, 2011*

_____. *Çağ ve Nesil 8, Izmir: Nil Yayınları, 2011.*

_____. *Çağ ve Nesil 9*, Izmir: Nil Yayınları, 2011.

_____. *Emerald Hills of the Heart: Key Concepts in the Practice of Sufism 2*, New Jersey: Light, 2004

_____. *Enginliği ile Bizim Dünyamız*, Istanbul: Nil Yayınları, 2011.

_____. *Fasıldan Fasıla 1*, Nil Yayınları: Istanbul, 2011

_____. *Fasıldan Fasıla 2*, Nil Yayınları, Istanbul, 2011

_____. *Fasıldan Fasıla 3*, Nil Yayınları, Istanbul, 2011

_____. *Fasıldan Fasıla 4*, Nil Yayınları, Istanbul, 2011.

_____. *Fasıldan Fasıla 5*, Nil Yayınları, Istanbul, 2011.

_____. *İnancın Gölgesinde, 1, Izmir: Nil Yayınları, 2011.*

_____. *İnancın Gölgesinde, 2, Izmir: Nil Yayınları, 2011*

_____. *İrşad Ekseni, Istanbul, Nil Yayınları, 2007.*

_____. *Kalbin Zümrüt Tepeleri, 1, Izmir, Nil Yayınları, 2011*

_____. *Kalbin Zümrüt Tepeleri, 2, Izmir: Nil Yayınları, 2011.*

_____. *Kalbin Zümrüt Tepeleri*, 3, Izmir, Nil Yayınları, 2011

_____. *Kalbin Zümrüt Tepeleri*, 4, Izmir, Nil Yayınları, 2011.

_____. *Key Concept in the Practice of Sufism* 1, https://www.fgulen.com/en/

_____. *Key Concept in the Practice of Sufism* 2, https://www.fgulen.com/en/

_____. *Key Concept in the Practice of Sufism* 3, https://www.fgulen.com/en/

_____. *Key Concept in the Practice of Sufism* 4, https://www.fgulen.com/en/

_____. *Kirik Testi, 1*, Izmir: Nil Yayınları, 2011.

_____. *Kirik Testi, 2*, Izmir: Nil Yayınları, 2011.

_____. *Kirik Testi, 3*, Izmir: Nil Yayınları, 2011.

_____. *Kirik Testi, 4*, Izmir: Nil Yayınları, 2011.

_____. *Kirik Testi, 9*, Izmir: Nil Yayınları, 2011.

_____. *Ölçü veya Yoldaki Işıklar*, Istanbul: Nil Yayınları, 2007.

_____. *Pearls of Wisdom*, available at https://www.fgulen.com/en

_____. *Prizma 1*, Izmir, Nil Yayınları, 2011.

_____. *Prizma 2*, Izmir, Nil Yayınları, 2011.

_____. *Prizma 3*, Izmir, Nil Yayınları, 2011.

_____. *Prizma 4*, Izmir, Nil Yayınları, 2011.

_____. *Prizma 5*, Izmir, Nil Yayınları, 2011.

_____. *Prizma 6*, Izmir, Nil Yayınları, 2011.

_____. *Prizma 7*, Izmir, Nil Yayınları, 2011.

_____. *Prizma 8*, Izmir, Nil Yayınları, 2011

_____. *Ruhumuzun Heykelini Dikerken*, Izmir: Nil Yayınları, 2011.

_____. *Sonsuz Nur 1*, Istanbul, Nil Yayınları, 2007.

_____. *The Messenger of God: Muhammad*, New Jersey: The Light, Inc., 2005.

_____. *The Statue of Our Souls: Revival in Islamic Thought and Activism*, New Jersey: The Light, Inc., 2005.

_____. *Toward a Global Civilization of Love and Tolerance*, New Jersey: The Light, Inc, 2004.

_____. *Ve Gaybın Son Habercisi*, KDD, *Yeni Ümit*, Istanbul, 2003.

_____. *Zamanın Altın Dilimi*, Izmir: T.O.V. Yayınları, 1997.

Gundem, Mehmet. *My interview with Gülen*, Milliyet, January 27, 2005

Ebaugh, Helen Rose. *The Gülen Movement: A Sociological Analysis of a Civic Movement Rooted in Moderate Islam*, London: Springer, 2010.

Ho, Engseng. *Graves of Tarim*. Berkeley,University of California Press, 2006.

Ibn Arabi, *Tafsir al-Qur'an*, www.altafsir.com

Ibn Kathir, *History of the Prophets*. Translated by Muhammad Mustapha Geme'ah, (Riyad: Darus salam, n.d

Ibn Kathir, *Tafsiru'l Qur'an al-Karim*, www.altafsir.com

Ibn Khaldun, *The Muqaddimah*, trans. by Franz Rosenthal, chapter I and II, http://www.muslimphilosophy.com/ik/Muqaddimah/Chapter1/Toc_Ch_1.htm retrieved 10.14.2015

Ibn Ashur, *At-Tahrir Wat-Tanwir*, www.altafsir.com.

Ibn Sa'd, *Tabaqâtü'l-Kübrâ*, Beirut, 1957.

Ibn Shaddād, Bahā' al-Dīn. *The Rare and Excellent History of Saladin*, London, Ashgate,2002.

Imam Rabbani, *Mektubat Tercümesi*, Hüseyin Hilmi Işık, Istanbul, Hakikat Kitabevi, 2014.

Kabbani, H. Muhammad, *Classical Islam and the Naqshbandi Sufi Tradition*, Fenton, MI, Islamic Supreme Council of North America, 2004.

Kandehlevi, Muhammed Yusuf, *Hayatu's-Sahabe*, Istanbul, Akçağ Yayınları, 1982.

Koc, Dogan. *Strategic Defamation of Fethullah Gülen: English vs. Turkish*, Lanham, Maryland, University Press of America, 2012.

Koksal, M. Asim. *Islam Tarihi*, available at http://www.canibim.com/islamtarihi.php. Retrieved 26.08.2015

Kazuo, Morimoto, Introduction, in *Sayyids and Sharifs in Muslim Societies: The Living Links to the Prophet*, ed. Kazuo Morimoto, London, Routledge, 2012.

Lewis, Franklin D. *Rumi - Past and Present, East and West: The Life, Teaching and Poetry of Jalal al-Din Rumi*, London: Oneworld Book 2008.

Macdonald, Donald, "The life of al-Ghazzālī, with especial reference to his religious experiences and opinions," *Journal of the American Oriental Society*, Vol 20, (1899): 71-132.

Maluf, Amir. *The Crusaders Through Arab Eyes*, USA: Al-Saqi Books, 1984.

Masud, Khalid. "The obligation to migrate: the doctrine if hijrah in Islamic law" in *Muslim Travellers: Pilgrimage, Migration, and the Religious Imagination*, Eds Dale F. Eickelman & James Piscatori, London: Routledge, 1990.

Metcalf, Barbara, "Islam and Women, the case of the Tablighi Jama`at," *SEHR, volume 5, issue 1: Contested Polities, 1996* http://web.stanford.edu/group/SHR/5-1/text/metcalf.html. Retrieved 7.10.2015.

Michel, Thomas, *Insights from the Risale-i Nur: Said Nursi's Advice for Modern Believers*, New Jersey, Tughra Books, 2012.

Michon, Jean-Luis. "The Spiritual Practices of Sufism," cited in *Islamic Spirituality Foundations*, edited by Seyyed Hossein Nasr, New York: Crossroad, 1987.

Monroe, K.R. *The Heart of Altruism*. Englewood Cliffs, NJ: Princeton

Press, 1996.

Morimoto, Kazuo, Introduction, in *Sayyids and Sharifs in Muslim Societies: The Living Links to the Prophet*, ed. Kazuo Morimoto, London, Routledge, 2012.

Nursi, Said. *Asari Bediyye*, Istanbul: Envar Nesriyat, 2012.

_____. *Al-Mathnawi al- Nuriyyah*, trans. Huseyin Akarsu, New Jersey, 2008.

_____. *Damascus Sermon*, trans. by Şükran Vahide, Second revised and expanded edition Istanbul, Sözler Neşriyat, 1996.

_____. *Tarihceyi Hayat,* Istanbul, Sözler Neşriyat, 1993.

_____. *The Flashes*, trans. Şükran Vahide, Istanbul, Sözler Nesriyat, 2002.

_____. *The Letters,* trans. Şükran Vahide, Istanbul, Sözler Nesriyat, 1996.

_____. *The Rays*, trans. Şükran Vahide, Istanbul, Sözler Publications, 2006.

_____. *The Words*, trans., Şükran Vahide, Sözler Publications, Istanbul, 2001.

Özdalga M. Elizabeth, "Worldly Asceticism in Islamic Casting: Fethullah Gülen's Inspired Piety and Activism." Critique: Critical Middle Eastern Studies, *Critique*, Vol. 17 (Fall 2003): 61-73.

Özdemir, İbrahim, *Bediuzzaman Nursi's Approach to the Environment*, 2006, available at http://www.nur.org/en/intro/nurlibrary/Bediuzzaman_s_Approach_to_the_Environment_123.

Özdemir, Şemsinur, *Hoca Anne ve Ailesi*, Istanbul, Ufuk Yayınları, 2014.

Özalp, Mehmet. "Muhammed Fethullah Gülen" in *Great Spiritual Leaders: Studies in Leadership for a Pluralist Society* edited by Seforosa Carroll, William W. Emilsen, Canberra, Barton Books, 2014.

Ramadan, Tariq, *Islam, the West and the Challenges of Modernity*, translated by Said Amghar London, The Islamic Foundation, 2001.

Rushton, J. Philippe. "Genetic similarity, human altruism, and group selection," *Behavioural and Brain Sciences*, 12, 1989.

Rubin, Michael, "Turkey's Turning Point," *National Review Online*, April 14, 2008, http://www.nationalreview.com/article/224182/turkeys-turning-point-michael-rubin

Rumi, Mawlana Jalal Din, *Mathnawi*, book 4, http://www.sacred-texts.com/isl/masnavi/msn04.htm

_____. *Mathnawi*, book 6, http://www.sacred-texts.com/isl/masnavi/msn06.htm

_____. *Discourse of Rumi (Fihi Ma Fihi)* , trans. by Arthur J. Arberry, Iowa:Omphaloskepsis, 1999.

Qutb, Sayyid. *In the Shade of the Qur'an.* Available at http://www.kalam-ullah.com/shade-of-the-quran.html

Russsell, Tony & Cutler, Catherine. *The World Encyclopedia of Trees.* NY, Lorenz Books, 2003.

Saritoprak, Zeki. "Fethullah Gülen and His Theology of Social Responsibility," in Ismail Albayrak, ed., *Mastering Knowledge in Modern Times: Fethullah Gülen as an Islamic Scholar,* New Jersey: Blue Dome Press, 2011.

Sahiner, Necmettin. *Son Şahitler,* http://www.nur.gen.tr/en.html.

Sertkaya, Süleyman. *The Sirah Genre: An Evaluation of Fethullah Gülen's Approach,* unpublished dissertation, Australian Catholic University, 2016.

Shadchehr Farah Fatima Golparvaran, *Abd al-Rahman Jami: Naqshbandi Sufi, Persian Poet,* unpublished Dissertation, The Ohio State University, 2008.

Shama'il Muhammadiyah, http://sunnah.com/urn/1803040.

Simsek, Osman. *İbretlik Hatıralar.* Izmir: Işık Yayınları, 2010.

_____. *Yanık Yürekler.* Izmir: Işık Yayınları, 2010.

Tittensor, David. "Islam's Modern Day Ibn Battutas: Gülen Teachers Journeying Towards the Divine," in *British Journal of Middle Eastern Studies,* 42:2 (2015): 163-178.

Toynbee, Arnold J., "A Study of History, in William Eckhardt, Civilizations, Empires, and Wars," *Journal of Peace Research,* Vol. 27, No. 1 (1990): 9-24.

Toynbee, Arnold J. & Daisaku Ikeda, *The Toynbee-Ikeda Dialogue: Man Himself Must Choose.* New York, NY: Kodansha,1976.

Ünal, Ali. *Fethullah Gülen'le Amerika'da Bir Ay.* Istanbul: Nil Yayınları, Istanbul ,2001.

_____. *M. Fethullah Gülen, Bir Portre Denemesi.* Izmir, Nil Yayınları, 2002.

Ünal, Ali & Alphonse Williams, *Advocate of Dialogue: Fethullah Gülen,* Fountain, Fairfax, 2000

Valerievna, Izbullaeva Gulchehra. "The Theory and Application of Utilizing Jalal-Ad-Din Rumi's Spiritual and Moral Views." *Creative Education* 5, no. 18 (10, 2014): 1678-1683.

Yavuz, Hakan & Esposito, John L. *Turkish Islam and the Secular State: the Gülen Movement,* Syracuse: Syracuse University Press, 2003.

Yazır, Elmalılı Muhammed Hamdi. *Kur'ani Kerim Tefsiri,* http://www. kuranikerim.com/telmalili/nuh.htm

Yücel, Salih, "Fethullah Gülen: A Spiritual Leader in a Global Islamic Context," *Journal of Religion and Society,* Volume 12, (2010): 1-19
_____. Spiritual Role Models in Fethullah Gülen's Educational Philosophy, TAWARIKH: International Journal for Historical Studies, 3(1) (2011): 65-76.

Yücel, Salih & Selma Sivri, "Said Nursi's approach to the environment: A spiritual view on the book of universe," *Quarterly Insights* (4) (2009) 77-96.

Yücel, Salih & Albayrak, Ismail. *The Art of Coexistence: Pioneering Role of Fethullah Gülen and the Hizmet Movement* ,New Jersey, Tughra Books, 2014.

Wehr, Hans. *A Dictionary of Modern Written Arabic,* edit by J. Milton Cowan, third edition, New York: Spoken Language Services ink. 1976.

Websites

http://fgulen.com/en/

http://fgulen.com/en/fethullah-Gülens-works/thought/towards-the-lost-paradise/24463-towards-the-world-of-righteous-servants

http://www.isikcollege.vic.edu.au

www.altafsir.com

www.herkul.org

Al-Adab Al-Mufrad, http://sunnah.com/adab/6/12

Dogu, Ergil, *Fethullah Gülen and the Gülen Movement in 100 questions.* http://islamiccenter.org/environment-and-natural-living/
_____. "What is his perspective on the environment and natural living?" http://fgulen.com/en/Gülen-movement/fethullah-Gülen-and-the-Gülen-movement-in-100-questions/48368-what-is-his-perspective-on-the-environment-and-natural-living

Fontenot, Karen and Fontenot, Michael. "Fethullah Gülen as a Trans-formational Leader." Available at https://www.fgulen.com/en/

Gülen-movement/conference-papers/Gülen-conference-in-wash-ington/26453-fethullah-Gülen-as-a-transformational-leader-ex-emplar-for-the-golden-generation

Gülen, Fethullah, "People of Service," http://www.fgulen.com/en/

_____. "Baskanlik Kimin Hakkı," www.herkul.org

_____. *Adanmış Ruhlar ve İktisat-İstiğna Mesleği*, http://www.herkul.org/kirik-testi/hesabini-verebilecek-misin/

Erol, Mustafa K., "Are we doing enough to save the environment?" Available at http://www.Gülenmovement.us/are-we-doing-enough-to-save-the-environment.html

http://web.stanford.edu/group/SHR/5-1/text/metcalf.html

Lexilogos Arabic Dictionary, http://www.lexilogos.com/english/ara-bic_dictionary.htm

Özkök, Ertuğrul, "28 Şubat kararları uygulanabilseydi bugün darbe girişimi olmazdı," 19 Ekim, 2016, http://t24.com.tr/haber/ertu-grul-ozkok-28-subat-kararlari-uygulanabilseydi-bugun-darbe-gi-risimi-olmazdi,365898

http://www.kuranikerim.com/telmalili/nuh.htm

http://www.kalamullah.com/shade-of-the-quran.html

http://www.qtafsir.com/

Newspapers and magazines

Gülen, Fethullah, *Yeni Ümit*, V. 32, 1996.

_____. "Fena Fillah," *Sızıntı*, May, Iss. 376, 2010.

_____. "Mukaddes Göc," *Sızıntı*, October, 1985.

_____. *Sızıntı*, September, 1979

_____. "Bence Tam Ağlama Mevsimi," *Yağmur Dergisi*, October, 2002.

_____. *Sizinti*, January, 1993.

_____. "Bir Aynadır Bütün Varlık, *Yağmur Dergisi*, July, 2003.

_____. "Mukaddes Goc," *Sızıntı*, October 1985.

_____. *Sızıntı*, January, 1993, Vol 3, Issue 19

"A Farm Boy on the World Stage", *The Economist*, March 6, 2008

The Age, June 16, 2008

The Herald, June 16, 2008

Today's Zaman, April 19, 2009

The Economist , January 21, 2008

Milliyet, Mehmet Gündem 8-29 Ocak 2005

Rubin, Michael, "Turkey's Turning Point," *National Review Online*, April 14, 2008

Filkins, Dexter, "Turkey's Thirty Year Coup," *The New Yorker Magazine*, October 17, 2016

Lizette Borreli, "Cry It Out: 6 Surprising Health Benefits of Shedding a Few Tears," May 19, 2015 medical daily, http://www.medical-daily.com/cry-it-out-6-surprising-health-benefits-shedding-few-tears-333952

Index